Had I the Wings

Had I the Wings

THE FRIENDSHIP OF
BACHMAN AND AUDUBON

JAY SHULER

THE UNIVERSITY OF GEORGIA PRESS   ATHENS AND LONDON

Published by the University of Georgia Press
Athens, Georgia 30602
© 1995 by Jay Shuler
All rights reserved
Designed by Betty Palmer McDaniel
Set in 10.5 on 14 Fournier
by Tseng Information Systems, Inc.
Printed and bound by Thomson-Shore, Inc.
The paper in this book meets the guidelines for
permanence and durability of the Committee on
Production Guidelines for Book Longevity of the
Council on Library Resources.

Printed in the United States of America

99 98 97 96 95 C 5 4 3 2 1

Library of Congress Cataloging in Publication Data

Shuler, Jay.
   Had I the wings : the friendship of Bachman and
Audubon / Jay Shuler.
      p.   cm.
   Includes bibliographical references (p.   ) and index.
   ISBN 0–8203–1705–5 (alk. paper)
   1. Bachman, John, 1790–1874.   2. Audubon, John James,
1785–1851.   3. Naturalists—United States—Biography.
4. Ornithologists—United States—Biography.   5. Animal
painters—United States—Biography.   6. Lutheran Church
—South Carolina—Clergy—Biography.   I. Title.
QH31.B13S48   1995
508'.092'273—dc20
[B]   94–25422

British Library Cataloging in Publication Data available

To Martha, Dale, and Ted

Contents

Illustrations

*D*URING A CAMPAIGN TO PRESERVE swamp forests in the low country of South Carolina, I decided to write about John James Audubon, the noted ornithologist, and his friend John Bachman, a Lutheran pastor of Charleston, South Carolina. To bolster the debate with the forest managers, we needed to know what the southeastern swamps were like before clear-cutting, cultivating, draining, and damming destroyed many of them and altered the primeval settings of others. I learned that the almost vanishingly rare Bachman's warbler—the female discovered in 1832 and the male in 1833 by Bachman, and named for him by Audubon—had nested in one of the swamps we were defending. Had Bachman written a letter telling Audubon of his discovery of the warbler? If so, had he described the swamp as well?

After reading almost fifty of Bachman's letters, I came upon the one I hoped to find. Happily, by then the issue had been settled with the foresters. Most of the swamp habitat associated with Bachman's warbler had been set aside as wilderness, and I was caught up in the friendship of the two naturalists. To my surprise, I discovered that in the numerous books celebrating Audubon, his friendship with Bachman had merely been touched on, or even belittled, though Bachman made substantive contributions to Audubon's *Ornithological Biography,* was his partner in producing *The Viviparous Quadrupeds of North America,* and gave pivotal advice and assistance to Audubon during the troubled last decade of his career. Both *Ornithological Biography* and *The Viviparous Quadrupeds of North America* would have been far different works without the benefit of Bachman's insight and labors— *The Quadrupeds* might even have foundered.

By contrast to the attention given Audubon, writers have largely neglected Bachman. A biography of Bachman, undertaken by a grandson and ultimately completed by Bachman's youngest daughter, Catherine Bachman, was published in Charleston in 1888. A fine unpublished doctoral dissertation by Raymond M. Bost (1963) focused on Bachman's Lutheranism. A brief but keen biography by Claude H. Neuffer and a few sensitive biographical sketches exhaust the list (Happoldt 1960).

But Audubon and Bachman wrote reams about themselves. Fortunately, much of their voluminous and revealing correspondence has survived. Replete with accounts of their activities, and peppered with questions and answers about their personal and professional lives, this material is the equivalent of a long and intimate conversation. Some of the letters quoted in this book have not previously been used in interpreting the lives of Audubon or Bachman.

My goal is to portray the dynamic Bachman-Audubon friendship by recounting elements of their backgrounds, their experiences, and the shared works of science and art that inspired it. I also hope to draw attention to Bachman's influential station in American science.

Acknowledgments

I AM GRATEFUL to all who helped me with this book, and there were many: Brook Meanley, who in 1978 suggested that I write it, Mike Harwood and Mary Harwood, Ted Rosengarten and Dale Rosengarten, Trudy Rosen, Albert Sanders, Eloise Potter, Georgiana Grimball, Edward Dwight, G. Edmund Gifford, Jr., Anne Coffin, Jane Greely, Richard Haymaker, John Muller, Dave Catlin, Peter Machonis, Laura Townes, David Chamberlain, the William Coleman family, Thomas Morrison, Heyward Horry, William Grimm, John Dennis, Raymond Bost, John Lofton, Katharine Gilliard, Nancy Pringle, Sharon Bennett, Ditty Abrams, William Baldwin, Lester D. Stephens, and William Zimmerman, heir to Audubon's passion for painting birds and his gift of friendship—the substance of this book.

In 1979 the Charleston Scientific and Cultural Educational Fund supported my tour of museums in Henderson, Kentucky, New York, Philadelphia, Washington, and Boston. On this tour I saw the bulk of Audubon's original paintings and read much correspondence, obscure pamphlets, and other papers. Without this generous send-off I could not have written this book.

For access to their libraries, I also thank the following institutions with which John Bachman was associated: St. John's Lutheran Church, the Charleston Library Society, the College of Charleston, and especially dear to Bachman, the Charleston Museum.

This list would be longer but for my forgetfulness and papers lost to hurricane Hugo. For those whose names should have appeared here, but do not, I apologize, and thank you nevertheless.

APSL	American Philosophical Society Library
CMBA	Charleston Museum, Bachman and Audubon
COPP	Library of the College of Physicians
CPL	Cleveland Public Library
EA	Eliza Audubon
HUHL	Harvard University, Houghton Library
JB	John Bachman
JJA	John James Audubon
JWA	John Woodhouse Audubon
LA	Lucy Audubon
MA	Maria Bachman Audubon
MM	Maria Martin
SIA	Smithsonian Institution Archives
SJLC	St. John's Lutheran Church of Charleston
VA	Victor Audubon
WCFP	William C. Coleman, Family Papers
YUBL	Yale University, Beinecke Library

Had I the Wings

Chapter 1

A WALK THROUGH CHARLESTON

T HE MORNING OF 17 OCTOBER 1831 was unseasonably warm. Bubbles of humid air detached from the sun-bathed roofs of Charleston and drifted skyward. Vultures, flapping and sailing, used the updrafts to boost themselves to heights from which they scanned docks, streets, butcher stalls, and corners of walled gardens overgrown by exotic plants for carrion and garbage. The sharp-eyed gliders spiraled lazily above low-flying herons that stroked the air like oarsmen toward saltmarsh feeding grounds along the coast, here and there veering to avoid steeples that projected through city treetops like chalk fingers.

Like the birds in the sky, John James Audubon had set out from his rooming house to survey the Carolina landscape for what it might offer him (Audubon 1969, 1:143). His hazel eyes acknowledged the buoyant birds, then lowered to appraise brick walls that edged the streets. The walls, their gates locked, screened houses and gardens of wealthy citizens. Opened, the doors would give access to piazzas of houses set endwise to the street and even with the edges of the sidewalk.

As Audubon crossed the street he sank into sand that almost topped his shoes. His easy stride was broken. On reaching the sidewalk on the other side, he lengthened his step for another block.

A trying voyage from England, where he had spent the better part of five years publishing *The Birds of America,* had brought him to New York. From New York, he and two helpers had proceeded by boat and coach, sleeping at intervals in boardinghouse beds shared with strangers. The last leg of the trip before reaching Charleston, on rutted roads through pine woods and swamps, was dismal in Audubon's estimation—"no birds, no quadrupeds, no prospects (save that of being Jostled)" (1:143).

His assistants were Henry Ward and George Lehman. Ward was a taxi-

Self-portrait, in pencil, by John James Audubon.
From *Audubon and His Journals,* vol. 1 (New York:
Scribner's, 1897).

dermist, the youngest son of Englishman J. J. Ward, a "bird-stuffer to the King" (Audubon 1900, 1:284). Young Ward's duties were to collect birds and preserve their skins to be sold in England to help defray the costs of the expedition. Lehman, an artist Audubon had met in Pittsburgh when both were penniless, painted backgrounds for some of the birds that Audubon drew. He had worked for Audubon before, in the forests of Pennsylvania.

In South Carolina, the Audubon party found the Peedee River in flood so high it took three hours to cross it by canoe. The three men suffered the worst jostling while traversing the Santee River delta on a causeway made of logs embedded crosswise in the mud. Fifty miles onward, they pulled up at the ferry dock on the east bank of the Cooper River, and saw Charleston across the estuary.

The weary travelers hailed the city with "unfeined delight," crossed the harbor, and settled at once into an expensive boarding house, too tired to scout for less costly lodging. Audubon arose early the next morning. Refreshed by a night in a bed he did not have to share, he left his assistants to sleep late while he went out to canvass the city.

As usual before setting off in search of new birds and subscribers for *The Birds of America,* he had collected dozens of letters of introduction to important people he would seek out along his way. A practiced salesman, he relied on numerous prospects to compensate for few successes per call. Thus he was not surprised by the result of his first Charleston encounter and wrote to his wife, Lucy: "I delivered my letters to Mr. Lowndes who received me as all strangers are when they present a letter of that kind and we parted" (Audubon 1969, 1:143).

The sun climbed higher and he set off again under the live oak and pride-of-China trees that lined the streets and shaded the sidewalks, his long graying hair bouncing lightly on his shoulders. The handsome, athletic stranger may not have looked it, the way he marched down block after block of Pinckney Street (now named Rutledge Avenue), but at forty-six he worried about growing old, afraid he might not live to finish *The Birds of America,* begun eleven years earlier in a desperate scheme to redeem his fortune after bankruptcy and imprisonment in frontier Kentucky.

Though slightly stooped, he was taller than most of the people he brushed past—men on their way to offices on Broad Street; sleepy-eyed sailors groping back to the docks after a night on the town; and Negroes, most of them slaves, a few of them free, and some, slave-owners themselves. He "pushed almost out of town" to reach the home of the Reverend Samuel Gilman, a Unitarian minister educated at Harvard and author of "Fair Harvard," the school song. "There I found a man of learning, of sound heart and willing to bear the 'American Woodsman' a hand" (1:143).

Gilman put away what he was doing and accompanied Audubon back up Pinckney Street to help him find more reasonably priced rooms. Within a block or so, they came abreast of John Bachman's big new house surrounded by trees, flower and vegetable gardens, and an extensive poultry yard and aviary.

Of all Charlestonians, Bachman was the one Audubon should meet, not for rented rooms, but for his knowledge of birds and his contacts with the rich and influential men of the community. Everybody knew of Bachman's interest in the natural sciences. Certainly Gilman knew—his church and Bachman's were next door on Archdale Street, and both men were members of the Charleston Philosophical Society.

The seventeenth of October was a Monday, for Pastor Bachman a day of rest. Gilman and Audubon could not have walked past Bachman's house without observing whether he was at home. When Audubon and Gilman reached the business district, they found better rooms and returned to the street. There Gilman caught sight of Bachman on his horse and called out for him to come and meet Audubon. On hearing the name, Bachman dropped the bridle, leaped from the horse, and bounded to the sidewalk. Audubon later wrote that Bachman gave him "his hand with a pressure of cordiality that electrified me" (Herrick 1968, 2:9).

Audubon looked into Bachman's steady eyes, studied his strong ingenuous face, and saw that "all he said was good and true; and although he spoke of my labors in terms far exceeding what is due to them, I listened to him pretty well assured that he did not intend me to play the part of Gil Blas," the gullible protagonist of a popular French novel. His doubts melted. "Mr. Bachman!! why my Lucy Mr. Bachman would have all of us to stay in his house." Bachman made it clear that Audubon and his men should use his home on Pinckney Street as freely as they would their own "encampment at the headwaters of Some unknown Rivers," and that they

Portrait of John Bachman painted by his son-in-law John
Woodhouse Audubon, ca. 1837. Courtesy of the Charleston
Museum, Charleston, South Carolina.

should stay with him not less than three weeks. "Could I have refused his kind invitation? No! It would have pained him as much as if grossly insulted." On hearing that, Audubon was off to round up Ward, Lehman, and baggage and to move into Bachman's spacious house (2:9).

In the face of Audubon's acceptance of the invitation to move into Bachman's house that steamy day in mid-October, Bachman saddled up and wove swiftly through the streets of Charleston to warn his household to prepare for the strangers. Harriet Bachman and her unmarried sister, Maria Martin, were thrown into a flurry of planning, giving instructions, and dashing from floor to floor to see that their orders were carried out by the servants. With three stories, fifteen rooms, and wide piazzas that stretched the length of the second and third floors, the house was big enough to absorb the guests. Beneath the piazzas, a brick pavement connected house and garden. The lush greenery struggled to be formal, but reflected instead a tendency of the gardener to sacrifice aesthetics for utility.

The guests who had appeared on such a short notice were admitted to the house through tall, narrow, double-doors set with tiny diamond-shaped panes of glass, opening between the piazza and the main hall. They were ushered at once into the formal parlor to meet the family. A crystal chandelier hung from the high ceiling, and its multiple reflections sparkled between three tall mirrors set on the paneled walls.

Introductions done, Audubon took the tour. He was shown "a room already arranged for Henry to skin our birds—another for me and Lehman to Draw," he wrote to Lucy, "and a third for thy Husband to rest his bones in on an excellent bed!" (Audubon 1930, 1:143). Thick masonry walls, which supported the upper stories, kept the "low-ceiled" ground-floor rooms cool. The sills of windows created seats that overlooked the garden. One of the rooms contained nothing but a huge stone tub for bathing. Hot water was piped in from a brick oven outside that took "immense effort" to fire up. The heart of the ground floor was Bachman's study—a library, office, and refuge into which he and Audubon settled for a torrent of talk (Rose 1927). Though both had been in Philadelphia in 1804, they had not previously met.

Bachman had some "capital anecdotes" to tell about their mutual Philadelphia acquaintances, Alexander Wilson and George Ord, but in the end,

Audubon's plans for completing *The Birds of America* dominated the conversation. Bachman became so enthralled with Audubon's project that he wanted everyone in Charleston to know about it. They took a break from talk to write an article for the *City Gazette and Commercial Daily Advertiser* announcing Audubon's arrival. On 19 October 1831, only twenty-four hours after Bachman and Audubon were introduced, Charlestonians read the Lutheran pastor's impression of his new friend:

> Mr. Audubon.—We had yesterday the pleasure of an introduction to Mr. JOHN JAMES AUDUBON, THE CELEBRATED ORNITHOLOGIST, and the worthy successor of the adventurous and enthusiastic Wilson. Mr. AUDUBON has a fine speaking countenance, a scrutinizing and intelligent eye, and features in general, strongly marked with the industrious habit called for by his occupation, while they glow with the enthusiasm necessarily awakened by the poetry—the oriental—of his peculiar undertaking. He visits our section of the country with the view, not only to patronage, but also with the enriching of his work with such ornithological specimens, as the well known abundance of our Southern Plumage, so readily promises. His fame in this pursuit, so generally and widely known, renders any remark upon the character of his mind, perfectly unnecessary. He is spoken in terms of the highest eulogiums, by the foreign Reviews and journals, and independently in our own country has met with a reputation, not less high than well merited. MR. Audubon, we are given to understand, proposes to pass through the Southern states to Florida, and to pass six months in exploring that peninsula. He will then pursue the line of the coast of the Gulf of Mexico to the mouth of the Sabine, ascent Arkansas to its headwaters, thence to the Rocky Mountains, and descend the Columbia River. This tedious, difficult, and perilous journey, Mr. AUDUBON has undertaken for objects purely scientific; and we have a right to expect from his researches through extensive regions of the country, considerable and inestimable additions to our present stock of ornithological knowledge.

Audubon had supplied the rolling American itinerary he hoped to complete, and Bachman surely wrote the glowing personal description and the depiction of Audubon as a scientist. Both contributions were bound to impress the readers of the *City Gazette and Commercial Daily Advertiser,* though Charlestonians who had purchased the work of Alexander Wilson decades earlier may have thought Bachman's claim that Audubon was Wilson's "worthy successor" a little excessive. Certainly Audubon was the successor to Wilson in Bachman's life, and Bachman soon learned not to praise Wilson too much in Audubon's presence, lest he find himself "like a toad under the harrow" (JB to JJA, 22 September 1833, WCFP).

Thus rich Charlestonians, to whom the article was addressed, could be excused if they missed the main point. Bachman failed to tell them what Audubon most needed them to know—that a great artist had come to Charleston to sell them a spectacular collection of hand-colored bird engravings that would stand as a monument to their taste and means; instead, he made it sound as though Audubon were soliciting funds for a scientific expedition. This promotional blunder may explain in part why the number of subscriptions for *Birds of America* from South Carolina, by comparison with, say, Georgia and Massachusetts, ultimately disappointed both men.

But the blame for Audubon's slow start in selling *Birds of America* was not entirely Bachman's. Seduced by his wholehearted adoption into the Bachman family, Audubon failed to capitalize on his first weeks in Charleston, neglecting to solicit subscriptions when he was yet a novelty and interest in his work was at a peak. From the start Audubon saw Charleston as a place to paint and write, to enjoy a wealth of bird life and the warmth of Bachman's household. These left little time for the relentless canvassing he imposed on other cities.

The new friends slipped into a routine that Audubon described in a typically enthusiastic letter to Lucy. "Out shooting every Day—Skinning, Drawing, Talking Ornithology the whole evening, noon and morning," Audubon wrote on the last day of October, "in a word my dear Lucy had I thee and our Dear Boys along I certainly would be as happy a mortal as Mr. Bachman himself is at this present moment, when he has just returned from his Congregation—congratulated me on my days work and now sets amid his family in a room above me enjoying the results of his days work" (Audubon 1969, 1:144).

Audubon was naive to think that Bachman had suspended moral judgment by congratulating him for working on Sunday. The Sabbath of a pastor and the Sabbath of others were not equivalent—in time Bachman would explain the difference to his friend. But Audubon was correct in judging the praise, bestowed in the drawing room *en passant* between services at St. John's, and a few hours of rest upstairs in his house, as thoroughly sincere.

A painting of a yellow-crowned night heron had won Bachman's praise. The drawing glowed with pigment not quite dry. Delicate plumes cascaded down the heron's back. The bird looked up and over its shoulder as though alarmed, and plumes from its crown swept down behind it on the page. Its beak was parted, suggesting a guttural squawk. Bachman, in Audubon's company, had seen precisely that setting during one of the trips they had taken into the wilds around Charleston. He had shot that very heron with Audubon at his side. Audubon's drawing of the heron and Bachman's delight in it were the culmination of their first week together, a week so filled with happiness it would stand as a high point in both their lives (C. Bachman 1888, 129).

During those weeks after they first met, their love for pursuing birds was charged by their enjoyment of each other's company. As though they were boys, they killed birds by the hundreds, matching the atavistic joy of cave dwellers who worshipped the game they hunted and decorated their caverns with colorful renderings of them.

The unrestricted killing of birds and mammals in the early nineteenth century was a common pastime of American men. The supply of birds seemed inexhaustible. To be a man, to win a reputation in the community as a provider, was to have and use the motivation and the skills required to kill wild things. Beyond the sport of it, vicariously for Bachman and directly for Audubon, shooting birds served down-to-earth needs: choice specimens for Audubon to use as models, and the excess, skinned and sold in the booming English market for such things, to finance Audubon's travels. During his first month in Bachman's house, Henry Ward fleshed 280 birdskins of sixty species (Audubon 1969, 1:147).

"Do you not remember, as if it were yesterday," Bachman wrote to Audubon the next winter, "with what triumph we brought down the first 'Blue Herons'? With what a shout we made the Forest echo, when we

Yellow-crowned Night Heron. Courtesy of the Thomas Cooper Library, University of South Carolina.

picked up the 'Yellow-crowned Heron,'" which Audubon had been so anxious to draw. Bachman reminded Audubon, "How we rejoiced when, after taking so wide a tour over the 'Charleston Bridge,' at last we found out where the 'White Cranes' fed; how you cheated me out of a shot; and how we hung the fellows by their long necks on the bushes" (C. Bachman 1888, 130).

Having had his say to Audubon, Bachman pulled a fresh sheet and addressed it to Audubon's younger son, John Woodhouse. "Just ask your father whether he remembers Chisolm's pond—when I missed, I always had an excuse, that my gun was too short, and when he did so, he always said that the Cranes were a Quarter of a mile off." From Chisolm's pond, Bachman and Audubon turned to other Charleston marshes where they shot little blue herons in addition to common egrets (129–30).

When it became obvious that their stock of water birds would satisfy the market for their skins in London or elsewhere, Bachman led Audubon out into the country to collect "Carrion Crows [black vultures] and Turkey Buzzards," which the birdskin buyers also found attractive. They crossed the Charleston Bridge, which spanned the Ashley River, and made their way a few miles upstream to the buzzard roost in a swamp wood on the edge of the river. The friends sneaked through the undergrowth on ground covered with droppings and molted feathers. At the heart of the copse the stench became almost intolerable.

Somber files of the scavengers hunched overhead on branches, shoulder to shoulder, unconcerned. Never hunted, highly regarded as street cleaners, and within the city protected by law, they lacked the experiences that would have made them fear the men then penetrating their redoubt. They watched with disinterest as Audubon and Bachman stationed themselves, raised their guns, and aimed where the birds were packed most tightly (Audubon 1967a, 1, 18).

Thunder in the copse—as for a few minutes the hunters banged away. Bodies thumped down through the branches, but some of the naked-headed birds managed to launch heavily into slow flight, "hissing, grunting, disgorging." The survivors flapped higher and higher, struggling beyond range of the guns, battling the compliant air for altitude (1967, 18).

Bachman and Audubon turned over about twenty corpses to Henry

Ward, who skinned them and dumped the denuded bodies at the foot of Bachman's garden. When their fellows sailed down to cannibalize them, Audubon and Bachman put science above the law, and bagged additional vultures for Henry to skin.

The skinning room became one of the curiosities of the city. Men dropped by to watch the English dandy with the swift scalpel. Dressed as though he were hosting a dinner party, he fretted that his costume was not elegant enough for Charleston gentlemen. Even Bachman's tall austere cook, Thomas, slipped out of the kitchen when he could to stand quietly in the doorway absorbing Henry's techniques, anticipating a day when birdskinning might be his assignment (C. Bachman 1888, 101).

The heat hung on, and after a few weeks the supply of birds to serve as models and specimens slowed. With little to occupy them in the skinning room, Audubon took Henry Ward into the field, where he proved to be as effective with the gun as with the knife. Unfortunately though, his English complexion was not up to the rigors of the semitropics. His employer commented, "We had the weather extremely hot and in all excursions the sand flies have tormented us at a round rate." Because of the sweating and bugbiting, "Henry's Face and Legs have been rendered so sore that the poor Fellow could hardly walk and his Skin is now coming off from all over him—he was fairly frightened and thought he was going to die; he is now much better" (Audubon 1969, 1:147).

Audubon discovered that he did not have to leave the lot in Cannonsborough, a relatively new residential district, to study birds. For several years birds had wandered between the house, the garden, and the aviary in the poultry yard near the slave quarters. Bachman had captured some of these birds himself, friends had supplied others, and the Charleston market afforded a wide selection of local and foreign species. At various times the Bachman aviary was home to cardinals, painted buntings, blue grosbeaks, passenger pigeons, anhingas, and others native to South America and Europe. A ruddy turnstone, Maria Martin's personal pet, had the run of the dining-room table. At meals the bird patrolled the white linen for tidbits as though the cloth were a stretch of mirrored sand lying between the waves and the dunes of a barrier island beach, preferring boiled rice or bread soaked in milk to creatures of the sea (Audubon 1967a, 5:233).

Bachman was very successful in raising ducks to serve on his table. His daughter reported that "one year he raised over three hundred" (C. Bachman 1888, 325–26). In time he published a pamphlet on his method, which recommended feeding the birds buckwheat bran and boiled fish. A farmer following his instructions brought three thousand ducks to the Charleston market in the course of a summer. Translated into French and German, Bachman's pamphlet was used in Europe "especially along watercourses where fish could be obtained" (to JJA, 21 October 1842, WCFP).

Birds invaded Bachman's study. He had wondered if bobwhites could be bred in captivity, which aviculturists before him had tried and failed. Hatched by a bantam hen, several of his bobwhites became so tame they trailed the pastor about the garden and followed him into the study. When Bachman settled at his desk to write, as he did almost every day from four to eight in the morning, the most confiding of the quails settled beside him and nibbled his fingers. If he laid his pen on the desk to free his hand to rub his eyes, this bird would pick the pen up and scamper out of the door with it (Audubon 1967a, 5:63).

Originally housed in the aviary, a brown thrasher, which Audubon called a "Ferruginous Mocking-bird," was given the freedom of the garden. It learned to watch for Bachman to come outdoors with a spade in his hand. While Bachman dug, the thrasher lurked at his heels to snap up tidbits from the turned turf. It became so companionable it slept in the study perched on the back of Bachman's chair, the one with the wide arm that doubled as his writing table. When the study door was left ajar one evening, the vigilant Bachman cat slipped in and ate the thrasher (3:11).

A pair of pileated woodpeckers had better luck. Bachman kept them in his study from the summer of their capture as nestlings into the unusually cold winter that followed. Their home was a cage made of live oak as strong as iron. But the woodpeckers incessantly tested the bars, and one frigid dawn, the hour when Bachman habitually came to his desk to study and write undisturbed by his numerous household, he opened the door and a woodpecker flew from a shattered bookshelf and shot to freedom. The woodpecker left behind went on "hammering away" at Bachman's library as though the owner were not present. Bachman released it, too. Its wide wings cupped the cold air as it bounded to a garden tree where its cell mate waited. As though savoring their freedom, the pair hitched in step around the trunk, and as upon a secret signal took off and vanished into a landscape of smoking chimneys and walled gardens, pale under a rare Charleston dusting of snow (4:227–28).

For all the pageant of birds at Cannonsborough, it was the aviary of Dr. Samuel Wilson that gave Audubon the subject of one of his first Charleston paintings. Dr. Wilson, a year younger than Bachman—and a friend and medical school classmate of Audubon's friend, Dr. Richard Harlan of Philadelphia—lived across Archdale Street from St. John's Lutheran Church (Audubon 1969, 1:148). He and Bachman became friends soon after Bachman settled in Charleston, and the doctor shifted his church affiliation from Episcopalian to Lutheran. Dr. Wilson also adopted Bachman's passion for birds. His wife had died the previous winter, and the lonely physician was drawn to the busy Bachman home.

Audubon was told about Dr. Wilson's ground doves. Someone had collected a pair and their helpless young, and Wilson had purchased them, nest included. Despite the shock of captivity, the doves settled down in the doctor's aviary and without a break took up feeding their squabs. What was more, when that brood fledged, the old doves produced a second nestfull. The opportunity to paint three generations of common ground doves, a species for the first time available to him for inclusion in *Birds of America,* was irresistible. The doctor's doves won Audubon over as "the sweetest birds" he had ever seen, and the composition he designed for them reflected that feeling (1:146).

Excursions into anthropomorphism show up in a number of compositions Audubon devised for *Birds of America,* his work in Bachman's drawing room being no exception. The roles of the friends who frequented the studio—not including George Lehman and Henry Ward, whom Audubon treated as servants—suggest the roles Audubon may have assigned his doves to play in the painting. Like the dove with the squab snuggled against her, Maria Martin routinely mothered the children in her house. Maria Martin also was a close friend and admirer of Bachman and Audubon, the two males displaying bright feathers at the top of the picture. And the wistful gaze of the lonely dove at the left center matched the mood of recently widowed Dr. Wilson.

Ground Dove. Courtesy of the Thomas Cooper Library, University of South Carolina.

Thirty-five years old, since the age of nineteen a member of her brother-in-law's household, art unfolded before Maria Martin on a grand scale. To that point, her experiences as an artist were limited, confined to production of such things as a velvet handbag decorated with carefully painted flowers. Now, a noted artist sat at her side, eagerly teaching her all he could (C. Bachman 1888, 97–98).

Outside the drawing room, in the garden, stood a vigorous young magnolia with shining leaves and cones from which red seeds dangled on snowy threads. Fall flowers bloomed along the walkways. Inside, Maria Martin was lost in concentration as she struggled with depicting the young ground dove, her first bird "painted from life," with Audubon as her instructor. At this point, one bird at a time was enough for her, and she omitted the motherly adult the squab snuggled against, as well as the three male doves perched above.

In one of his weekly letters to Lucy, Audubon credited himself with painting fifteen birds in Charleston during October and November of 1831, and Lehman with finishing them with "views Plants &c," for a total of five drawings (Audubon 1969, 1:147). One background was a full-fledged landscape. Behind a pair of long-billed curlews, Lehman hung a gray watery sky, setting off the harbor, the Charleston skyline, the saltmarsh, and a mud flat. To amuse Eliza, Bachman's second daughter, Lehman deftly brushed a portion of this scene—the city skyline—on a page of a small notebook in which she collected sketches, poems, and sayings (Sanders and Ripley 1985, 51).

Three of the paintings with backgrounds by Lehman can be identified. One is the leafy branch laden with eight green oranges for the ground doves; the others—a green-briar vine for the yellow-crowned night herons and the powdery thalia on which Audubon placed two golden-crowned kinglets—are simple floral decorations set against the white paper (Audubon 1966, plate 236).

Audubon knew that Lucy would welcome news of this productive flurry of painting. Lehman, and Henry Ward as well, had to be paid whether or not they produced. During their twenty-three years of marriage Lucy had suffered through one family financial debacle after another, the low point the bankruptcy of 1819 when Audubon was jailed as a debtor (Herrick 1968, 1:260).

By mid-November, the productivity of the Audubon team in the field and drawing room abated. No "new" birds turned up for Audubon to paint, and Lehman had no backgrounds to draw (Audubon 1969, 1:149). As for Henry Ward, Audubon had showed poor judgment in hiring him in the first place. The pampered young Englishman was devious and irresponsible. His efficiency in serving his employer depended on close supervision, which Audubon was not inclined to give (1:103).

George Lehman, on the other hand, was a man of substance, a professional artist whom Audubon had met in Pittsburgh in 1824 when both were struggling free-lance artists. Seeking, like Audubon, a better market for his art, he accompanied Audubon on a raft down the Ohio River until river-life proved less profitable than he had hoped it would be. When the two artists teamed up in 1829 on Audubon's first return to America from England to replenish his supply of bird portraits, Lehman had demonstrated competence and hard work (1:97). He might have been even more valuable had Audubon been able to teach him his method of drawing birds.

Chapter 2

BACHMAN'S YOUTH

ERE AND THERE, through breaks in the trees shrouding the high hills just south of Schaghticoke in New York, the glittering waters of the Tomhannock and its tributaries were visible. At the foot of the hills, the Tomhannock merged with the Hoosack, and near the juncture of the two streams, tall waterfalls plunged into deep-shaded glens from which giant trees soared beyond the clutch of loggers. One of these glens was a favorite retreat of Johny Bachman, born 4 February 1790 in nearby Rhinebeck. Occasionally, he retired to the hidden place to meditate (C. Bachman 1888, 20; the spelling of "Johny" is taken from an inscription on a flyleaf, to John Quitman, 23 December 1847, APSL).

The sloping fields that skirted the hills and streams were tended by settlers, mostly German, English, or Dutch in origin, and about three thousand slaves of African descent (Bachman 1850, 213). Johny's mother, Eva, came from Germany. His great-grandfather, George Bachman, a native of Switzerland who emigrated to England, came to America in 1753 as secretary to William Penn. Johny's older brothers were Henry and Jacob, who was named after his father. His only sister, the youngest of the Bachmans, was named for her mother.

Johny and his father's slave, George, "whose delight it was to accompany his young master into the woods, and to assist him to entrap animals and birds," were particularly close (C. Bachman 1888, 17). In an indelible childhood memory Bachman was riding through the countryside in a horse-drawn sleigh with George holding the reins. The temperature had plunged. Both riders were lightly dressed, but George wrapped the child in a buffalo robe. After a time of tense groping through the storm, George found the Bachman farmhouse, pulled up to it, and dashed in with his young friend in his arms. Telling the tale many years later, Bachman noted that though *his* ears and nose were "frozen," George, without benefit of the buffalo robe, seemed quite unaffected by the subzero cold (Bachman 1850, 213).

The first of many naturalists John Bachman would count as friends, George was also his first mentor. The black man was a tireless hunter, his interest in the out-of-doors extending beyond mere tracking and killing animals. Bachman recalled that George not only "knew many quadrupeds and birds, but was well acquainted with their habits" (Audubon and Bachman 1989, 90). He remembered that when his interests in natural history turned to serious study, "George was always anxious to aid us in our pursuits."

Bachman's passion for wild places grew stronger as he matured. Repeatedly, in the quiet times of years to come, the views and music of the Hudson River below its juncture with the Hoosack would play through his mind: "river ice thunderously breaking up in spring; long trains of duck and geese . . . crackling along the open water"; and "the wild pigeons and all the birds of heaven made every string of a boy's heart vibrate with joy" (JB to Paul S. H. Lee, 3 September 1827, CMBA). He wrote that from his earliest boyhood, he had an irrepressible desire for the study of natural history (C. Bachman 1888, 15).

Johny sensed, however, that his hard-working neighbors took a dim view of his fascination with nature. Besides, they regarded nature study a waste of time. Pioneer farmers generally held that woods should be cleared, prairies plowed, rivers controlled, and their denizens either eaten at the table or killed as pests. Bachman mused later, "Such were the prejudices existing in those early, unenlightened days against the supposed trifling pursuits of Natural History, that I pursued my investigation by stealth and labored without those guides which numerous scientific works now provide" (17).

When he did discover some "scientific works" in a shop in the nearby town of Troy, the barrier to obtaining them was neither parental nor neighborly opposition, but lack of money. He and George set up a trap line, hoping to catch, skin, and sell the fur of beaver and other animals, and earn enough in the long run to buy the books (18).

Whatever his neighbors may have thought about nature study, his parents nevertheless supported Johny Bachman. Jacob Bachman, after all, permitted his slave to use his time trapping and selling the beaver skins. Eva Bachman went so far as to prepare the "spare room" for her son's study, and bestow on him the special privilege of a cozy fire on cold nights. Reading before the fire gave the young naturalist knowledge with which to test his own ideas in the woods and fields. Before long, with George at his side, he had acquired an "extensive collection of plants, birds and quadrupeds" (18).

But George was not the boy's only teacher. From earliest childhood Bachman was exposed to parental training, and when he reached twelve, Anthony T. Braun, the new pastor of the Lutheran church in Schaghticoke, undertook his formal education (Bost 1963, 9).

Funded as a professor by the estate of Pastor John Christopher Hartwick, who had made a fortune buying and selling Indian lands, Braun's duties under Hartwick's will were to teach languages and introductory sciences to persons who planned to study religion seriously (8). But as Bachman had not yet declared his intention to be a pastor, his first studies under Braun probably were restricted to languages and science as well as assisting with services in St. John's Lutheran Church at Schaghticoke. These were interrupted when he left New York to further his education in Philadelphia.

Young Bachman, about twelve years old, was awed by the urban landscape and the one hundred thousand frenetic people of Philadelphia. By comparison to the well-spaced farmhouses of his home village, here were rows of "private buildings" that stretched from "the Delaware to the Schuylkill" (C. Bachman 1888, 154). Most of the Philadelphia buildings were crowded three-story tenements of red brick, ornamented by steps of white marble. The streets, paved with pebble-stone, were cleaner than any in Europe.

In those wonderful streets, Bachman would recall that "old, fat, huckstering, independent, sturdy dames looking out keenly for the pennies" plied their "one-horse carts filled with churns of milk, and eggs, butter, chickens, and vegetables" (C. Bachman 1888, 154). The sidewalks were a foot higher than the cobble streets so that passengers alighting from carriages could step onto them without being spattered by mud.

Philadelphia was the cultural and scientific heart of the English-speaking New World, home to numerous medical doctors, naturalists, and artists.

European scholars visiting America frequently included Philadelphia on their itineraries.

Already absorbed in natural history studies, John Bachman moved easily into the circles frequented by these men and was inspired and learned from them. By May of 1804, Philadelphia had become familiar to the fourteen year old from Schaghticoke. He was in school Monday through Friday. On Sunday he went to church. And he often could be found on Saturday and during vacation in Bartram's garden, "the usual resort of botanist."

The garden grew at Kingsessing, the Bartrams' twenty-acre estate on the banks of the Schuylkill River just south of town. There John Bartram and his sons had successfully transplanted numerous interesting American plants from places as diverse as Florida, Louisiana, and the shores of Lake Ontario, which Bartram and his son William had scoured for botanical curiosities.

Almost all of the trees of eastern North America were represented in the Bartram garden. In addition to trees, rare and spectacular shrubs blossomed profusely, none more striking than *Franklinia,* a camellia-like beauty father and son had discovered on the banks of Georgia's Altamaha River. Within a few decades of discovery, *Franklinia* had vanished from the wild, surviving only as descendants of plants the Bartrams had cultivated.

Of John Bartram's sons, it was impractical William who had spent the most time searching for plants, and after his father died, it was William whose unflagging interest kept the garden going. Indeed, it was William's constant presence in the garden as much as the glorious collection of botanical rarities that made it a mecca for naturalists. His father had died before his popular and influential book *Travels Through North and South Carolina, Georgia, East and West Florida* (1791) was published.

Bachman began to visit the garden when he was about thirteen years old. William Bartram was then a bent old man in tattered clothes, his contented face shaded by a floppy hat while he patiently broke clods in a flower bed (Savage 1970, 178). He was famous, yet he rarely crossed the boundaries of Kingsessing, even to travel the short distance to Philadelphia for meetings of the American Philosophical Society, of which he was a founder. And apparently, Johny Bachman never became a familiar of William Bartram, perhaps because of the great discrepancy in their ages.

Early in his stay in Philadelphia, Bachman made friends with Alexander Wilson, a Scottish immigrant twenty-two years older than he, and like himself, a newcomer to the garden, yet to make his mark as an ornithologist. Handsome, and with shadowed eyes, Wilson's life was marked by more than its share of conflict and sorrow. His father was a smuggler. His mother a pious woman who wanted her boy to study for the ministry. After his mother died, his stepmother pressed the boy to herd sheep and then to sign on as an apprenticed weaver.

All the while, Wilson yearned for fame as a poet. His verses won recognition, though not in the way he had hoped. A long dramatic ballad, "Watty and Meg," was published anonymously and most readers assumed that Robert Burns was the author. The pamphlet sold unbelievably well, more than one hundred thousand copies, and the publisher rewarded Wilson with a greatcoat, a useful gift because by then the consumptive poet had been locked in prison for writing "The Shark, or Long Mill Detected," a political poem about a Paisley mill owner and how he bled his workers (241–42).

On his release he decided to seek a climate kinder than that of Scotland. A disappointment in love, a theme of his unhappy life, may have reinforced his decision. With more than three hundred other emigrants, the twenty-eight-year-old poet and his sixteen-year-old nephew, Wil Duncan, pressed onto the ship *Swift* for a long, slow, and brutally crowded voyage to America under conditions as hazardous as those on slave ships.

In mid-July of 1794 the *Swift* anchored in the Delaware estuary near the little port of Newcastle, and Wilson and his nephew continued on foot to Philadelphia. Wilson thought that a red-headed woodpecker he shot during the thirty-mile walk was the most beautiful bird he had ever seen. He found employment with Alexander Lawson, a Scottish immigrant like himself, who owned an engraving shop in the city. Restless and homesick, Wilson soon moved on, for a while peddling cloth in New Jersey. Not until the autumn of 1796, as headmaster of Elwood School in Milestown, outside Philadelphia, did he enjoy a measure of contentment. He learned German, the language of his pupils, and mastered the violin, a skill that brought companionship with other musicians. To prepare for his classes and to further his education, he read late into the night.

A scandalous love affair triggered a midnight flight from the village and loss of the best job Wilson ever had. Abandoning everything but his greatcoat, he retreated to a log cabin in backwoods New Jersey and was unhappy there also. In less than a year he returned to Philadelphia, jobless and despondent. His rescue came early in 1802 in the form of yet another call to teach, this one at Gray's Ferry, a mile down the Schuylkill from Bartram's garden, on the opposite side of Philadelphia from Milestown.

Though he had dreaded his return to teaching, Wilson was entering the happiest period of his life. His friend and former employer, the printer Alexander Lawson, suggested he learn to draw, and William Bartram encouraged him to study birds. In the summer of 1803, Wilson combined bird study and drawing when he shot an owl and stuffed it for use as a model. Other models—some living—were brought to his cottage by students. He took up painting birds with the headlong devotion he had given to poetry.

In March of 1804, despite having no experience to speak of in ornithology or painting, Wilson presumed to inform Lawson that he was going to collect, draw, and publish portraits of all the birds of North America. Lawson, a practical man, told him he was crazy.

At this juncture, at the very beginning of his audacious project, the consumptive Wilson needed to identify birds in the field, a skill he had yet to acquire. William Bartram, more or less confined to the garden by old age, assisted Wilson as best he could. However, a young naturalist who had begun to frequent Bartram's garden at about the same time as Wilson suffered no such limitations. Though yet an adolescent, John Bachman had learned to identify the birds of Schaghticoke and Philadelphia by sight and by song as well (JB to author of *The Birds of Long Island*, 4 May 1844, CMBA).

Identifying birds by their songs was practiced by few naturalists of the time. Perhaps Bachman had read about it in a book he purchased from the book shop in Troy and tried it out in the woods. *The Natural History of Selborne* by the great English observer of nature, Gilbert White, had been published in 1789, a year before Bachman's birth, and was widely sold. In it, White wrote of distinguishing between bird species similar in appearance but dissimilar in song.

During the time Bachman frequented Bartram's garden, he also met

Alexander Von Humboldt. On 20 May 1804, in route to France, a ship bearing the great scientist docked at a Philadelphia wharf. Within a week of his arrival the leaders of the city decided that this young but already famous naturalist should confer with President Thomas Jefferson. Charles Wilson Peale, distinguished portrait painter, was appointed Humboldt's escort to Washington.

On the return of Peale and Humboldt three weeks later, a list of Philadelphia men who were eminent in literature and science was compiled and each was sent an invitation to a dinner honoring Humboldt at Peale's Natural History Museum. John Bachman surmised that, though just fourteen, he had been honored with an invitation because he frequented Bartram's garden and studied birds with Wilson (C. Bachman 1888, 391).

On the appointed night, the precocious naturalist climbed the stairs to the second story of the statehouse in downtown Philadelphia and entered the long, narrow, high-ceiling room that housed Peale's collection. Gray marble fireplaces faced each other from either end of the hall. Light from five brass candelabra, each bearing seven candles, played on the guests and illuminated a huge mastodon skeleton, eleven feet at the shoulder, the prize of the Peale collection. Feeling as though he were a guest of honor, Bachman noted that besides himself, among the invited naturalists were only "the two Bartrams, Wilson the Ornithologist, Lawson his engraver, George Ord, and a few others" (390–91).

Introductory speeches were brief: the evening was devoted to the great man. Instead of a long formal dissertation, Alexander Von Humboldt conducted a relaxed question and answer session. For five years Humboldt and his companion, A. J. A. Bompland, had explored Central and South America collecting vast numbers of plants, animals, and rocks. Humboldt's observations about the ways that the physical components of the environment influence the distribution of living things predated the concept of ecology, and may ultimately have been more important than his spectacular collections.

Young Bachman was impressed by Humboldt's knowledge and warm personality, and in turn, Bachman impressed Humboldt. According to Bachman, they met daily for the remainder of the scientist's stay in Philadelphia, and before Humboldt sailed, "He inserted my name in his notebook." Not until Bachman's tour of Europe thirty-four years later, in Berlin in August of 1838 (Happoldt 1960, 157), would they see one another again, but they exchanged letters and Humboldt regularly sent copies of his works to Bachman as they "successively appeared" (C. Bachman 1888, 391–92).

During Bachman's vacation at Schaghticoke later in the busy summer of 1804, he shot and skinned seven or eight jays of a species he had not noted before. He took one of the skins back to Philadelphia and gave it to "the esteemed author of 'American Ornithology,'" thus becoming "the person who first gave intimation to Mr. Wilson that the species [Canada jay] was to be found in the Union," a fact that Audubon later inserted in the text of *Birds of America*. Audubon also wrote that "my friend, the Rev. John Bachman, informed that one caught in a snare that had been set for the common partridge" (Audubon 1967a, 4:121).

Audubon did not mention Bachman by name in the account of the Canada jays (nor did Wilson credit Bachman in the account published later in his *American Ornithology* [1808]), but the location of the observation, "in the upper parts of the State of New York," the citing of Wilson's *American Ornithology,* and the pointed preemption of Wilson's discovery of the jays, points to Bachman. Further, Bachman's daughter Catherine quotes her father as saying, "I was intimate with Alexander Wilson, the pioneer of American Ornithology, and furnished him with the rare birds existing in the Northern parts of New York" (C. Bachman 1888, 94).

Bachman may have influenced Wilson to visit this area. At dawn on an Indian summer day in October in 1804, Wilson and his companions, Duncan and Isaac Leech, the latter a student from Milestown, set off through the forests and streams of the state of New York, sometimes walking, sometimes paddling a little skiff they had rented. They saw several birds they could not identify, including "a white-tailed, dapple-breasted hawk," which an onlooker assured Wilson was "the white-tailed [bald] eagle" (Cantwell 1961, 129).

After visiting Niagara Falls, Wilson and his friends turned homeward, and on 22 November 1804, a heavy snowstorm overtook them. In the snowy trees, Wilson saw four fluffy gray-and-white birds that matched the skin Bachman had given him. Wilson shot three of the birds, and on reaching Philadelphia in December displayed their skins as birds new to the Union. He later learned that Canada jays were quite common in the northern states (127, 132).

ABRUPTLY, WHEN JOHN BACHMAN was about sixteen, he began to cough blood so profuse and bright he thought he had burst a blood vessel (JB to MM, 27 October 1840, CMBA). When the eminent physician, Dr. Benjamin Rush, examined him, he "was given over [given up]," and his treatment, the bleeding and purging that Rush used for most diseases, was terminated.

Thus Bachman was forced, "just as he was about to gain the goal of his ambition," to leave the Philadelphia school he attended without graduating. Wan and despondent, he set off for his parents' farm in upstate New York, made it safely there, and for half a year lay in bed, nursed by his mother. The coughing gradually subsided, his strength slowly returned, and at last he could tramp the woods with George again (C. Bachman 1888, 20, 189).

The years Bachman had spent in Philadelphia associating with naturalists and scientists had changed his view of nature. He no longer focused solely on building up collections of objects; now he also investigated nature's processes and recorded the results in his journal (Audubon and Bachman 1989, 80).

At home in Schaghticoke in March of 1808, with George as his assistant, he began an investigation of weasels, addressing the question, "in what manner their change from brown in summer to white in winter was effected?" (to JJA, 18 February 1833, WCFP). He would test two hypotheses—either the brown hairs of summer dropped in fall and were replaced by white ones, or the brown hairs gradually faded to white. His field work included capture of several weasels, a task made easy by the lust of the bloodthirsty little predators for the raw meat with which Bachman baited his traps.

His observation that hunters in the area were killing so many rabbits disadvantaged by the deep snow it seemed that the population would be wiped out diverted Bachman's attention from the weasels. He decided to capture rabbits sufficient to guarantee a breeding stock, and to hold them for release in the spring. But they were hard to catch until it occurred to

Bachman that he and George might use the weasels already in their cages to help them snare the rabbits.

He and George set off through the snowdrifts with a dog, a strong sack, and a box containing several weasels, each leashed with a cord. The dog put up a rabbit, which darted to the safety of a hollow tree. George and Bachman fished the smallest weasel out of the box, and urged it into the cavity. Frightened, it resisted. The next weasel, itself newly caught, immediately darted in and killed the rabbit—hardly the desired result! George took the fierce little creature to the farm and filed down its teeth. From then on the bold but dull-toothed predator would scoot into the hollows where the rabbits had taken refuge, and the rabbits would bolt out and into the sack that George stretched over the entrance hole. He caught twelve one morning and fifty in about three weeks.

Bachman called off the project. He and George had caught so many rabbits that obviously the rabbits were, after all, in no danger of being wiped out by hunters (Audubon and Bachman 1989, 80).

About a year and a half had passed since Bachman left Philadelphia. His health seemed restored, and considering his options for a career, he decided to read for the law. Idly, his law books set aside for the moment, he thumbed through his father's copy of *Luther on Galatians* and the words, "Thou art no more a servant, but a son, an heir of God through faith," came to him.

He walked up into the hills to "a seat under the shadow of a rock near a stream of water, [which] was for several successive summers our favorite resort for retirement and reading." Giant trees backed by the cliffs edged the stream. About a dozen black squirrels dodged around the trunks and in and out of hollows (Audubon and Bachman 1989, 114).

In this quiet spot, Bachman prayed that his Lord tell him what to do, and the answer that came to the young man was to go and preach to others the glad tidings that had set him free.

Bachman asked to be confirmed. After Pastor Braun administered the rite he invited the neophyte to move into his home in West Sandlake to facilitate his studies (C. Bachman 1888, 20–21).

Bachman's studies with Braun did not interfere with his investigations of local plants and animals. Tempted by a light, early snow, he went into the forest to search for the northern hare. Instead, he found footprints of a more interesting mammal, one he could not identify, though he suspected it was a bear, "a species which even then was scarcely known in that part of the country." He tracked the animal for five miles before darkness prompted him to turn toward home. Snow fell through the night and continued to fall for two more days. Bachman gave up the chase, concluding that the bear had denned up for the winter, and that his chance to collect it "had passed by" (Audubon and Bachman 1989, 92).

Several weeks later George greeted Bachman with news that he had picked up the trail where the creature had crossed a road recently cut through the forest. The partners put their dogs on the trail and followed them to an isolated cabin. Nearby lay the body of a dead horse. Signs proved that foxes as well as the mystery animal had feasted there.

After gorging, the animal had set off on a circuitous path toward the Hoosack River, the route Bachman had taken less than a month earlier when he had first seen the footprints. George and Bachman followed and this time no storm turned them back. They found the animal's den under huge rock slabs on a steep slope beside the frozen river (92).

The hounds rushed in and just as quickly backed out to lick their wounds. Their frantic barking was met by snarls from the cave, and significantly, "a strong and very offensive smell." By prying away a slab Bachman cleared a shot at a shadowy form crouching in semidarkness. To his surprise, it was not a bear he had killed, and for a time he thought he had discovered a dramatic unnamed species. He could not be sure, however, until he returned to the Philadelphia area to study under the Reverend Frederick Mayer. There he would consult Buffon's *Historie Naturile generale et particulare,* and determine that he had shot a "Glutton," or wolverine, not a new species after all, but a rare wanderer from the far north, known for its strong skunklike odor (Audubon and Bachman 1989, 92).

After the conclusion of Bachman's religious training under Braun in West Sandlake, he was instructed in theology by Pastor Frederick H. Quitman of the Lutheran church in Rhinebeck. Born in Germany, Quitman was a graduate of Germany's prestigious University of Halle.

Quitman's influence on Bachman never faded, though Bachman did not study long under him. Frustrated by the lack of employment opportunities in upstate New York, the young student decided to defray his expenses by teaching school. Consequently, he sought out a teaching job at Frankfort, just "east of Philadelphia," near enough to the city for him to study under the Reverend Philip Frederick Mayer, a son-in-law of Quitman. In less than a year Bachman became dissatisfied with his position at Frankfort and began to seek another, one nearer to Mayer's church. The only incident Bachman recorded from the Frankfort interlude was his capture of an exotic featured star-nose mole, his interest in natural history as strong as ever (216).

On a brief excursion into Philadelphia in the spring of 1809, Bachman called on old friends, Wilson and Wilson's nephew, Duncan. Aside from friendship and shared interests, Bachman's meeting with Wilson and Duncan was significant for practical reasons. The Scot and his nephew knew that the post at Elwood School at Milestown, where both had taught, was vacant. They urged Bachman to accept the job if it were offered. It was and Bachman was hired (C. Bachman 1888, 22).

Giant cherry trees shaded Elwood School, west of Frankfort "on Bristol Turnpike, a short distance above Dark Run Lane." The one-story, wooden school building had been enlarged several times as the student body had grown. On Sundays, when a willing preacher happened to be in the neighborhood, services were held in the school, as there was no church nearby. As often as not, however, the students had to walk to church, either at "Germantown on the one side, or Frankfort on the other" (411–13).

Bachman boarded at Mr. Culp's house, a wayside inn that doubled as a weaving shop. Hardly a homey residence, it was, nevertheless, a refuge to the lonely young teacher. He soon made friends with an older Milestown couple, and the woman became for him "a mother when I was far from home." Bachman wrote years later, "I imagine I still see her gentle, quiet face, and hear her sweet welcome." Her garden was one of the most beautiful he had ever seen, bright with tulips, narcissus, and anemones cultivated by her own hand. The flowers were full of fragrance and beauty. "The passion for flowers is contagious, and I found it extended to several others in the neighborhood." It extended to Bachman as well, and a love of gardens enriched the remainder of his life (411–12).

As much as Bachman enjoyed Milestown and its surroundings, he had little enthusiasm for his pupils. They were of all ages, sizes, and sexes, a bewildering mix for one young teacher to instruct as they disliked such basics as Latin, French, and German—precisely the subjects that Bachman had to teach (412). Not much older than the recalcitrant youngsters, he found it difficult to control his classes. But Milestown was close enough to Philadelphia for Bachman to continue his studies with Mayer and to stay in touch with old friends.

The flow of time had lifted Wilson's banishment from Milestown. He "visited us occasionally from Philadelphia," Bachman recalled, "and I always joined him on Saturdays in looking for specimens in Ornithology" (413). Wilson had published the first volume of his *American Ornithology* in 1808 and had undertaken a midwinter trip to the South, collecting birds and selling subscriptions to his work, expected to run to ten volumes. Both goals for his southern tour had been accomplished—subscription sales had been especially brisk in Charleston and Savannah (Savage 1970, 266–67).

Now Wilson faced publication of volume 2, again writing, collecting and painting birds, and selling subscriptions almost single-handed. He reserved for himself the difficult and costly task of etching the copper plates, though he assigned the coloring of the prints to others.

His need for new birds and more money became so pressing that he undertook a second winter journey in January of 1810, when Bachman was at the midpoint of his year at Milestown. Traveling alone and mostly by foot, Wilson reached Pittsburgh in February, purchased a little boat, and paddled through sleet, snow, and floating ice on a route that took him hundreds of miles down the Ohio and Mississippi rivers. After many diversions and some frightening incidents, he made his way to New Orleans and the balmy Gulf of Mexico, wandered through the Southeast, and returned to Philadelphia in August, completing a journey that would have tested the strongest of men, not to speak of the frail and ailing naturalist (280).

Wilson had seen things few would ever see again in the primitive, doomed, American forests. Big Bone Lick in Kentucky, with its all but inexhaustible deposits of mammoth and bison skeletons, was rich in primeval visions. There the sky was all but closed one day by a flock of passenger pigeons he estimated to number "two thousand, two hundred and thirty million, two hundred and seventy-two thousand" (277). One day he saw a dense flock of Carolina parakeets, their plumage speckling the large tree they perched on with iridescent green, orange, blue, and yellow. In a coordinated maneuver, the parakeets lifted from the branches and fluttered down to carpet the earth with their color (273–74).

On his return to Philadelphia, Wilson surely was pleased to talk with his friends about the birds he had seen, but apparently he did not mention, even in the privacy of his closely held journal, what happened in a store near Louisville. There, a long-haired merchant with a local reputation as a naturalist, studied Wilson's engravings closely, and seemed poised to subscribe, when his partner muttered in French, "Yours are better." The merchant, John James Audubon, then pulled several of his own paintings from under the counter and spread them for inspection. Audubon did not subscribe to Wilson's work after all—perhaps he could not afford it—but before Wilson continued on his journey, Audubon discussed ornithology with him and guided him through the local countryside (274–75).

Travel-worn, Wilson returned to Philadelphia in August, his health failing and finances faltering. Nevertheless, he wrote and painted and etched copper plates to the limits of his strength. One gray November morning in 1811, he was sitting in his room painting the "White-headed Eagle" when a visitor appeared. The gaunt Scot looked into a familiar face. John James Audubon had trekked east to borrow money for a business venture, and had seized the opportunity to return the call Wilson had paid him in Louisville. Despite Wilson's addiction to his work, he left the eagle on the table and escorted Audubon to the exhibit rooms of the famous artist Rembrandt Peale. Featured in the exhibit was a painting of Napoleon crossing the Alps (Audubon 1900, 2:203).

Wilson meant to please by showing Audubon around, and Audubon found the exhibit interesting, but he had not sought out Wilson merely to guide him around an already familiar city. A leisurely discussion of ornithology, bird paintings, and Wilson's progress in publishing them would have been far more stimulating. As it was, Audubon felt slighted by being rushed off to Peale's studio. He would not forget the slight, imagined or real, nor would he forget the vivid image of the eagle that Wilson was carefully finishing. A fierce but unnaturally slender raptor clutches a nondescript little fish in its claws. The essence of Wilson's *tableaux* would appear in Audubon's *Birds of America* nearly two decades later, a bold composition, this eagle, correct in every proportion, and its prey, a large voluptuous catfish animated by Audubon's genius (Audubon 1900, 2:203).

Desperate to complete *American Ornithology* before his death, Wilson painted, coughed, wrote, and sold subscriptions. Friends helped him, but Wilson had so distanced himself from people that he could count them on the fingers of a hand: his cousin Wil Duncan, William Bartram, his confidante Sara Miller, the peculiar George Ord, twenty-five-year-old heir to a Philadelphia fortune, and John Bachman.

In August 1813 the ill-starred Scotsman collapsed and died suddenly, having just published the seventh volume of *American Ornithology* and with the eighth underway. Bachman recalled watching him die "by inches with poverty neglect & mortification." Wilson, little known during his life, won fame on his death. "They [some Philadelphia naturalists] remind me of the wife that first broke her husbands heart," Bachman would write to John Woodhouse Audubon twenty years later, "& then jumped into his grave desiring to be buried with him" (to JJA, 25 March 1835, CMBA).

Ord took up Wilson's work as though it were his own. He finished the eighth volume and wrote the ninth himself, completing what was hailed at the time as the finest work on birds yet published (Cantwell 1961, 258).

By summer 1810, Bachman had left Milestown to teach at the school of St. John's Lutheran Church of Philadelphia. Failure to maintain discipline—he sent a letter to the vestry complaining about the behavior of his students—boded ill for his future there, and an item in the minutes of a Board of Trustees meeting of July 1811 refers—not to John Bachman—but to a "Charles Stellwagon" as the school "Preacher" (Bost 1963, 63–64). Bachman remained in Philadelphia despite the loss of his post, however, and was listed as a communicant at the Good Friday service at St. John's in 1812, continuing his theological training under Philip Frederick Mayer (65).

When Anthony Braun, pastor of the Gilead pastorate, died in March 1813, Bachman was invited to replace him (86). Bachman had been under Mayer's instruction in or near Philadelphia for more than three years, supporting himself mostly by teaching. He had earned a "simple licence to preach" and was delighted with this opportunity to return to the community of his childhood. As the busy new pastor of the Gilead pastorate, he baptized forty-eight babies during the eighteen months he served his first pastorate, yet he still found time to study natural history (88).

In Schaghticoke that summer Bachman watched a pair of woodchucks readying their den for hibernation. Wondering if indeed it were true, as one authority had written, that "their burrows contain large evacuations in which they deposit large stores of provisions," he marked the spot for later inspection.

A light November snow softened the air, and frost had begun to creep into the soil when he turned his attention back to the burrow. George opened it and Bachman inspected the fat torpid rodents snug in a nest about twenty-five feet from the entrance, but he found no stored provisions. Continuing the experiment, he buried the woodchucks under a haystack. The female died during the first sharp cold snap, but the male survived and Bachman transferred him to the cellar where he slept the winter through.

In fine shape when Bachman looked at him late in February, he was nowhere to be seen two days later. The groundhog had roused from his winter "sleep" and wandered off, demonstrating to Bachman's satisfaction that "there was certainly no necessity for a 'store of provisions' for him" (Audubon and Bachman 1989, 20).

At some point during the crowded months of Bachman's first pastoral year, "mild, amiable, pious" William Duncan spent a week at Schaghticoke. Duncan and his uncle had lived in America for seventeen years, each the other's only relative and closest companion. Now Wilson was dead, and in this time of loss it was natural for Duncan to seek out the young pastor who had been the friend of both. He brought Bachman a gift, an India ink drawing of the Milestown schoolhouse, a token of their years in Philadelphia (C. Bachman 1888, 413). Duncan was perceptive. Bachman had indeed begun to miss literate city-people who could satisfy, as Mayer had expressed it, Bachman's "laudable thirst for information" (Mayer to B. A. Markley, 30 September 1814, SJLC).

Church, social affairs, and natural history experiments all were abruptly interrupted in the spring of 1814 when consumption struck Bachman again. Hemorrhaging of his lungs, which had driven him from school, resumed with such strength that he was advised to seek a southern climate. Risking a voyage during the late summer and early fall hurricane season, he was at sea for several months. "I took a voyage to the West Indies, and recuperated greatly," he wrote (C. Bachman 1888, 26).

While Bachman was in the Caribbean, out of touch with the rest of the world, the vestry of St. John's Lutheran Church of Charleston, South Carolina, communicated with both Frederick Quitman and Frederick Mayer requesting help in securing a pastor. For three years their congregation had been without one, depending on an Episcopal priest to conduct Sunday services. Mayer and Quitman recommended three young pastors, none of whom would accept the call. Despite Bachman's excellent qualifications neither Quitman nor Mayer had considered him as a candidate, thinking him "so comfortably settled" in his home community that offering him the post would be fruitless; "but in this instance," Mayer wrote to Charleston after Bachman had returned from the Caribbean and accepted the position, "my expectation was agreeably disappointed" (Mayer to Vestry, 29 September 1814, SJLC).

Mayer attributed Bachman's acceptance of the Charleston call to the "Severity of his labours," to his service of three churches, and his longing to associate with intellectual people. Bachman may also have had in mind the benign Caribbean climate that had brought him remission and the similar climate in Charleston (Mayer to Vestry, 29 September 1814, SJLC).

The people of the Gilead pastorate reacted to the news that Bachman was leaving them with disbelief. They insisted that rather than resign, he should accept a nine-month leave of absence, hoping that his health would improve and that he would return to Schaghticoke (Bost 1963, 94).

Chapter 3

THE MARTINS OF CHARLESTON

O N 17 DECEMBER 1814, John Bachman began the long stagecoach ride to South Carolina. He had received from the vestry of St. John's Lutheran Church a letter of credit to finance the journey and the advice that "this is the most favorable season for a journey to Charleston"—meaning, of course, the most favorable season for avoiding the deadly storms and fevers that haunted the Carolina coast in warm weather (Vestry and Wardens to JB, 14 October 1814, SJLC).

Bachman stopped off at Rhinebeck to attend a meeting of the Ministerium called especially on his account, and in the old church where he had been christened, he accepted ordination bestowed by the "learned and eloquent" Dr. Quitman. "A boy can pitch a pebble [from the Rhinebeck church]," he wrote to Quitman's son years later, "to the humble stone house where I was born" (inscription on a flyleaf, to John Quitman, 23 December 1847, APSL). Quitman's son by then had become a general in the army of the United States.

Bachman also visited Philadelphia on the way, and preached at the church of his "ever faithful friend," the Reverend Mayer. Then he was fully committed to a tortuous twenty-nine-day journey overland to Charleston.

Eight times along the way the coach broke down or overturned. In addition, America was at war with Great Britain again, and Bachman saw fresh graves and smoldering ruins in the vicinity of Baltimore and Washington (C. Bachman 1888, 27). Arriving in Charleston early in January, he watched its citizens work on defense lines "around the land-side of our city—even ladies went there with hoes and spades" to cheer the men. Bachman joined the effort, "for it was our common country to be defended" (C. Bachman 1888, 28).

The congregation settled down expectantly on the January Sunday in the

St. John's Lutheran Church of Charleston when John Bachman preached his first South Carolina sermon. They were prepared to see, hear, and judge the young man who would fill the pulpit that had been without a pastor for four troubled years. One woman noted her impressions: "His height was medium; his figure slender; his complexion fair; features regular and eyes blue. He looked very young—though in his 25th year. His voice was strong clear and sweet. When the services were ended, we stopped to be introduced, and his bright smile immediately won our hearts" (29).

The Martins—the two unmarried sisters, Harriet and Maria, and their mother, Mrs. Rebecca Solars Martin—were among the families Bachman met. The deceased grandfather of the sisters, John Nicholas Martin, had played a pivotal role in the early history of St. John's.

John Nicholas Martin and his rural German family had joined a group of Bavarian emigrants bound for America and had landed in Philadelphia in September 1754. A short time later the group moved to North Carolina. After about two years, the colony found a permanent home at Dutch Fork, South Carolina, an area between the Broad and Saluda rivers, near the site of the future capital of the state (Townes, no date, no page numbers).

Pastor Martin served several small Lutheran churches in the community, and in November 1763, he took charge at St. John's Lutheran Church in Charleston for a brief tenure. In 1767 he was called to a growing Lutheran community located about midway between the sea and the South Carolina mountains.

Only seven years after he had left Charleston, however, Pastor Martin returned to preach again at the Archdale Street church. He established a farm on the outskirts of the city for his wife, Ann Catherine, two daughters, and five sons, all named John. The youngest, John Jacob, a babe in arms when the family first came to the city in 1763, would make a name for himself before he left Charleston (C. Bachman 1888, 10–11).

Charleston was among the first colonial cities to be attacked by British forces trying to put down the American Revolution in 1776. The Martin farm lay across the path that the redcoats took to approach the city. To forestall enemy use of the farmhouse, the American defenders burned it. Out-maneuvered, the British withdrew, and Martin rebuilt. The redcoats returned in 1780, and this time it was they who torched the house. The enemy chose to ignore Martin and his church—perhaps in deference to German mercenaries in their own forces. But when Martin had the temerity to refuse to pray for their king, they boarded up the church, confiscated his property, and banished him. Then, in a seesaw campaign for Charleston, the king's men were repelled, and again John Nicholas Martin rebuilt his farmhouse. He died in it in July 1795, surrounded by descendants (Townes, no date, no page numbers).

At twenty-six, John Jacob Martin, hard working and widely respected, married Rebecca Solars, a widow two years his junior who brought with her "a decent competency, for he himself had nothing" (Stroble 1825, 4). Within twenty years he had nursed the Solarses' nest egg into a fortune. Among several children was a daughter, Harriet, born 8 October 1791, and her sister, Maria, born 6 July 1796.

In 1810 Jacob Martin fell desperately ill. His family urged him to take a tour of the North. He did, and in Baltimore he met Elizabeth Pennington and fell in love. Unwilling to give up his family, his mistress, his community, his lucrative career, and his prominent place in society, he brought his mistress to Charleston and housed her in "a secluded part of the city" (Stroble 1825, 4–6).

After a while, gossip began to spread about the arrangement, and word of it eventually reached Pastor Martin Strobel, a son-in-law and nephew of Jacob Martin. Strobel tried to put down the rumors, hoping the affair would run its course, but those "pests of society, tale-bearing old women," were not content until Rebecca Martin "became possessed of the fact." Charleston became too small a place for the lovers, who fled to Philadelphia (6).

Strobel commented in a footnote about the affair that "Mr. Martin, previous to his leaving Charleston, did settle considerable real and personal property upon his family." However, Pastor Strobel was not impressed. "This was nothing more than justice. They [Jacob Martin's wife and daughters] would much rather have lived in poverty with him, for they desired no other wealth, than the happiness his reputation and kindness afforded them" (6).

Although Charleston was braced for war when John Bachman first arrived on 10 January 1815, a peace treaty had already been signed with England. Word of the treaty had traveled so slowly that no one in the city knew about it, and the suffering of the people went on for several months after the war was officially over.

Winter, too, relaxed. The return of spring and the presence of a talented young disciple of Martin Luther in the pulpit seemed to awaken the congregation from four dormant years, and sixty-four people were confirmed to the faith at the Easter service (C. Bachman 1888, 27–29).

With its dark interior, naked beams, a chancel without rails, and a tiny pulpit that hung like a bird nest high on a wall, the half-century-old church could no longer adequately serve the congregation. Before Bachman arrived, plans for a larger and grander St. John's had been commissioned from Charles Fraser, a distinguished Charleston artist and architect. The Fraser plans envisioned a white-columned church as elegant as any building in the city, a reflection of the good taste and wealth the congregation had achieved in the new country. One deft architectural nod to the Lutherans of rural Germany was added later—a fluted, onion-shaped cupola topped by a sharp spire.

Sweltering days and buzzing clouds of mosquitoes in 1815 brought an early summer outbreak of the dreaded stranger's fever whose victims turned yellow and often died. The wise old men of St. John's had not ceased to fret about the health of their thin, pale minister. They urged Bachman to leave Charleston for the duration of the sickly season.

He declined. In time of trouble, he insisted, he would stand with his people. The vestry countered with a resolution to close St. John's for three months. Bachman read the fiat from the pulpit, laid the paper down, and made a defiant personal statement—for so long as the doors of St. John's remained closed, he would conduct services in a vacant chapel that he had rented with his own money for all who wished to attend (C. Bachman 1888, 31–32).

A message from Schaghticoke that his father had suffered a stroke and was not expected to survive broke the impasse between Bachman and the vestry. Now he must go north, compelled by duty to his father. Episcopalian bishop Theodore Dehon agreed to preside in Bachman's absence at the laying of the cornerstone for the Fraser church, scheduled for August 1815 (32, 35).

Bachman found his father remarkably cheerful, and if he had not known that his disorder was "a lingering and dangerous one," the son would have had hope for the father's quick and complete recovery. He settled down and as best he could, comforted his old parents and ministered to the Gilead pastorate. These Lutherans had neither sought nor found a new pastor—they still considered John Bachman their own.

One of the first things Bachman's old father told him was that on the next Sunday he should preach on *marriage*. Sunday came and Bachman was prepared. Even before the service began, however, fifteen couples marched into the church. They answered the ritual questions put to them by the surprised pastor and joined hands to be pronounced "man and wife." The poised, thin minister was told that ever since it had become known that he was on the way to Schaghticoke, "Some had delayed their weddings, and others hastened their preparations" (31–32, 34).

Despite the comfort John Bachman gave his parents and his Gilead congregations by his presence, Bachman longed for news of cold weather in South Carolina, which would allow him to return to Charleston. As he explained in a letter to one of his friends there, "I can assure you that though my native spot is dear to me, yet nothing could induce me to remain [in Schaghticoke]. Charleston I consider as my home; and unless the inhabitants treat me with greater neglect than they have heretofore done, they will have to keep me for life" (34–35).

On 23 January 1816, just a year after John Bachman had taken over the pastorate of St. John's, he and Harriet Martin married in the historic oft-restored Martin farmhouse. After the wedding, Pastor and Mrs. Bachman moved into the parsonage on Cannon's Bridge Road.

There had been indications of their attachment even before he went to New York to visit his ill father, probably everyone in the congregation knew that John Bachman and Harriet Martin had become very good friends. The young pastor had been naive enough to trust the delivery of his love letters to young Jacob Schirmer. The boy made no secret of his commission.

Even so, there were reasons beyond requited love that caused the congregation as well as Harriet Martin to be pleased. The three Martin women now had a male to protect them for the first time since Jacob Martin and Elizabeth Pennington fled Charleston. The laws and the judiciary of the time offered women little protection for their persons or properties. Even the strongest woman needed a trustworthy man as a guardian, and John Bachman radiated authority and trust.

As for Bachman, he too had reasons beyond love to celebrate his wedding. By marrying Harriet Martin he sealed membership in the Lutheran community of Charleston, and a great deal of property and money came under his control.

Maria Rebecca was born to Harriet and John Bachman on 19 December 1816, and Mary Eliza a little more than a year later. By early summer of 1827 the parsonage in the western part of the city was quite crowded. Bachman babies appeared every fifteen months on the average. And the household also included Maria Martin and her mother, Rebecca Martin. Even from the outside, the parsonage had a look of runaway fecundity, ringed by flourishing vegetable and flower gardens, duck pens, and a chicken yard lorded over by a chanticleer so insistently vocal that the neighbors complained.

Jacob Bachman of Schaghticoke died on 11 March 1824, but word of his death was so long in reaching Charleston his son did not undertake the long trip home for the funeral. Not until three years later was Bachman required to go north to help settle his father's estate. Expecting to return within six weeks, he left his protégé, John G. Schwartz, in charge of the church (C. Bachman 1888, 44).

Harriet Bachman stayed with her family. She bore responsibility for seven daughters, including Clara and Ellen, the sickly twins still in their matched hand-woven cradles. Already Cordelia, John, and Henry had died in infancy, and Harriet felt unwell most of the time, several months into her eleventh pregnancy.

Maria Martin accompanied her brother-in-law to New York. Summer and its fevers had returned, and to travel alone was to risk illness in the doubtful care of strangers. Maria had been at Bachman's side as long as Harriet had been. Maria sewed for the children, taught them French and reading, and pitched in when hard work had to be done. She told stories, sang, and made up lyrics and poems that amused adults and the children. Small—at her heaviest she weighed barely a hundred pounds—she was not truly beautiful. She could, however, summon a reserve that let her blend in with the crowd. Or she could play the perfect hostess or traveling companion, vivacious and witty, the center of attention.

From the moment John Bachman and Maria sailed from Charleston until they departed the ship in New York they labored under the shadow of illness and death. Bachman had hardly closed his eyes for his first nap on the ship when Margaret Bowen, a child of Episcopal bishop Nathaniel Bowen, fell ill, lapsed into a coma, and died. Faced with burying her daughter at sea, Mrs. Bowen was disconsolate. To avoid the traumatic ritual in a hostile setting, Bachman circulated a petition among the passengers to give up cold drinks despite the heat of the season, in order that the ice aboard could be packed around the small body. Bishop Bowen, who had preceded his wife and daughter to New York, met his wife at the dock, and their daughter's funeral was held on land (45).

Until the child was buried, Bachman had not realized how nearly exhausted he was, but he had little time to dwell on it. He reserved a coach leaving for Schaghticoke early the next morning. His rest that night was cut short by the stage driver who "knocked us up at 3 AM." They boarded the coach, which wound endlessly on dusty roads through mountainous terrain. At journey's end, Bachman thought it remarkable that despite so trying a trip by ship and coach he was still in excellent health (45–46).

His mother, however, was on crutches after a fall and was living with his sister. The doors and windows of the old home had been nailed up. The executors of his father's estate carefully explained that there could be no settlement before the harvest brought some money into the community, a circumstance at least two weeks off. Depressed by the "melancholy scenes," Bachman and Maria Martin prepared to board the packet boat *Albany* for a voyage, "if I may use that expression," Bachman said, up the recently completed Erie Canal (46).

The Erie had been open to travel less than two years when John Bachman and Maria Martin set off to float the length of the canal from Albany to Buffalo. Canal-boat travel was a pleasant novelty—no waves, potholes, broken wheels, axles, or tipped coaches, only a dreamy glide behind mules that plodded along several hundred feet ahead of the packet. "The boats pass each other almost as easily as wagons in King street," Bachman wrote. Katydids, birds, and even rustling leaves were heard by the attentive naturalist; occasionally the muted sounds of village life also reached him. Several times the canal itself soared across turbulent rivers on aqueducts so nearly perfect that Bachman marveled at them more as art than engineering (47, 68).

The narrow craft was gently propelled by horse power through the countryside at a sedate four miles per hour. Purple milkweed, columbine, and other summer wildflowers leaned out from the banks almost close enough for the passengers to touch. Every now and then their perfume drifted over the flatboat. His interest in botany aroused, Bachman leaped ashore while the packet paused in the locks. He plucked blooming specimens and presented them to Maria to preserve for him. In the middle of that pleasant first outing on "Clinton's Ditch," he thought of Harriet and took half an hour to write to her (46, 68).

At Lockport, twin sets of five locks promised a change in the temper of their journey. In mighty twelve-foot rises one of the sets lifted the canal boat sixty feet to the crest of a rock ridge where the canal had been cut astride a six-mile ridge to Buffalo on Lake Erie. Three of those miles had been gouged from solid rock. John and Maria had left quiet water behind.

" 'Tis folly to attempt a description" of Niagara Falls, the pastor wrote to friends in flat Charleston, where gentle tides eased in and out of an estuary several miles wide. "The great waters of the Erie have been congregated together, pressed into a narrow space, roaring and foaming angrily to be released, and they come with one awful plunge, tumbling down—down the dark abyss. The earth trembles, the spray arises up the heavens, forms itself into clouds and passes away" (68, 69).

John and Maria lingered at Niagara Falls for several days before boarding a balky steamboat that took them from Buffalo down Lake Ontario to the St. Lawrence River. The boisterous lake made Bachman as seasick as he had ever been at sea. The boat was forced to take refuge in a little port for the better part of a day to wait out a blow. On the lake again, the engine kept breaking down, intermittently leaving the boat dead in the water, rolling and plunging with every monster wave, while below the crew fumbled with a troubled boiler. Fortunately, the hull of the craft was well designed, and though Bachman was uncomfortable, he never doubted that the boat would weather the storm. Finally, a favorable gale pushed the travelers toward their destination; otherwise, Bachman mused, they might never have cleared the lake (48).

They entered the St. Lawrence with its "beautiful, romantic views"— a medley of rocky shores, widely separated log cabins dwarfed by giant hemlocks, more than a thousand islands, some towering like castles and others aligned like village cottages along a lane, and tumultuous rapids. The boat shot down one nine-mile stretch in twenty exhilarating minutes. The lighthearted Canadians "sang, laughed, and jumped." Caught up in the excitement, the clear voice of Maria Martin rang out above the rest with "the boat song." It was the climax of the trip. Bachman and Maria would treasure their memory of that passage down the rapids as the most exhilarating in all their travels (69–70).

On 7 August 1827, satisfied that his mother need not want for money for the rest of her life, John Bachman walked out of the final meeting of the executors of his father's estate. That assurance, however, was not sufficient to dispel the sadness of cutting the last material ties with his boyhood. The silent deserted old home itself seemed lonely. Bachman's heart ached with the contrast of his happy trip with Maria and the aura of old age and death in Schaghticoke. He longed to see his children and Harriet (51, 54).

Before John and Maria departed for Charleston, they made courtesy calls. On 8 August he and Maria boarded a steamboat up the Hudson to visit an uncle, and spent a night in his home. Bachman slept badly. The next day he rode to Rhinebeck on an obstreperous horse to call on Frederick Quitman, then just three years short of ninety. Bachman returned to his sister Eva's home with a slight fever. By nightfall his fever had risen, and he awoke on 11 August shaken to realize that he was very ill. He and Maria decided to flee upstate New York and try to reach New York City to obtain suitable medical assistance (51, 54).

They dashed to the river to catch the next steamboat, but the craft had pulled away from the State Dock at Rhinebeck just minutes before they arrived, and they watched helplessly as it wheeled into the current and pointed downstream. Back in town they managed to find a bed where Bachman could rest until the next boat, scheduled to take passengers across the river in the afternoon.

A heavy summer storm pelted the Hudson in the afternoon. Prospective passengers packed onto a launch dispatched to pick them up from the Rhinebeck bank of the river. Water lapped over the deck boards, frightening everyone. But the launch struggled safely across, and the steamboat docked on schedule.

Bachman was so weak that crewmen had to half-lead, half-drag him aboard. The sight of a man so obviously ill panicked the other passengers, who took to their heels "like a flock of frightened sheep." Unfortunately, to reach the bunk assigned to him, Bachman had to be dragged past the passengers again. Again they bolted. Sick though he was, Bachman wryly observed that some of these people would have leaped over the rail had they continued to be chased (55).

Hardly had Bachman reclined on his bunk than the captain of the steamboat loomed over him with questions. Fearing that because he was ill he would be ejected from the ship, put off at some forsaken spot where no one could help him, Bachman answered questions the only way he could—frankly.

The captain left without giving a hint of what he might decide to do. He was not present, fortunately, when Bachman fainted, revived, and fainted again. With each loss of consciousness Bachman became more desperate. The expulsion from the steamer never took place. But the threat, his unabated fever, and his lapses of consciousness, led to "a most dreadful night" (55).

At sunrise the steamboat docked in New York and Maria Martin sent a note into town asking for help from Mr. Mortimer, whom they had met on the *Albany*. Mortimer insisted that Bachman be taken to his home, where he could be nursed. Barely conscious, the pastor managed to rouse himself and declined the offer, which he feared would endanger Mortimer's family. Instead, Bachman and Maria moved into the Broadway boarding house of Mrs. Waldron and called one of New York's most skilled physicians to treat him.

The doctor prescribed cupping—"a horrible operation," in which a glass vessel emptied of air by a flame was clamped over a fresh cut on Bachman's forehead. Bachman's blood slowly flowed into the vacuum. The treatment worked, he thought—"It greatly relieved my head—the principle seat of the disease" (55).

At first, Bachman hoped that the fever would subside promptly and that he and Maria could sail to Charleston, but it was unrelenting. He suffered a burning thirst and a throbbing headache, and to his physician's consternation, the fever took on a "typhoid form," a turn that moved the patient beyond his skills.

"At last," Bachman recalled, "my eyesight was gone—the whole world was shut up in darkness." He knew from wide pastoral experience that in such cases death followed blindness. "The conviction flashed over my mind—here your earthly pilgrimage is to be brought to a close." It seemed strange to be dying, to be torn from his wife and seven "interesting children." Then he remembered the biblical promise that widows and fatherless children would be taken care of (55–56).

He had lived with Harriet for almost twelve years. Her devotion and affection had made those years the happiest of his life. Never had two people lived more harmoniously together. To die so far from her and the little girls seemed terrible. He tried to think about his will. In the past decade there had been many changes in his property. He lost the thought, the details of his property out of reach of his feverish mind (55–56).

"Is my heart right with God?" He had been "rather wild" in his young days. Reconstructing the scene later as he wrote in his journal, he began a list of his transgressions, thought better of it, and inked them out. He was comforted by the thought that he had early "commenced the study of divinity, and undeviatingly pursued the path of integrity and usefulness." He was thinking more clearly. "Through the mercy of a Savior, I hoped I could look forward to the salvation of my soul." At that moment, Bachman felt "an inexpressible satisfaction and joy within." He was in the hands of his God, and "nothing that this world can afford, can ever be equal to it. There were no forebodings, no fears, no doubts, and I was enabled inwardly to say, 'Oh death, where is thy sting. Oh grave, where is thy victory'" (56–57).

Six days later, on the night of 23 August, an excruciating pain settled on the back of his neck. Through the pain, the soft light of dawn flooded the room. "Great God—I could see! I looked, and looked again, and the light seemed to come upon me like an angel's visit, to bid me live" (57).

By 31 August, he felt so much better he decided to write a cheering letter to Harriet about something that had taken place outside the room of his struggle with death. Maria, who had never left his side, had asked a friend to help get him to "Thornburn's establishment for rare plants." A chair was brought out at Thornburn's and Bachman long contemplated the beauty of living things. When he had absorbed all he could from where he sat, he and the chair were shifted to another spot. His mind traveled the globe as he mused on the exotic collection—"the Indian Rubber, with leaves still larger and more glassy than the Magnolia Grandiflora—a Cactus Triangularis in full bud—one plant from South America, whose leaves, colored by nature, formed a handsome flower" (58).

A letter from New York could be mailed and delivered in Charleston in five days if consigned to a swift packet that sailed at once and caught favorable winds. Or a letter might languish for weeks after posting, or vanish. The letter that reached Charleston on Sunday morning, 26 August 1827, was one of the swift ones. It brought to Bachman's adopted city the first word of his terrible illness (63).

Schwartz, the student Bachman had left in charge, read the letter and reacted quickly. The congregation was gathering at St. John's for the Sunday service, but Harriet Bachman had not yet arrived. Schwartz cancelled the service and raced to the Bachman residence, hoping to reach Mrs. Bachman before she left the house (63).

She was at home, and he told her the news. Devastated, she kept to her room for a week, Schwartz spending much of that time trying to "sustain and cheer her." She was, he wrote, "in a state of suspense as distressing as it was awful." It may have been just as well that "the mails were constantly failing," for the tidings in the letters from New York "would only have served to extinguish the least glimmering of hope" (63).

Every day, praying for mail with better news, Schwartz and Bachman's closest friends, Dr. Samuel Wilson and the merchant William Kunhardt went to the post office. Crowds of anxious people gathered there daily in hopes of a letter. The outpouring of love and concern for John Bachman so moved the impressionable Schwartz that he wrote, "I think that I could die easy and happy, if I had such a congregation weeping for me, and praying for my welfare" (64–65).

Bachman's convalescence in New York stretched from weeks into months. Despite being "yellow as a pumkin" and suffering from partial loss of vision, he and Maria bravely attempted a tour of New England to pass the time constructively. They ventured as far north as Boston. Frequently fever frightened them along the way, but in each incident the fever soon subsided, and at last, late in November, news reached the exiles of a heavy frost in Charleston, ending the sickly season. Soon after, they boarded a packet and sailed for home (73).

Chapter 4

A CHILD IN FRANCE

$\mathcal{A}$S A CHILD IN FRANCE, Audubon loved to draw. From the beginning, his favorite subjects were the birds, mammals, and plants he found in the fields and woods around his father's chateau near Nantes. In 1803, at age eighteen, Audubon left France to live at Mill Grove, a Pennsylvania farm his father had bought to spread the risks entailed by sizable investments in Haiti.

A New World filled with the birds of America inspired Audubon to search for a way to draw them in more lifelike positions than he had achieved in France. First he hung dead birds from strings tied to their feet, with their wings unfolded prettily and tails spread to expose their marking. But Audubon was dissatisfied and dismissed his renderings as signs used by people who sold poultry. He came closer to success with a pair of phoebes nesting in a cave in the bluffs of Perkioming Creek, which flowed through his father's property (Audubon 1900, 2:526).

Seated on a rock in the cave, Audubon made sketch after sketch of the perky little birds as they flitted between nests inside and feeding grounds outside. These drawings he rejected, too. Empty outlines devoid of detail, he called them. He learned in the grotto, though. Forced to look closely at the wild phoebes, he comprehended that they typically "sat uprightly, now and then glancing their eyes upward or sideways, to watch the approach of their insect prey." He was but a step from writing, as he did later in his article on drawing birds, "The better I understood my subjects, the better I became able to represent them in what I hoped were natural positions" (2:526).

Searching for a way to pose his elusive subjects, he tried propping dead birds on a table or the ground. When that failed, he tried stringing them up like puppets. With cork and wire he constructed bird manikins, but the results were laughable.

At dawn one summer day, though, he leaped from his bed convinced he had the answer. He saddled up and rode five miles to Norristown to buy wire. The store had not opened, so he bathed in the river and then returned to make his purchases. Back in Mill Grove in time for the tenant's wife to offer him breakfast, he grabbed his gun instead of eating and ran off to kill the first bird that he saw, a kingfisher on Perkioming Creek.

The kingfisher became his first subject drawn according to his new system, the one he would use for the rest of his career. He impaled the body with a sharp wire and pinned it in a lifelike posture against a piece of soft board that he had marked off in squares. He positioned the head with a wire through the skull just above the beak. Smaller wires positioned the feet, and pins steadied the toes and spread the feathers of the tail and wings. Once he had achieved the pose, he drew the bird on a sheet of paper that he had lightly marked in squares the same size as those of the board. He measured the bird carefully, ensuring that his finished drawing was exactly life-size.

But the method did not ensure an animated or dramatic pose, or even a pleasing composition. The skill to create these things came to Audubon gradually. Not until he set off down the Ohio River in 1820 after his bankruptcy and incarceration, hoping to recoup by publishing his bird paintings, did his gift for design emerge fully.

Petite Maria Martin, distracted from domestic concerns by the amazing activity in the low "ceiled" drawing room, was not forced immediately into the intricacies of the flesh-and-wire sculpture perfected by Audubon. He set up the birds for her to paint. Her model set up, Maria Martin persevered until she had sketched the outline and painted the color. Her early drawings may have lacked the crisp execution of Audubon and Lehman, but Audubon urged his pupils on with generous praise.

The Pinckney Street drawing room hit its stride with the golden-crowned kinglets perched on the powdery *thalia*. George Lehman drew the delicate portrait of the wildflower, among the rarest in the South, and Audubon the tiny vibrant kinglets. Their crowns of yellow and flame complemented the blue-violet of the *thalia* blossoms and echoed in miniature the shape of the large, bright, and many-ribbed leaf picked in Philippe Noisette's garden, located on ten acres about a mile northwest from Bachman's house on Pinckney Street (Audubon 1967a, 2:167).

Noisette's touch must have seemed magical to Charleston flower lovers. He bred an especially beautiful hybrid rose bearing lavish bunches of pink blossoms. Philippe's brother Louis, also a horticulturist, promoted the rose in Paris. Another brother, Antoine—not a rose breeder—lived in Nantes, the home of several Audubon relatives. Noisette's rose became an international favorite, a fit subject for the premier painter of roses, Pierre-Joseph Redoute (E. Bull 1969, 72, 76–77).

By October 1831, Noisette's luxuriant garden west of Charleston was well established. He had won trophies from local natural history clubs and amassed a large herbarium of dried plants. Nor were his natural history interests limited to plants. He built a collection of insects and snakes preserved in bottles filled with spirits of wine (Will book number h. 101, 1834–39, Philip S. Noisette, 29 January 1835, Charleston).

Noisette and Audubon shared aspects of their backgrounds. Both were Frenchmen who became Americans, and both were naturalists with Santo Domingo (the island today consisting of Haiti and the Dominican Republic) backgrounds. Philippe Noisette's six children were mulattoes; their mother was the black slave Celestine with whom Noisette openly resided in Charleston. Audubon was the only white child among half a dozen mulatto children his father, Jean Audubon, begot in his Santo Domingo (the Haiti component) country home.

Audubon was born on 26 April 1785. His mother was Jeanne Rabine, lately of France (Ford 1988, 21–23). In fragile health throughout her pregnancy, she died in early November just six months after the birth of her son. The other children in Jean Audubon's house were born to a Santo Domingo woman of color, Catherine Bouffard. A few months before Mademoiselle Rabine died, Catherine Bouffard became pregnant again and bore that child in the spring of 1786. A year later, she gave birth to yet another of Jean Audubon's children. This child she named Rose, after her favorite sister. Rose Bouffard had a light complexion, a match for that of her half-brother, Jean Rabin.

Despite Jean Audubon's thriving business and growing family, his prospects in Santo Domingo were threatened. Slaves outnumbered mulatto and white masters by nine to one and were increasingly rebellious. With a gift for testing the wind and taking the right tack, Jean Audubon sold much of his property, bought a ship, loaded her with sugar, and sailed to New York, where he sold the cargo and invested the proceeds in Mill Grove, a Pennsylvania plantation.

Unrest and violence erupted in Santo Domingo while Jean Audubon was in Pennsylvania. France, itself unstable, was in no position to intercede against the slaves on the side of the slave owners. Jean Audubon returned to the island to organize a militia with other men of property. Concluding when he got there, however, that the revolt would not be put down and that the island would never be safe for whites, he returned to France, leaving Jean Rabin behind, as well as Catherine Bouffard and his other children, the youngest a daughter born a few weeks before he sailed.

In France, the monarchy crumbled. Paris convulsed, blood flowed in the streets. From the relative safety of Nantes, Jean Audubon waited as the French revolutionaries set up and cut down one government after another. Once more he pondered his course and prevailed on several of his friends compelled to visit Santo Domingo for business reasons to bring Jean Rabin and Rose home when they returned. Jean Audubon's French wife agreed to take the children from Santo Domingo into her care.

Childless in two marriages, Anne Moynet Audubon, nine years older than her husband, opened her heart to the little boy and his half-sister. The Audubons left Nantes, a city with potential for political violence as the revolution spread, and settled near Coueron, a quiet village a few miles from their former home.

To Anne Audubon, the boy was Prince Charming. She dressed him in the fanciest clothes, supplied him with money, arranged *carte blanche* at the Nantes candy store, and enrolled him for lessons in violin, fencing, dancing, and drawing. When he was eight, he and Rose were legally adopted by the Audubons. At fifteen, he was baptized as Jean Jacques Fougere Audubon (Herrick 1968, 1:61–62).

At eighteen, the son of Jean Audubon became subject to Napoleon's draft. His father, rather than allow him to risk his life in service of the self-anointed emperor, arranged passage for his heir on a ship bound for America. After landing in New York, Audubon pushed on to his refuge, Mill Grove, his father's property near Philadelphia (Audubon 1900, 1:15–16). Standing on the bank of Perkioming Creek, the weary young traveler could look over the fields and meadows that swept uphill to a big solid house of native stone. He liked what he saw of the United States and soon anglicized his name to John James Audubon, a sure sign that he saw his future in the English-speaking New World.

Soon after Audubon's arrival, the William Bakewell family, lately of Connecticut and England, took up residence at Flatland Ford, which shared a boundary with Mill Grove. Young Audubon pointedly scorned the English newcomers, a people who had twice imprisoned his father. But in the privacy of the woods, where Audubon had gone exploring and William Bakewell hunting, they met by chance and Audubon acknowledged Bakewell's friendly greeting. The Englishman subsequently called on Audubon at Mill Grove, and John James bridled his horse and cantered over to Flatland Ford to return the visit.

Only Lucy Bakewell, the oldest of the children, was at home when he came. A year younger than her caller, she was poised enough to pull two chairs to the fireplace and bid him sit down. They chatted and fell in love (1:17–18).

Meanwhile, in France, Jean Audubon arranged a business partnership for young Audubon and Ferdinand Rozier, the mature and level-headed son of an old business friend. The partners would operate a basic supply store for settlers in Kentucky. This satisfied the Bakewells that John James could support their daughter, and both families gave their blessings to the marriage.

Lucy and John James were wed in the living room at Flatland Ford on 5 April 1808, and three days after the ceremony set off on a taxing journey by coach and riverboat to Louisville, Kentucky, where Audubon and Rozier had located their business. On the way, the stagecoach upended, painfully bruising Lucy. But after floating on an overcrowded and unstable flatboat down the stormy Ohio River to Louisville, the young couple settled into quiet married life in the hotel Indian Queen.

Between 1826 and 1838, while Audubon traveled back and forth between England and America publishing and selling subscriptions to *Birds of America,* he encouraged the impression that he was an incompetent businessman who focused more on the beauties of nature than the virtue of making money. In one of Audubon's stories, he and the hired clerk left

Rozier and wandered off to hunt in the forests and fish along the streams. In another tale, Audubon rode his horse toward Philadelphia. When an interesting bird flew across the road, Audubon left the horse—which was loaded with moneybags—and dashed after the bird. These and other tales, intended to amuse, created curiosity and helped the partners to sell their goods.

Though inflated by Audubon's imagination, the fantasies were fashioned on frames of fact. No doubt Audubon and the clerk did leave the store to hunt and fish, but both Audubon and Rozier also stood to profit from their efforts. As Audubon pointed out after a successful trip, "there lies fish enough for ourselves and our neighbors" (2:213).

Nor was Audubon usually absent from the store. Lucy complained to an English cousin that she had too few books to keep her occupied while her husband spent long hours at work. And we have the word of both Wilson and Audubon that he was standing solidly behind the counter the day the Scot came in to sell subscriptions to his book (2:200–201, 224).

Long after Audubon left Kentucky, stories circulated in Henderson about the day he dived off the bow of a steamboat, swam its length underwater, and popped up safe astern. Kentuckians appreciated that it took a strong and resourceful man to make dangerous, but vital, restocking trips from Louisville to the east coast, and they would have noticed that Rozier, by his choice, rarely stepped beyond their store's front door (Herrick 1968, 1:253).

Audubon accommodated Rozier. When the stodgy Frenchman suggested that they move their business downriver to Henderson to escape competition from eastern merchants pouring into Louisville, Audubon concurred because he "longed to have a wilder range," he claimed. But Henderson, when they got there, was more primitive than either had expected, "the country so very new, and so thinly populated that the commonest goods only were called for." Rozier again agitated to move, this time to St. Genevieve on the Mississippi, a town of French-speaking settlers (Audubon 1900, 1:30).

In December 1810, with the assistance of John Pope, the store clerk, the partners packed barrels of whiskey and other stock, loaded a flatboat, and set off downriver for St. Genevieve in threatening weather. A heavy snowstorm enveloped them before they rounded the first bend. At Cash Creek, ice trapped their boat and held them fast for twenty days before loosening its grip. Ice halted them again on the Mississippi as they were poling their vessel upstream. They pitched camp on the bank at the Great Bend at Tawapatee Bottom, using their sails as tents. For Audubon, six weeks of waiting for a thaw was an enchanting interlude. He spent his time watching wolves stalk swans on the ice, he hunted to supply the camp, and he communed with Indians who came to trade. At night the Indians sat in a circle around the campfire and listened to Audubon's violin and John Pope's flute (Ford 1988, 81).

As for Rozier, he spent the month and a half shivering in his tent until at last the frozen river broke free with a heart-stopping roar. A moving wall of ice and water nearly swept the camp away. Then the waters calmed and ran swift and sure again, and the traders poled on upriver to St. Genevieve, where the frigid winter had set up a windfall for them. Ice had cut off the town from the outside world, and prices for the few goods available there had skyrocketed. The flatboat and its load of whiskey were as welcome as flowers in spring. Thirsty townsfolk eagerly purchased for two dollars apiece bottles of whiskey that had cost Audubon and Rozier twenty-five cents a barrel.

The music of spoken French went straight to Rozier's heart. He pronounced on the spot that here he would live for the rest of his life. Thirty-four years old and unable to speak English, he would not budge. Audubon insisted just as strongly that he would not force Lucy to part from their friends in Henderson to set up shop in alien St. Genevieve. The two men thus decided to dissolve their partnership. All of the stock stayed with Rozier, with Rozier paying Audubon for his share, partly in gold and partly in notes. Audubon then purchased a beautiful horse and returned to Henderson (Audubon 1900, 1:31).

With the gold, Audubon and his brother-in-law, Thomas Bakewell, set up a business distributing frontier staples, such products as pork, lard, and flour. Had war not flared again between the United States and Great Britain, in June of 1812, Bakewell and Audubon's firm might have succeeded. But English warships cut off goods in route to New Orleans. Once more, Audubon dipped into capital and opened a store in Henderson. Without partners to contend with, the modest venture prospered. Audubon purchased a log cabin and a few acres of land, the first home he and Lucy had owned.

But Audubon invested heavily in a sawmill, and in 1819 the mill failed. Creditors seized his house and land, his household goods, drawings, everything except his clothes and that frontier necessity, his gun. He left the gun with Lucy and walked to Louisville to be jailed.

Within a few days he was set free, having paid what he could and declaring bankruptcy. Deeply depressed, he closed his eyes to birds and his ears to the songs that had always lifted his spirits before (Herrick 1968, 1:257, 260–61).

A free man, he walked to Shippingport, a pleasant village on the Falls of the Ohio five miles below Louisville. A number of affluent French immigrants lived there, among them James Berthoud, a French aristocrat turned barge builder. Berthoud had treated Audubon as though he were a son, visiting Audubon in Henderson to give him support before he went to jail. Tragically, James Berthoud had died suddenly in Audubon's home a few days after Audubon left Henderson to surrender to prison. Audubon now wanted to give his condolences to Madam Berthoud before he left the area (Ford 1988, 105).

He stepped into the familiar Berthoud living room, pausing a moment to study a charcoal portrait of James Berthoud that hung on the wall. He had drawn the picture in happier days. Without work or capital, a financial pass that seemed hopeless, it occurred to him that perhaps he could draw portraits for pay (106–7).

He posted a notice that he was available and was amazed at how many people seemed to want an artist to capture the features of loved ones at the handsome fee of five dollars a sketch. This small success at the low point of Audubon's life, like the tremulous note of a February chickadee, was a suggestion of spring in a long winter. Even so, the supply of sitters dropped off once the pent-up demand for likenesses had been satisfied.

A few acquaintances tried to help him find employment. One of them, Robert Todd of Lexington—whose daughter, Mary, would marry Abraham Lincoln in 1842—wrote to Cincinnati College recommending that they hire Audubon to teach drawing and French, and mentioned in passing that Audubon had "nearly finished [painting] a collection of American birds, and is anxious to see Wilson's Ornithology to ascertain whether or no there is any bird . . . which he Mr. Audubon has omitted to paint" (109).

The college did not hire him, but Todd's effort bore fruit in the form of an offer from a trustee of the college, Dr. Daniel Drake. The hard-put portrait painter was invited to join the staff of Cincinnati's newly founded Western Museum, which its director, Dr. Drake, described as "a complete school for natural history" (Herrick 1968, 1:305). Audubon's job required that he prepare mounted birds and fish for the rapidly expanding natural history collection.

A bonus, from Audubon's point of view, was the museum's possession of a copy of Alexander Wilson's *American Ornithology*. Dr. Drake had met Wilson in 1810, shortly before Wilson's call on Audubon in Louisville, and thus was familiar with Wilson's work and was an ideal sounding board on which Audubon could test the notion that *he* could make money by painting and publishing a collection of American birds, one surpassing Wilson's (1:205).

In June of 1819, attempting to improve the reputation of the institution he had founded, Dr. Drake told an audience that Audubon had painted a large number of birds not in Wilson's works and some that were unknown to science. Unfortunately, Dr. Drake's speech, with its claim to have on its staff the successor to Wilson, did not raise enough money for the museum to pay its bills. Audubon's salary fell into arrears. Lucy secured a position teaching school to make up for the lost income, and Audubon organized a private art class and drew portraits when commissioned. But none of these stopgap efforts to support his family disguised his failure.

In a dozen years of marriage, he had gone through the capital his father had given him, had borrowed from his in-laws and lost the money in doubtful business ventures, had painted portraits and that petered out, and had worked for the Western Museum and not been fully paid for his efforts. Some of these reverses were bad luck, some the result of an unstable economy, some of scoundrels who stole from him, some of friends who let him down, and some of his own shortcomings. Whatever the combination, his family was suffering and he saw only one hope to recoup. Lucy must support herself and the boys with her teaching, while he set off into the wilderness to paint birds and eventually publish a book on the birds of America.

In his journal Audubon wrote of his departure: "THURSDAY-Ohio River Oct-12th, 1820. I left Cincinnati this afternoon at half past 4 o'clock, on Board of Mr. Jacob Aumack's flat boat bound to New Orleans—the feeling of a Husband and a Father, were My Lot when I kissed my Beloved Wife & Children with an expectation of being absent for Seven Months" (Audubon 1929a, 3).

Seeking redemption, Audubon followed the same course Wilson had taken after visiting Henderson more than a decade earlier. Audubon knew that to outstrip his rival he had to paint birds better than Wilson, discover birds Wilson had missed, and observe their habits and write skilfully and entertainingly about them.

Audubon was confident of his ability as a painter, but as a writer, his assurance sagged a bit. Wilson had already won a reputation for fine prose, while Audubon, judging by his journals and letters and accounts by people who knew him, wrote vividly and with charm, but with less literary acumen in both French and English. Nor was Audubon's knowledge of birds encyclopedic. That first day on the river he saw but could not identify so common a bird as a hermit thrush.

His notes show how consciously he pitted himself against Wilson; how pointedly he probed for chinks in his predecessor's reputation. Audubon shot an immature male yellow-rumped warbler in excellent fall plumage that day, and as he drew a picture of it, he recalled that Wilson had erred in calling a bird of the same species the "Autumnal Warbler." As though rehearsing his new role, Audubon announced to himself and his journal, "I feel perfectly Convinced that Mr. Wilson made an error in presenting his Bird as a new spicy [species]." For Audubon to remember such a small detail about Wilson's writing showed that he had learned Wilson's work well (4).

Audubon recognized that he would need help to produce *Birds of America*. Probably that was why he had boarded the flatboat with a potential assistant, "Joseph Mason a Young Man of about 18 years of age good family and naturally an amiable Youth" (3).

Actually, Mason was only thirteen when he set off down the Ohio with

Audubon. Perhaps Audubon overstated the boy's age because he felt a twinge of guilt for subjecting a child to so rigorous and uncertain a journey as this one promised to be. As for Mason, he and his family were poverty stricken, and the boy was more likely to be fed in the wilds with Audubon than at home with them. Audubon explained in his journal that Mason "is intended to be a Companion, & a Friend." He did not record at that point that the boy, who had been one of his art students in Cincinnati, might assist him with the paintings (3).

The flatboat and its passengers drifted through a wetlands wilderness about to be swept away by a wave of settlers. Audubon sensed as much. The great swamp forests were obstructions to the pioneers. They viewed the Indians who fished the river and hunted the forest as a menace. But here and there clearings and small settlements intruded on the bluffs, minor aberrations in a wild environment where bear and wolves still roamed freely. As Audubon and Mason drifted downstream on the flatboat, they viewed ivory-billed woodpeckers and Carolina parakeets almost daily.

Aumack tied up the flatboat for a few days in Natchez, a bustling town with a population that Audubon estimated at two thousand. On one of the streets of Natchez, Audubon chanced to meet his affluent friend, Nicholas Berthoud, son of James Berthoud and the same age as Audubon. Berthoud carried on the family trade of barge and boat building, and had become the husband of Lucy's sister, Eliza. He transacted business up and down the river from Shippingport to New Orleans.

Audubon and Joseph eagerly accepted a suggestion that they board one of Berthoud's flatboats about to leave for New Orleans. On this craft, Audubon and Jo sailed in comfort and style, though Audubon, in his excitement, had left the portfolio containing his paintings on the dock.

On 7 January 1821 Audubon wrote: "At New Orleans at Last—We arrived here about 8 o'clock this morning; hundreds of Fish Crows hovering near the shipping and dashing to the Watter like Gulls for food—uttering a cry very much like the young of the Common crow when they first leave the nest" (111).

IN NEW ORLEANS, hoping to paint portraits for a living, Audubon happened to meet John B. Gilly, an old acquaintance. Gilly did not commission a portrait, but he let Audubon draw one "purposely to expose it to the Public." Audubon accepted the offer and happily recorded the results: "It is considered by everyone who Knows him to be perfect." Gilly's friends responded with commissions, but as his supply of sitters diminished, a summer of heat and mosquitoes descended on the city. Audubon despaired of reconstructing his life (120).

At that point, Mrs. James Pirrie, one of his patrons, suggested that he might like to accompany her and her daughter 125 miles up the Mississippi to Oakley, their plantation in the Louisiana hill country. There he would teach sixteen-year-old Eliza half of each day, and he and Joseph could work as they pleased the rest of the time. Mrs. Pirrie would pay him sixty dollars a month and provide their room and board. Although in Oakley Audubon would not be collecting new birds full time in the Rocky Mountains or East Florida, he would not be marooned in steamy New Orleans either (159).

Audubon and Mason took passage to St. Francisville on the *Columbus*. As the steamboat churned up the river, Audubon toyed with the thought of passing by St. Francisville and traveling all the way to Kentucky for a reunion with Lucy. But that would have interrupted his mission to publish the *Birds of America*. Audubon and Mason disembarked as scheduled, climbed the high bluff at "Bayou Sarah," and after a meal at the home of Mr. Benjamin Swift, whose son John would become a close friend of Audubon, began the walk to Oakley.

The enchanting countryside diverted Audubon from his troubles. Blossoms of yellow poplar, holly, beach, and magnolia scented the air, and flowering trees sheltered thousands of warblers and thrushes. Swallow-tailed and Mississippi kites swooped low through the leafy branches to snatch insects and newly hatched birds from their nests. Five miles of walking through this paradise ended all too soon.

The artist arrived at Oakley a troubled man, lonesome for his family, struggling to find his way after failing in business and having barely survived as an artist in New Orleans. So were the Pirries a troubled family. At the plantation house Audubon was greeted by James Pirrie, the hard-drinking but sympathetic master of the place.

Most of the four productive months Audubon and Mason lived at Oakley were happy ones. Audubon piled up more than twenty paintings that he would publish eventually. Some of them—for example, the weightless swallow-tailed kite with a sinuous garter snake in its talons—are among his finest.

Like Audubon, Joseph Mason matured as an artist at Oakley. His Swamp Snow-ball (*Hydrangea quercifolia*) fits without a seam in an Audubon composition with a wasp and a yellow-throated vireo. In fact, Mason's work in his early teens; the muscadine grapes that accompany Audubon's summer tanagers—the winged elm with the Bewick's wren, a bird not yet described that Audubon collected just before departing Oakley—rivaled any botanical paintings yet produced in America.

As astonishingly polished as Mason's botanical backgrounds were, and as richly deserving of credit, he could hardly have produced them without Audubon at his side, constantly advising, even at times taking the brush to retouch the painting in progress, until his birds and Mason's backgrounds seemed the work of one hand. Mason learned his craft by executing Audubon's vision. The youth would continue his career as an artist into maturity, but his reputation ultimately rested on the work done as a lad with Audubon in Louisiana.

In the fall, Eliza became mildly ill, and any illness afflicting the last Pirrie child living at home was enough to throw her parents into intense anxiety. In due course it became clear, to Audubon at least, that Eliza had passed the crisis and no longer was in danger. With little sympathy for her overly solicitous parents, Audubon complained that instead of getting her up and about, Eliza's family kept her in bed and stuffed her with food.

Eliza's doctor declared that Audubon, himself, was bad for her. He forbade her to resume lessons with him, or even to see him except during regulated appointments. Audubon concluded that the doctor had romantic as well as professional motives and refused to listen to him. Mrs. Pirrie, trusting the doctor, perhaps fearing for her daughter's life, dismissed Audubon on 10 October 1821. Audubon's arrogance melted. He begged to stay on at Oakley for eight or ten days to get his observations, notes, and lists of birds in order. Bedeviled James Pirrie sided with Audubon, and permission was granted to delay the departure.

The truce between Audubon and Mrs. Pirrie was short-lived. Tensions built until the moment that Audubon and Jo Mason took their leave. Audubon bid Mrs. Pirrie and her older daughter, Mrs. Smith, a chilly good-bye, and the lovely Eliza received little better. "My Pupil Raised from the Sopha and Expected a Kiss from Me—but None Were to be disposed of, I pressed her Hand and With a general Salute to the Whole Made My Retreat." Feeling much the injured party, he loaded his possessions on a wagon and he and Mason "vaulted our Saddle and Left this abode of unfortunate Opulence without a Sigh of regret" (196).

Although he no longer admired the house of Pirrie, he hated to turn his back on the "sweet Woods" around the plantation. Anticipating what lay ahead for him—the fetid air of crowded New Orleans—he longed to fill his lungs with "the purer air that circulates through" the woods and take it to the city (197).

The struggle to stay afloat in New Orleans resumed at once. Rival artists spread rumors to discredit him. Money owed him was difficult if not impossible to collect. A friend fresh from Louisville reported that Lucy was planning to catch the first steamboat for New Orleans. Audubon longed to see his family again, but days passed by with no sign of his wife. Presently, he received a disheartening letter from her. The next letter was more cheerful, but it was an old one that had been delayed in the mail. Hoping she would turn up, he met steamboat after steamboat, only to walk downcast from the docks.

Over the years, flirtations notwithstanding, Audubon's love for Lucy endured. He parted from her reluctantly when *Birds of America* demanded it, then strived to bring the family back together as soon as he could. Lucy tried too, but her husband's financial ups and downs eroded her confidence. From her point of view, no sooner would she settle into a routine that would assure shelter and food for the family than she was called on to plunge into the unknown again. Yet somehow, the friendship and passion of their marriage survived, and just before Christmas of 1821 his wife and sons arrived in New Orleans.

Lucy brought with her the drawings that Audubon had left behind when he boarded Aumack's flatboat at Natchez—James Berthoud had rescued them—and Audubon was surprised and disconcerted to see that they were not up to the work he had done since. Missing from the early work was the ease of execution that more than a year of intense drawing and painting in Louisiana had given him. His powerful feel for design and drama had emerged in the interim. Even as he frowned at the Carolina parakeet from his Henderson days, he unpacked the huge sheet of seven agitated little parrots he had painted at St. Francisville and laid the two versions side by side.

In the hill country of Louisiana, cotton planters were enjoying new wealth and wanted their children to have the advantages of a suitable accent, literacy, and culture. Mrs. Robert Percy had invited Lucy Audubon, English-born and educated, to come to Beach Woods plantation just north of St. Francisville and start a school there. Mrs. Audubon would be paid one thousand dollars a year and provided with a house. Her students would include the Percy children, her own son John, and other children of the community. The Audubons decided to leave the house they had rented on Dauphine Street and accept the offer at Beach Woods.

The school thrived with Lucy in charge. Audubon taught there briefly, but he and Mrs. Percy clashed over the color of her daughter's cheeks in a portrait Audubon was painting. The cheeks were "jaundiced" in Mrs. Percy's opinion. Audubon hotly insisted they were a good likeness, and was ordered off the plantation. When he returned secretly a few days later and spent the night with Lucy, he was found out. Her husband evicted from her bed (Ford 1988, 142), Lucy watched him go. Despite the humiliation, she could not bring herself to give up the security of her position at the Beach Woods school for the periodic disasters she had come to expect with her husband.

Audubon and Joseph Mason wandered up the river as far as Natchez, where they parted in August 1822. Joseph's father had died, and the boy wanted to go to his mother. Audubon gave him a gun to shoot game, and paper and chalk for drawing portraits for pay during the long walk to Cincinnati. They had been companions for almost two years. They had seen hard times, but even these Audubon remembered fondly: "He drew with me; he was my daily companion, and we both rolled ourselves together on bufaloe robes at night." Mason returned Audubon's affection, regarding his mentor as his "greatest friend" (Herrick 1968, 2:69).

In the spring of 1824, having drawn many birds since parting with Joseph Mason, Audubon took about one hundred of his paintings to Philadelphia, hoping to arrange for their publication. He arrived in the city practically unknown and soon would learn that he had chosen a poor place and time to try to publish the work that he hoped would eclipse Wilson's *American Ornithology*.

At twenty-one, Charles Lucien Bonaparte, nephew of Napoleon, was in town to publish *his* expanded edition of Wilson's book. Bonaparte had asked Titian Peale to draw the new birds that had turned up since Wilson's death, and Alexander Lawson to do the engraving and printing. Bonaparte saw Audubon's lively paintings and asked to include some in his book. But with Peale's commission threatened, local opposition stormed into the frey, catching Audubon off guard. Lawson challenged Bonaparte, saying, "You may buy them [Audubon's drawings], but I will not engrave them." Wilson's former employer found fault with almost every aspect of Audubon's work. "Ornithology requires truth and correct lines—here are neither!" George Ord, the friend who had completed *American Ornithology* after Wilson died, also disparaged Audubon's work (1:327–30).

But Philadelphia's natural history community was not entirely against Audubon. A few there accepted his genius and responded to his charm. They would be invaluable allies: Thomas Sully, an English-born portrait painter, praised the exotic woodsman; Dr. Richard Harlan, an ambitious physician and zoologist, enlisted on Audubon's side; Edward Harris, cultivated and rich, won Audubon's undying gratitude by buying some early drawings that Audubon was offering at fire-sale prices, then pressing an additional one hundred dollars into the artist's hand with the comment that men like him should not be without funds. Even Rembrandt Peale, brother of Titian, strayed from the family fold to commend Audubon's works of art.

Toward the end of Audubon's summer in Philadelphia, he visited Mill Grove. He and several other men were chatting with Samuel Wetherhill, who had purchased the estate, when thoughts of the past suddenly overcame Audubon. Abruptly he grabbed his hat and ran through the woods and down the path to the grotto on the banks of the Perkioming where he had once sketched phoebes, and where he and Lucy had exchanged vows of love. The cave had collapsed, replaced by remains of a quarry. Audubon looked up and gave thanks that the sky had not changed (1:335).

DURING THE TWO YEARS following Audubon's return to Louisiana he managed to boost his folio to more than two hundred paintings and, with

Lucy's help, to save one thousand dollars, enough to allow him to sail in the summer of 1826 from New Orleans to Liverpool, in search of an English printer for *Birds of America*.

Surely no one who boarded the *Delos* on 18 May 1826 in New Orleans was prepared for a summer spent crossing the Atlantic (Audubon 1967b, 4–5). At sea for ninety stultifying days, cut off from the work that had sustained his enthusiasm for so many years, Audubon read every book he could find. He sketched the sailors and his fellow passenger, John Swift of St. Francisville, who had brought along eleven gallons of whiskey to share with everyone.

In a haze of alcohol, Audubon perceived the most mundane of incidents as macabre. A tin lamp swung hypnotically from the ceiling and the jaw of a shark tacked to the wall glowed brightly in his dark cabin. Mice ran about—cockroaches darted out of holes—maggots popped from chunks of cheese and flopped on the table. He wrote long passages of sex and flatulence, and became so introspective that he advised diarists who might read his journal to do as he did and write "all he sees, all he thinks, or all— yes, out with it, all he does" (33–34).

The blue devils of depression that haunted him throughout the voyage of the *Delos* escorted him onto the docks at Liverpool. Customs men went into deep huddles before clearing his paintings and other possessions. He was dismayed at how his eyes burned and he could hardly breathe in the town where heavy coal smoke poured from the chimneys of every house and factory.

Lucy's sister, Ann, had married Alexander Gordon, a New Orleans businessman now living in Liverpool, and Audubon called at his office. Gordon at first did not appear to recognize him, but they had a brief conversation that ended when Gordon said that Audubon might drop by the office again sometime—not the slightest hint that he might be welcome in his home. Audubon wondered in his journal what he had done to deserve such treatment. "Ah, that is no riddle, my friend, I have grown poor" (45).

Audubon called on influential people in Liverpool, hoping to interest someone in subscribing to *Birds of America*. Attempting to deliver letters of introduction, he was repeatedly told that the person he wanted to see was out. He was getting nowhere. After three days, on a dismal Sunday, he got drunk in his room, opened his journal, and again followed his pen through pages of sex, profanity, and hints of his own illegitimacy (45–51).

By Tuesday, though, all had changed. "Burst my brains, burst my coarse skull, and give the whole of your slender powers to enable me to describe my feelings this day." Richard Rathbone, one of Liverpool's most prominent citizens, had read his letter of introduction, admired his drawings, and arranged for a dinner party to introduce him to the opinion makers of the city, not the least of whom was Richard Rathbone's brother, William, who like all the Rathbones was rich, Quaker, and cultured (54).

Audubon charmed the family. Down to the children, they seemed to love him. "Their youngest boy, Basil, a sweet child, took a fancy to me and I to him, and we made friends" (60, 119).

With Hannah Mary, a sister of Richard Rathbone, Audubon engaged in a flirtation that had the hallmarks of an adolescent love affair: soulful looks, romantic walks together through the countryside, and the exchange of sentimental little gifts. Hannah presented him with a penknife and he responded with a wonderfully evocative charcoal self-portrait inscribed "Almost happy" (127–28).

Liverpool's social life was livened by Audubon's presence. Captivating, unpredictable, and with a flare for the exotic word or gesture, he shocked the guests at one party by picking and eating a love apple (tomato), which they all thought was poisonous. The socialites were amused by his floppy, backwoods trousers of "good Harmony cloth," and his unconventionally long hair, groomed, he slyly proclaimed, with that frontier cosmetic, bear grease. One afternoon he turned up for tea at William Roscoe's and found a party in progress. Roscoe was a banker, poet, biographer, and the premier Liverpool patron of the arts. A group quickly closed around the newcomer. Between answering questions about wild America and his art, he responded to calls for imitations of turkeys, owls, and doves. Artistic Mrs. Edward Roscoe, daughter-in-law of the host, had to rise from her chair to make heard serious queries about the Audubon style of drawing birds (86–87).

The appetite of the group had been primed for tales of ferocious beasts and painted savages by Charles Waterton, an eccentric traveler who had been to North and South America, and had written a best-selling book,

Wanderings. Audubon affected an unwillingness to match Waterton's literary excesses and modestly confessed that he had never been assaulted by an animal larger than a tick or mosquito. It would be fun, though, he mused, alluding to one of Waterton's far-fetched stories, to have ridden "a few hundred miles on a Wild Elk or an Unicorn—or an Alligator" (87).

Waterton fancied himself a serious naturalist. When he heard about the parody Audubon spun at his expense, he added Audubon to a list of people to attack in print, at his convenience, because they criticized his work.

In late September, boosted by social and business triumphs in Liverpool, Audubon moved on to Manchester and then to Edinburgh, becoming increasingly known as he traveled. The prestigious Wernerian Society met and listened with interest to his papers on vultures, alligators, pigeons, and snakes. He may not have made a conscious decision to do it, but he took his cue from Waterton and selected material more for its entertainment value than its contribution to knowledge. After hearing Audubon's quickly written papers based mostly on notes from his water-stained journals, the Wernerian Society published them in its proceedings, and copies were distributed and read as far away as Philadelphia.

Initially, the rattlesnake paper caused the most excitement. To the poisonous pit viper Audubon attributed the ways of the harmless ratsnake, which climbs in trees in pursuit of prey and kills its victims by constriction. None of Audubon's Edinburgh audience was sufficiently conversant with American reptiles to mark the error on the spot, nor did Dr. Thomas P. Jones of Philadelphia when the paper came to him. As a former director of the U.S. Patent Office and a professor in an American medical school, Dr. Jones had a background that should have led him to question the story. Instead, it seemed to him just the sort of thing that would go well in the *Franklin Journal,* which he edited. He republished the article verbatim and claimed credit for writing it (Herrick 1968, 2:72).

Philadelphia naturalists hooted down the article, and humiliated, the editor recanted, identifying John James Audubon, not himself, as the source of the falsehoods. Then Jones sniffed that he should not be criticized just because he had not the time to review the piece before his printer rushed it off to the typesetter.

Unaware that his writing career had begun with a bang across the Atlantic, Audubon went about the business of showing his drawings around

Edinburgh. A book dealer was impressed enough to escort him to the shop of engraver William Home Lizars. Audubon had displayed only a few sheets when the distinguished Lizars exclaimed, "My God! I've never seen anything like this before." When he saw the peregrine falcon, Lizars fell silent for a moment and dropped his arms. "I will engrave and publish this!" (Audubon 1967b, 249–50).

Lizars copied the drawings on copper plates, huge because Audubon insisted his birds be published life-size as he had drawn them. The engraver achieved shading by the difficult technique of aquatint, in which rosin dust is applied over a line drawing previously etched on the plate. The art of the process is to coax the dust to just the right places in just the right amounts to produce shading. Then, the plate is struck, and the black-and-white engraving is pulled, both lines and shading ready for craftsmen to paint over with watercolors.

Everything fell into place. With copies of the first prints of *Birds of America* in hand, Audubon solicited subscriptions from rich and learned Englishmen, and from others who attended exhibitions of his work in Liverpool, Edinburgh, and Manchester. A hitch arose when Lizars withdrew from the project because he was pressed to switch his attention back to the works of Prideaux John Selby, who may have become uneasy over the magnitude of the ornithological star rising in his bailiwick. About that time Lizars's colorists went on strike, providing the printer with an excellent excuse to break his commitment just when Audubon most needed to deliver prints to his subscribers.

Fortunately, Audubon was in London selling subscriptions when he got the bad news and had the good luck to find a replacement for Lizars, Robert Havell, an unknown, but as it turned out, an equally skilled engraver and more reliable than Lizars. Audubon moved his operation to the English capital (318).

The American woodsman's stay in England lengthened to nearly three years. Plates were printed and delivered to subscribers in sets of five, which were called numbers: a large "elephant" size print, a middle-size one, and three small prints. As more and more numbers were issued, and the subscription list grew longer, it became clear that *Birds of America* would turn a profit.

Just as it seemed to Audubon that his business would succeed, he came to suspect that his marriage was failing. When Lucy wrote from America, which was seldom, it was most often to complain that he had neglected some duty, or to tell him of the burdens of rearing a family alone. She responded coldly to pleas that she come to England to resume her life with him, waiting for Audubon to prove that he could support her (Audubon 1969, 1:77–78).

The need to settle the issues with Lucy might of itself have made him go home. The necessity to paint more American birds for Havell to engrave made a prompt return a certainty. Only about fifty drawings ready for publication remained in his portfolio. Some of these combined birds with inappropriate plants, some were soiled, and others were just no longer up to his standards. Though he feared that his English subscribers, doubting his will to complete *Birds of America,* might cancel in his absence, he had to go (Audubon 1900, 1:297).

Henry Ward, a young taxidermist, accompanied him as far as New York. In Philadelphia, Audubon hired George Lehman to paint landscape backgrounds for his birds, and while there learned that the Ord circle of naturalists were criticizing the mockingbird and rattlesnake plate, mocking the snake's S-curved fangs Audubon had drawn. Not surprisingly, no one in Philadelphia subscribed to *Birds of America.*

Audubon would not give up his campaign to repair relations with Lucy. She responded to a letter he wrote to her at Beach Woods by expressing reluctance to leave Louisiana. Several letters later, however, she consented to meet him in Louisville. Not Lucy, but a young man came up to greet Audubon when he arrived, someone Audubon did not at once recognize. It was his son, Victor, at twenty-one a bookeeper for William Bakewell (1:62). Audubon had not seen him for nearly five years.

Lucy stayed put in St. Francisville. Determined to face her, Audubon took a Mississippi steamboat all the way to Louisiana. As he walked toward Lucy's house, he could hear a child fingering a piano. Preoccupied with the student, the teacher did not notice Audubon, who stood silently behind her listening to the music for a moment, then whispering her name. Audubon and Lucy fell weeping into each other's arms (1:63).

Lucy had to collect her accounts and dispose of her three slaves before she could leave for England. Audubon used the time, about two months, to draw and observe birds and to call on old friends. When at last they got underway on 7 January 1830, Audubon used the trip to good advantage. He stopped off in Washington and wheedled a subscription from the Library of Congress, the first subscription he sold in America. In Baltimore, he sold three more. He sold none in Philadelphia (Herrick 1968, 1:436).

A letter from William Swainson, an English ornithologist, awaited Audubon in New York. Swainson had paid young Ward to collect American natural history specimens for him, but Ward had not delivered any, and Swainson seemed to hold Audubon responsible. Actually, Audubon had seen little of Ward since the beginning of the trip. The young man had gone to Philadelphia, presumably to visit his taxidermist brother, Frederick. There he made excuses and doubled back to New York. Audubon heard later that in New York, Henry had joined a "lower cast" girl from London (1:431).

BEFORE BOARDING SHIP for England, Audubon met with Ward and wrote to Swainson. Audubon was not specific about what he found, but he assured Swainson that Henry was "doing extremely well if what he told me is true." Audubon was careful not to ruffle Swainson's feathers. The well-known nature writer and ornithologist had warmly prasied Audubon in a review, and they had exchanged letters. Audubon had visited Swainson and his family at their country home and had been impressed by him. Because the time was near when Audubon would have to write a text to go with the engravings, and would need help, he could see a role for the literate Swainson in his future (2:96).

Many things competed for Audubon's attention when he and Lucy landed at Liverpool, so he suspended his effort to find an editor for a while. Ann Gordon was ill. Lucy decided she had to remain in Liverpool to nurse her sister. With his wife occupied, Audubon hopscotched about England putting his business in order. Subscribers complained about the coloring of some of the engravings, going so far as to cancel subscriptions. Busily and effectively, Audubon charmed and calmed his problem patrons into staying aboard.

Audubon posted a long thoughtful letter to Swainson on 5 May 1830, recounting his voyage from New York and the bird paintings he had accumulated in America. He also confessed that he planned "to *write a book!*" which he would discuss further with Swainson when they met (2:96).

Swainson sensed that Audubon was opening a negotiation. "So you are going to write a book[—]'tis a thing of little moment for one who is not known . . . but much will be expected from you." He warned Audubon that George Ord had come to England to stir up trouble. Ord had tried and failed to have Audubon blackballed from election as a Fellow of the Royal Society. With enemies like Ord, chided Swainson, casting himself as Audubon's protector, Audubon had better make his publication unassailable (2:98).

Encouraged by this response, Audubon asked the widely published author if he would "bear a hand in the text of my work—my furnishing you with the ideas & information which I have and you to add the science which I have not." He went further and hinted that he and Lucy would move in with the Swainsons while they worked together. As though fending off an objection he expected Swainson to raise, Audubon assured him that he and Lucy would supply their own "wines, porter or ale" (2:102).

Swainson declined the offer, explaining that as an Englishman he could not take in boarders. As for working with Audubon, he would not be content to serve merely as editor. He wanted his name on the title page as author as well (2:104, 105).

Audubon was not yet sufficiently familiar with ornithology to appreciate Swainson's limits as a scientist; it was just as well that Swainson priced himself out of the job. The widely recognized Englishman believed in a system of classification more occult than scientific, holding that "all things that have life have been created on one plan, and this plan is founded on the principle of a series of affinities returning into themselves; which can only be represented by a circle." A strange and incomprehensible wrinkle was his belief in the inevitable recurrence of the numeral "5" in his taxonomy. Insertion of this mystical system in *Ornithological Biography* would have provided George Ord and others opportunities to ridicule Audubon, which they would have gleefully seized on (2:93–94).

An Edinburgh friend suggested that Audubon enlist William MacGillivray, a bright but little known zoologist who had written several very favorable reviews of *Birds of America* (Audubon 1900, 1:64). When asked to be Audubon's assistant, MacGillivray accepted Audubon's terms and they set to work with a rigorous schedule. Audubon rose from bed at four in the morning and wrote until ten or eleven at night. MacGillivray did not rise until ten A.M., but went on revising and editing what Audubon had written until two the next morning. Under such a regimen, the manuscript "went on incrasing in bulk, like the rising of a stream after abundant rains" (L. Audubon 1869, 205–6).

Within three months, Audubon and MacGillivray packed up a five-hundred-page volume of *Ornithological Biography* and turned it over to a printer. The one hundred species of birds covered in volume 1 were the same as those in the first twenty numbers of *Birds of America*. As Audubon had insisted, the prose was lively and entertaining, directed toward wealthy subscribers as well as impoverished scholars. Yet the scientific standards of the work satisfied most professional ornithologists, despite a few imaginative passages obviously intended to amuse. Audubon called these light adventures "Episodes," or "food for the idle," and had recycled the rattlesnake story in that capacity (Audubon 1969, 2:54).

During Audubon's writing marathon his thoughts again turned to America. He wrote requesting his Philadelphia ally, Dr. Richard Harlan, to locate George Lehman and hire him for another expedition. Henry Ward's New York liaison had played out, and he had turned up in England. Audubon hired him again with the view of meeting expenses by selling birdskins, which Ward would prepare for the lucrative English market.

In August 1831, just before he and Lucy boarded the *Columbia* for the voyage home, the first critical reviews of the new book appeared, generally praising the writing. But at Walton Hall, ancestral home of Charles Waterton, the reaction to volume 1 of *Ornithological Biography* was outrage. George Ord and Charles Waterton had found one another and convened at Waterton's grand estate to plan strategy. Ord was offended because he felt that Audubon had insulted Philadelphia in the introduction, and that the episode titled "Louisville in Kentucky" directly contradicted Wilson's claim that "literature and science" had no friend in that place. Actually, Audubon's version of Wilson's visit related many kindnesses that Audubon personally had bestowed on "the father of American ornithology" (Herrick 1968, 2:220–25).

What really stuck in Ord's and Waterton's craws was the literary and scientific merit of *Ornithological Biography*. It was a success, they admitted, but was *Audubon* the author? The book had to be a fraud, the work of a ghost writer whom they suspected was Swainson, not that of an illiterate backcountry American merchant! Even as Audubon and Lucy sailed toward New York, the disgruntled pair was fuming at Waterton's table, Ord scribbling sheet after sheet of fault-finding to use against their enemy Audubon when the time seemed right (2:87–88).

Chapter 5

PET OF EVERYBODY

NLY TWO WEEKS after he arrived for his first visit to Charleston in October 1831 and met John Bachman on a downtown street, Audubon informed Lucy that he was being treated like royalty. "I certainly have met with more kindness in this place than anywhere else in the United States—here I am the very pet of everybody, and had I time or Inclination to visit the great folk I might be in dinner parties from now until Jany next." But Audubon had "other fish to fry," the other fish being painting new birds, writing observations of their habits, and preparing birdskins for sale in London (Audubon 1969, 1:145).

His trips with Bachman into the field usually took place on Mondays and Tuesdays, Bachman's days off, when he put aside church duties and gave his all to Audubon. On Tuesday, 25 October, for instance, Dr. Henry Ravenell, an authority on sea shells, hosted Bachman and Audubon to "a splendid breakfast Dinner" and ferried them to Sullivan's Island and back in a "six oars boat." The next Monday, the friends drove with Dr. Wilson "9 miles shooting." This excursion was to Liberty Hall, a plantation northwest of Charleston and owned by Bachman's generous friend, Dr. Charles Desel. Bachman was so fond of the plantation, and hunted there so often and so freely, an author residing on a neighboring plantation mistakenly concluded that Bachman owned the Desel property (Irving 1842, 76).

Unlike the hunting parson, who felt practically disabled without a horse under him, Audubon preferred walking to riding, and with fresh memories of the pounding he had taken on the coaches between Richmond and Charleston, apparently he used the word "jostle" quite often (Audubon 1969, 1:143). Bachman began to call him "Old Jostle," a dig at Audubon's complaints and the five-year difference in their ages. He extended the metaphor by calling himself "Young Jostle," but he soon surrendered

"Young Jostle" to John Woodhouse Audubon, renaming himself "Jostle the third." Lucy became "Mrs. Jostle." However lightly conceived, this creation of a family linking Bachman and Audubon less than a month after they met clearly reflects the early closeness of their friendship (4 March 1833, WCFP).

The excursions to Sullivan's Island and Liberty Hall were a prelude to the friends' ambitious expedition to Cole Island in November. This trip was underwritten by one of Bachman's rich Charleston friends, William Kunhardt, a merchant and member of St. John's church, for whom Bachman had named his youngest son.

Situated south of Charleston behind an inlet separating the barrier islands of Folly and Kiawah, Cole faced the Atlantic through the gap. Tides rushed through the passage, building, tearing down, and rebuilding sand banks and bars. Some of the bars grew above the level of high tide, and there wind-blown dunes supported ranks of graceful sea oats. Safe from raccoons and other predators of the mainland, untold numbers of marsh and water birds rested and in season nested on the sandy islets.

Anticipating the Cole Island venture, Audubon wrote to Lucy, "We go there in the boat of a Friend called Connart who although no Sportsman is anxious for the progression of the Birds of America and gives us his boat— 4 negros to row and his clerk to Pilote us under my orders. Mr Bachman always goes with us [on the weekly expeditions], is an excellent shot and full of Life and spirits; we laugh & talk as if we had known each other for Twenty Years" (Audubon 1969, 1:147).

The party set out from Charleston early that morning, but because the "Pilote" was not at all sure of the route through the maze of creeks that led to Cole, delays and wrong turns added to the time and distance traveled and increased the opportunities to see birds. Cold air had flowed in from the north, breaking the heat and lending vigor to men and birds alike. Long-billed curlews, which Audubon had painted two weeks earlier, abounded in the marsh. Their extraordinarily long beaks were the perfect instruments for extracting fiddler crabs from their burrows in the mud and sand. The men observed no whimbrels, a somewhat smaller curlew years later to become common on the South Carolina coast while the long-billed curlews became rare.

Long-billed Curlew. Courtesy of the Thomas Cooper Library, University of South Carolina.

Suddenly Audubon was transfixed by the sight of "two noble 'birds of Washington' sailing majestically over the broad watery face" (Herrick 1968, 2:11). His acquaintance with the bird dated back to 1814, and his designation of it as a distinct species was the great delusion of his career.

Voyaging on the upper Mississippi, to pass the time Audubon had laid dreaming on the deck of the boat. The owner of the vessel, a Canadian, knew of his passenger's interest in birds, and when a great dark eagle sailed into view, the Canadian whooped. Audubon leaped to his feet. They watched the powerful bird until it sailed from sight, then Audubon listened enthralled as the older man explained that this huge raptor, which lacked the glint of gold in its plumage and whose head and tail as well as its body were black, was a species unknown to science (Audubon 1967a, 1:53).

Nearly two decades had passed since Audubon had first seen the great eagle, and Audubon had achieved renown as an ornithologist, but he still looked on the discovery of the bird of Washington as one of his most proud accomplishments. To him it seemed self-evident that the great raptor was no immature bald eagle. If nothing else, he argued, its size proved that. Its wingspan exceeded ten feet, he claimed, and the wingspan of the bald eagle reached only seven. The new species nested on cliffs, the bald always in trees. Unlike the bald, a petty tyrant that mugged ospreys, Washington's eagle plunged into the waters and came up with its own fish. If that were not enough, Audubon could tell Bachman that this greatest of eagles soared in curves more grand and sweeping than those of the bald.

Audubon explained why he named the eagle for George Washington:

> As the new world gave me birth and liberty, the great man who en-
> sured its independence is next to my heart. He had a nobility of mind,
> and a generosity of soul, such as are seldom possessed. He was brave,
> so is the Eagle; like it, too, he was the terror of his foes; and his fame,
> extending from pole to pole, resembles the majestic soaring of the
> mightiest of the feathered tribe. If America has reason to be proud of
> her Washington, so has she to be proud of her great Eagle. (1:55)

How providential that these fabulous birds, which Audubon himself had only rarely seen, should show up to display their uniqueness for Bachman. Now Audubon's learned new friend could gauge for himself that impressive wingspan, that graceful glide, that proud bearing. (Bachman seemed convinced, but doubts persisted in other quarters, and in a letter to Audubon dated 24 April 1837 [WCFP], he disassociated himself with their identification of Washington eagles at Cole Island. "I doubt whether it is found in the south—I think it must be a northwestern mountain species." And eventually Audubon's Washington eagle would prove to be the immature bald eagle after all.)

The hunters reached Cole about noon and whiled away several hours storing provisions in a "small summer habitation then untenanted." Afterward, they explored the island and shot such birds as tempted them. Toward sunset, the party separated into groups, the African Americans went off to the creeks to fish and gather oysters, while the white men stationed themselves at strategic places to intercept curlews that would fly over the island at twilight toward roosting places on Bird Banks (Audubon 1967a, 6:35–38).

The first curlews appeared while the light was yet bright. They whirred over in groups of about ten. As dusk gave way to darkness, the flocks became larger and passed in an unbroken rustling canopy of curlews, flapping, sailing, and flapping again, high above the dunes. On reaching Bird Banks between Cole Island and the sea, the birds dropped down without circling to inspect the sand. Guarded by rip tides, they seemed confident of their safety.

Knowing that barrels full of the succulent curlews would be welcome in Charleston, the hunters in their boat followed the stream of birds. But the instant that Audubon and Bachman stepped out of their little boat and onto the water-packed sand, the curlews roiled up and swung seaward above the sea oats. They put down beyond the range of the guns on the ocean side of the banks, where tremendous waves urged by the chilly northeaster cartwheeled from the open ocean. Curlews continued to pour from the marshes, but they kept a safe distance from the hunters, silhouetted by a thin band of light on the horizon. The light failed. No longer able to see their prey, the men returned to Cole Island and the vigorous fire awaiting them in the habitation.

Most of the party huddled at the hearth to heat their chilled hands. Audubon took over the cooking. Oysters and fish were roasted on hot ashes. Steaks brought from Charleston were broiled on sticks. Someone forgot the salt—Audubon demonstrated gunpowder as a substitute. The "villanous saltpetre" came from the powder horn mixed with charcoal. The hands and faces of the diners were soon smeared black. They had no plates or forks. "Good beverages" flowed freely. The men became so energized with "gaiaty, good appetites, and our hearts all right," Audubon wrote, "it was with some reluctance we spread our blankets, and arranged the fire preparatory to going to rest." Each reclined with feet to the coals, and soon was sleeping soundly, his arms serving as his pillow (6:37).

At dawn they rowed back to Bird Banks, and again the long-billed curlews flew when the sand crunched, this time over the estuary toward their feeding grounds in the salt marsh. Then a different flock of somewhat smaller birds flew in high from the north, passed to the south, and out of sight. A strong onshore wind had forced them inland from migration routes over the Atlantic. They came near enough, Audubon wrote, "for us to ascertain the species." He and Bachman had seen a flight of "Esquimaux Curlews" (6:46).

The party loaded Kunhardt's boat and returned to Charleston. For all the sport of Cole Island, not one new bird had been shot, and as much as Audubon had enjoyed it, from a professional point of view he judged the excursion to Cole a failure.

On Sunday morning, 7 November 1831, Audubon wrote his weekly letter to Lucy, this time complaining that he had been idle for a week and had begun to feel ashamed of the month of trouble he had imposed on the Bachmans. He anticipated an early end to "some of the happiest weeks of my life," and announced that John Bachman was willing to act as "my agent for my Work." Bachman would accept a stock of the first volume of *Birds of America* to be stored in his house, replenished from time to time, and shipped to subscribers as ordered. An even greater responsibility that Audubon imposed on Bachman was caring for the original paintings produced thus far on the expedition. Bachman would store them and dispatch them as needed in London for printing the second volume. He would also collect money from subscribers and shop for supplies, shipping the latter to Audubon at various outposts in the American wilderness. For these labors, Bachman would receive no pay.

The arrangement relieved Audubon of several nagging worries. Knowing Bachman "so well" and confident that Bachman was "uprightly good," he was "quite assured that all will go well with him" (Audubon 1969, 1–150), he wrote to Lucy. For Bachman's part, he was happy to serve a friend he loved. He could hope that, by accepting the care of Audubon's paintings, he would not have seen the last of the ornithologist, and that their intimacy would continue through new struggles and accomplishments.

Just before leaving Charleston, Audubon stopped by the drawing room to wire up a bittern for Maria Martin to draw. He and his helpers, Ward and Lehman, and Pluto, "a beautiful Newfound Land Dog" (1:148) given to Audubon by Dr. Samuel Wilson, departed Charleston at daybreak on Tuesday, 15 November on the *Agness,* a packet that made regular runs between Charleston and St. Augustine. Bachman waved goodbye to his friends at the dock, and then found a place to sit and compose a letter to Lucy as Audubon had requested.

Audubon had worried that the uncertainties of his expedition might discourage his wife. He had made progress in the six years since sailing to England; nevertheless, when he came to Charleston he had drawn less than half of the bird portraits required for *Birds of America,* and had sold far fewer subscriptions than necessary to finance the project *and* support his family. Only one of five volumes of text planned for *Ornithological Biography* had been published. He had to speed up the work. Over the next decade, Bachman's house became, in effect, Audubon's American home where he was always welcomed, where he stored his treasures, where a studio awaited him, and where he frequently returned to work and plan the moves necessary to complete *Birds of America.*

"I comply with a request of your kind and worthy husband," Bachman began, "who laid an injunction on me this morning that I should write to you." He assured Mrs. Audubon that her husband's hardy constitution would see him safely through the wilds of Florida. Meanwhile, he hoped that the people of Charleston would show their mettle by subscribing generously to her husband's work. He added, "The last has been one of the happiest months of my life."

Then Bachman opened his heart. "For the short month he has remained with my family, we were engaged in talking about Ornithology—in collecting birds—in seeing them prepared, and in laying plans for the accompishment of that great work which he has undertaken." Lucy need not doubt that Bachman was fully committed to Audubon's cause, that her husband had acquired a valuable ally. "Time passes rapidly away," Bachman concluded, "and it seems but as yesterday since we met, and now, alas! he is already separated from me—and in all human probability we shall never meet again" (C. Bachman 1888, 96).

Caught up in his own emotions, Bachman had forgotten Lucy's. A suggestion that Audubon might never return to Charleston was sure to alarm her, but he was compelled to write it, fearing that Audubon, who had appeared out of the blue to restore to him the joy and purpose of his youth might, just as unexpectedly, be taken from him.

In effect, Charleston was an island. What happened on the waterfront was so important to the city that its newspapers—each directed to a different political faction—regularly printed detailed shipping news. The names of arriving and departing passengers, letters addressed to Charlestonians, and incoming goods and the merchants who received them were listed for each ship, as well as scheduled departures.

William Kunhardt's countinghouse, a brokerage firm to which Bachman had his mail addressed, overlooked the bustling docks. On 2 December 1831 Bachman received a letter from Audubon and ducked into the firm office to read it and write his answer *immediately,* before the St. Augustine-bound *Agness* cleared the wharf. A letter put aboard on the second day of the month might be in Audubon's hands as early as the fifth or sixth. Bachman hurried. Foregoing his practice of carefully organizing his thoughts, he flitted from one subject to another. As he wrote, the crew hoisted the ship's sails to the accompaniment of creaking pulleys and would soon haul their lines and allow the *Agness* to swing out into the harbor.

"This moment your kind and interesting letter has arrived," he wrote. He told Audubon that the birds had come from the north on the heels of his departure for Florida, and if he had remained in Charleston there would have been plenty for him and his men to do. Someone had given Bachman a pair of wild turkeys. "Do examine into the Migration of Birds—do any birds remain in your part of Florida, that are not found here?" He had read more criticism of the rattlesnake story.

Among the scattered snippets Bachman tucked a spectacular promise. "I have gone carefully over my Ornithology, and have perfected myself in the Fringillas [sparrows and finches], and, I think that you will not catch me napping on that point—Would that I knew the Sylvias [warblers] as well. However the spring will do wonders and we will astonish you with new specimens." He was saying that he knew the sparrows and would study the warblers. Then he would be able to give Audubon the gifts dearest to his heart—new birds for *Birds of America* (C. Bachman 1888, 98).

He had done so many things for his friend and had taken over so much of the routine of his enterprise, Audubon could hardly fail to come back to Charleston—if nothing else, to collect the contents of the skinning room chocked with drying birdskins when Audubon left. Maria Martin had found storage somewhere in the crowded house for his drawings. Bachman had petitions circulating through the city for joint purchases of *Birds of America*. Bachman also stood ready to collect money owed Audubon, to attend to his mail, to buy and ship supplies, to discuss ornithology in long letters, and to stand ever ready to share with Audubon his home, his family, and his friends.

In a moment the *Agness* would be beyond Bachman's reach in the harbor. "They will not wait a moment longer for me, so dear Audubon, farewell" (C. Bachman 1888, 98).

MARIA BACHMAN, HER FATHER'S FIRSTBORN, was a few weeks short of her sixteenth birthday when he decided to take her with him to Sandy Run, a community near Columbia, South Carolina, for the December meeting of the South Carolina Synod. Besides attending to church business and following up on the effort to sell a *Birds of America* subscription to the state, he thought it was time to teach his daughter something of the world beyond Charleston (HB to JB, 14 December 1831, CMBA).

As the eldest child, Maria had shared some tumultuous times with the family. Infant brothers and sisters born every year or so were almost as likely to die as live. She remembered the family anguish when word came from New York that her father was near death, and then that after all he had survived. Even so, he did not return to Charleston for months. She saw the almost continous suffering of her ill mother.

The trip to Columbia was indeed educational. Young Maria learned that a fine horse could die unexpectedly on the road, that Lutheran families along the way would graciously take you in for the night, and that her father often stopped his horses to study the behavior of birds.

In the letter he would write to Audubon about his trip, he would tell of seeing a red-tailed hawk and an American kestrel perched on an oak. Presently the kestrel "made a dash among some snow birds [juncos], and as he was flying away with one, no doubt delighted with the anticipated feast, the Red Tailed took after him, made him drop the dainty bit, and caught it before it fell to the ground" (C. Bachman 1888, 99–100).

Cold wet weather plagued Bachman and his daughter on the long carriage trip home. Maria Bachman spent her sixteenth birthday, 19 December 1831, on the road, and the journey did not end until the bone-chilling night of 22 December had closed over Charleston. The next morning, a weary Bachman elected to let study and letter writing slide in favor of a day of rest.

Harriet Bachman and Maria Martin had other ideas. An Audubon letter had come while Bachman was away, and another the day he came home. The women insisted that he respond to their charming new friend at once. Bachman gave in and told Audubon of their demand, admitting that "this accords with my inclination." He weighed in with a little sermon of sorts. "Look here, my friend, before I forget it, why are you always talking of 'a load of gratitude'—now suppose we say no more about this. Your visit to me gave me new life, induced me to go carefully over my favorite study [ornithology], and made me and my family happy, We have, therefore been mutually obliged and gratified" (101).

ALTHOUGH AUDUBON HATED the sea—he lacked the stomach for it—the voyage to Florida had its bright moments. Bad weather forced the packet to shelter in St. Simon Sound, a bit of luck it turned out. He went ashore and encountered Thomas A. King, the owner of a plantation on the island. The planter invited him to dinner, and although a messenger from the *Agness* rushed up to the table just before the meal was served, and Audubon had to dash back to the packet lest the irritable captain of the *Agness* leave him stranded, King detained Audubon long enough to place his name on the *Birds of America* subscription list (Audubon 1969, 1:152).

A spartan St. Augustine boardinghouse was not easy for Audubon to adjust to after a month in Bachman's home, complete with an "amiable Wife and Sister-in-Law, Two fine young Daughters and 3 paires more of Cherubs." He disliked the old Spanish town and its environs intensely. It was in Audubon's opinion, "the poorest village I have seen in America," with little more around it than "the breaking Sea Surf in our Front and extensive Orange Groves in our rear—As far as I have been in the Interior of this place the Country is wretchedly sterile, Sandy and covered with almost impenetrable Spanish Swoard Plants" (1:156).

The unfriendly landscape gave him a glimpse of a new bird. After twice failing to shoot it himself, Henry Ward bagged it for him. Audubon described it as "a cross between a crow [black vulture] and a vulture [turkey vulture]," and promised Bachman that he would name it after him. In a letter to Lucy written on 29 November 1831, Audubon had puzzled over the strange hawk and his plans for naming it. "It is," Audubon wrote, "a kind of Exotic Bird probably very common in South America but quite unknown to me or to anyone else in this place—it is a mixture of Buzzard and Hawk and I have decided to call it Catharses Floridaniis." In fact, it was a caracara, common in South America as Audubon guessed, but already known to science. Obviously, Audubon had a hard time settling on a name for this bird (1:155).

Putting into motion a grand, if wildly impractical and terribly dangerous, plan to walk the beaches all the way from St. Augustine to the Keys, Audubon ignored the prospects of hostile Indians, storms, and rip currents. He and his men moved southeast along Florida's east coast. They stopped at several plantations, and elected to linger for a while at the estate of sophisticated, young, bored, and alcoholic John Bulow.

The jaded planter found Audubon amusing and seemed willing to go anywhere in pursuit of birds and do anything that struck Audubon's fancy. In a boat rowed by six of Bulow's slaves, they set off for an island noted for its breeding pelicans. Frigid weather—a blizzard by Florida standards—stranded them on the mud flats. For a while it appeared they might die of exposure, but furious bouts of pushing the boat across the mud and hiking through the storm brought them safely through. On Bulow's dock at last, Audubon sighed that their troubles had been "created for no other purpose but to punish us for our sins" (Herrick 1968, 2:15–20).

Quite unknown to Audubon, political contacts he had made in Washington on his journey south were finally bearing results. A copy of an order from the Secretary of the Navy of the United States directing "the officers commanding Revenue Cutters on the Charleston, Key West and Mobile Station" to assist Audubon, finally caught up with him at Bulow's plantation. He was overjoyed, and his solicitous host at once packed Audubon and his men in a wagon and sent them to St. Augustine to take advantage of the order (Audubon 1969, 1:172).

Lieutenant Piercy, commander of the U.S. schooner of war *Spark,* docked at St. Augustine, and presently found himself contemplating the bedraggled adventurers. The official letter specified that he "convey them to such other point within your cruising limits where the duties appertaining to the Revenue Service may lead you and where they may wish to go." Audubon specified the St. Johns River, and Lieutenant Piercy and the *Spark* set out across the short stretch of the Atlantic that separated St. Augustine from the mouth of the stream. A wild and sudden winter storm drove them back into port. On his second try, Piercy managed to enter the sluggish St. Johns River where the fresh snap of the sea was replaced by droning mosquitoes that called hungry mates to the feast (172).

The crew battled boredom by shooting bald eagles and alligators. One of the slaughtered alligators was so big, Audubon said, its blood ran the river red. Half the crew soon fell ill and blamed the stink of the river for it. A sailor accidently shot himself through the forehead. The river seemed determined to destroy them.

When Piercy decided he must flee to the familiar ocean, orders from the navy secretary notwithstanding, a bitter argument broke out. Audubon insisted they continue their exploration of the Florida interior via the *Spark,* and on losing the argument, he and his helper hired a skiff, loaded it with their possessions, including Pluto, the dog Dr. Wilson had given Audubon, and rowed up the fetid waterway even as Piercy and his men fled downstream toward the Atlantic.

After forty miles of twisting and looping and going nowhere, Audubon left one of his assistants on the bank with baggage, and Audubon and the other set out cross-country for St. Augustine, only eighteen miles as an exceptionally efficient crow might fly from where they had moored their little boat on the bank (Audubon 1900, 2:356–58).

Another stormy night compounded their difficulties, but with Pluto's nose to sniff out the trail, "used by Seminole Indians for ages," they reached the town about dawn (2:356–58). Their cross-country trip supported Audubon's earlier prediction to his wife, "My account of what I have or shall see of the Floridas will be far, very far from corroborating the flowery sayings of Mr Barton [William Bartram] the Botanist" (Audubon 1969, 1:183).

Pluto and the men boarded the *Agness* in St. Augustine on 5 March and set sail for Charleston. As usual, the weather was fine at the start of a voyage, otherwise the ship would have waited it out in the harbor. Passengers loitered on deck enjoying blue sky, blue water, and white sails that flashed on the horizon. One set of sails loomed larger and larger, and presently Audubon identified the *Spark*. Obviously Piercy had recognized the *Agness*.

The *Spark* pulled alongside and Piercy signaled that he wished to come aboard. He had secured a pair of magnificent tundra swans, perhaps in Norfolk while he had tied up for quick repairs, and he presented them to Audubon as a peace offering. Piercy whispered to Audubon that *he hoped* Audubon would not tell anyone "the reasons why I had left his Vessel."

The "Supurb pair of Swans" pleased Audubon but did not alter his opinion of their donor. "The man may have a good heart, but if his head like an empty box contains not brains enough to enable him to be a worthy Gentleman—the man and the head may go adrift from me" (1:184). (Audubon would not paint a tundra swan until 1838, when he had returned to London to complete publication of *Birds of America*. Actually, Florida is well south of the normal range of this species, but in Audubon's mind this swan was forever linked with the *Spark* and Florida, and when he drew one of the swans in London, he painted yellow water lilies native to Florida in the background.)

After their encounter on the high seas, the *Spark* scudded gracefully south toward St. Augustine and the *Agness* bucked full sail northeast toward Charleston. On 7 March 1832, just forty miles off Charleston, a gale forced the *Agness* back to Savannah, where Audubon went ashore to wait out the storm.

As he walked from the docks to a hotel, he felt the stares of pedestrians bemused by his tattered, dirty clothes, his neglected gray beard, and his imposing "Mustacios." He was not the least embarrassed. He regarded the stares as gestures of admiration accorded a romantic adventurer's triumphant return to civilization. As soon as he had stored his bags in his room, he marched off to find William Gaston, the businessman recommended by the Rathbones of Liverpool, who had handled Audubon's mail while he was in Florida. Gaston suggested that they get together at his home to look at Audubon's Florida drawings. Audubon was pleased that other guests had been invited, among them Colonel Keath of St. Augustine and Major John Eatton Leconte of the U.S. Army, a distinguished officer and well-known naturalist (1:184–85).

Audubon's windblown hair and sunburned skin testified to the hardships of the Florida wilderness. His marvelous birds, painted in the field only days earlier, testified to the grandeur of *Birds of America*. The centerpiece of his exhibition was the militant caracara, a subject he could not have better chosen to appeal to the military men in his audience. Audubon had solved a difficult problem in composing the picture. As he believed the bird to be a new species, he wanted to show the world the caracara's every feather. A way to do that was to paint two views of the same pose, one from the back and one from the front, representing two birds. Audubon assigned each image a role in a drama. The aggressor, with his back to the viewer, sets his mandibles as though snarling and narrows his eyes in an uncompromising glare as he dives toward his opponent whose vulnerable underside is exposed. The caracara on the defense draws back, beak agape, eyes wide and frightened. The bare faces of both birds glow blood red.

None of Gaston's guests put his name on the line just yet. The officers may have lacked resources to subscribe, and obviously when Gaston, one of Savannah's most successful businessmen hung back, they felt no pressure to step forward. Gaston supported a negative response by doubting that a subscriber could be found in all of Savannah, adding that he "had so many calls for his money that he could not do so" (1:185).

An unexpected chance to convince Gaston he should subscribe to *Birds of America* came to Audubon the next morning when he went to the merchant's office to reimburse him for expenses incurred in handling Audubon's mail. He had a conversation with Major LeConte about "the Philadelphians" who had abused Audubon with false allegations and unfounded criticism. As the Philadelphia story unfolded, Gaston's attitude changed and he signaled his clerk, who left the room for a few minutes. The clerk returned and Gaston lay a two-hundred-dollar check in Audubon's hand.

"My dear Mr. A.—I now Subscribe to your Work and would were it the last 200 I have," Gaston said. He escorted Audubon to the hotel and had Audubon's paintings displayed on the floor. Within an hour, two spectators had signed up and Audubon had six hundred dollars in his pocket (1:185). The conversation about Audubon's Philadelphia competitors did even more for Audubon than he realized at the time. Having taken Audubon's side against Ord and others, "that most extraordinary man Wam Gaston" became a zealot in Audubon's cause. In all, the merchant secured six *Birds of America* subscriptions besides his own. Further, Gaston ensured that Audubon would be paid in full by inserting a clause in sales agreements obligating the estates of subscribers for the complete work (Fries 1973, 197).

Meanwhile, Audubon's men boarded the *Agness* without him. He caught the mail coach to Charleston, electing jostling rather than *mal de mer*.

Bachman met the coach on 10 March 1832, and a dirty and disheveled Audubon jumped out and embraced his friend. At the house in Cannonsborough, Audubon found everyone well, including six-week-old Catherine, the fourteenth and last-born of John and Harriet's children. That night a lamp burned late in the study while the friends talked and talked after nearly four months of separation.

On Tuesday, the *Agness* entered Charleston harbor with Ward, Lehman, Pluto, and Audubon's baggage. The drawing and skinning rooms at Bachman's house were cleared for work; everything was set for a second productive Charleston interlude, including a tide of birds sweeping north along the coast. Snowy egrets were the theme of a crescendo. A few flew in from the south on 18 March. By the twenty-fifth, "thousands were seen in the marshes and rice-fields." Predictably, a snowy egret became the focus of Audubon's first big painting of the spring (Audubon 1967a, 6:163).

After completing the bird except for the fine white plumes, Audubon turned over the picture to Lehman for the landscape. A slate sky clears after a storm. On the horizon, nestled among live oaks, a red-roofed plantation house stands skirted by wide piazzas. A lake, called a "reserve" by the rice planters, reaches to the foreground, where the snowy egret stands on a muddy, weed-covered bank. With Lehman's share of the painting done, Audubon retrieved his brush and traced the plumes against the storm clouds.

A tiny figure of a distant hunter, stocky like Bachman, stalks the egret.

Indeed, he seems to be "the hunting Parson" himself, inserted in the composition by Audubon as an afterthought to a happy day in the field. (The snowy egret is the only published plate from *Birds of America* that contains a human figure. But in the published print, produced in London, someone has dressed up the hunter and topped him off with an elegant hat, a costume appropriate to the wealthy Englishmen who at that time were Audubon's chief customers for *Birds of America*.)

On her own sheet, Maria Martin copied that intricate painting to the last fine line—omitting the hunter. She betrayed her pride in her work by penciling on the back of her sheet, "March 26 1832. Copied from Mr. Audubon's picture" (Sanders and Ripley 1985, 75). Bachman's sister-in-law had learned a lot about watercolor during the six months she had known Audubon.

Less than a month later, Audubon tallied the accomplishments of his team during their second sojourn in Charleston: "9 beautiful Drawings and collected an immense deal of information." He had also won a *Birds of America* subscription from the Charleston Library Society, found several likely subscribers, and received payments collected by William Gaston. "This will ease my Lucy's mind I am quite sure," he wrote to his fretful wife, urging her to "depend upon my exertions for your comfort I think of nothing else," insisting she could expect results from his efforts "at no far distant period" (Audubon 1969, 1:193).

On Saturday, 13 April, the "U.S. Schooner MARION" came to Charleston. Audubon boarded her at once to meet her commander, Lieutenant Day, who impressed him as a "Gentleman." The officer and his vessel were under the direct command of James R. Pringle, a Charlestonian and Collector of the Port. The lieutenant could help Audubon only if Pringle issued the orders. To Audubon's relief, he recognized Pringle as a fellow dinner guest at the home of Joel Poinsette, whose power in the Union party extended to Washington. Pringle asked Audubon where he wanted to go. On hearing the answer, Pringle ordered the *Marion* to sail for the Florida Keys on Wednesday. "Thus my Lucy," Audubon chortled, "I will once more put to sea aboard a man of War and again visit that poor Country the Floridas!!" (1:193).

He left his latest drawings, which included such birds as the little blue heron, the lesser yellow-legs, and the boat-tailed grackles with a fine rendering of live-oak foliage by George Lehman, "in the hands and care of Mrs Bachman's Sister—Miss Martin a most kind Friend of ours believe me." He promised Lucy to avoid the poisonous night air of Florida by sleeping on the ship or camping on the beach. At either site he would enjoy a healthful sea breeze. After placating Lucy as much as he could with his pen, he asked Bachman to write to her as well (1:194–95).

Bachman complied, insisting that the Keys were not so unhealthy as generally thought. Audubon had become part of his family, Bachman wrote, and promised to pass on to Lucy any news he received about him. Having learned how depressed and anxious Audubon became when his work slowed down, and how his slowdowns upset Lucy, Bachman signed off with a reassuring observation, "During Mr Audubons last stay in our City he was generally kept well employed & was consequently in good Spirits" (21 April 1832, CMBA). In fact, Audubon's melancholia distressed Bachman, too.

The "Lady of the Green Mantle," as the smugglers of the Keys called the *Marion*, was anchored off Key West at sunset on 14 May 1832, and Audubon's party went ashore in a small boat. There Dr. Benjamin Strobel, naturalist, brother-in-law of Bachman's wife, and editor of the *Key West Gazette*, awaited them. Audubon declined Strobel's invitation to stay at his house in Key West overnight, insisting that he had to return to the *Marion* as he had promised Lucy. Nevertheless, he and Strobel saw one another almost daily until the *Marion* sailed north toward the end of May (Hammond 1963, 80:465).

Strobel had a newspaper to publish, but one day he deserted his desk and went with Audubon into the field. For twenty-one hours, they scrambled over mangrove roots, slogged through miles of shallows, and stumbled in knee-deep mud in search of birds, shells, and plants. "To Mr. Audubon this was an every day affair," Strobel reported to his readers, and indeed, not only did Audubon race through that day, he charged through the entire expedition in a state of exhilaration, collecting specimens and making notes that would spice *Ornithological Biography* with adventures and firsthand observations of little-known birds (80:466).

About one bird, Audubon was particularly curious. In Charleston, before he sailed, Bachman had shown him an odd specimen Strobel had sent from Key West, the head of a dove strikingly marked with a white band beneath the eye. Suspecting that the bird had not been described, Audubon was determined to collect it on this expedition (Audubon 1967a, 5:15).

The military community of Key West, responding no doubt to the letter from Washington backing Audubon's expedition, and influenced by Bachman's friends Joel Poinsette and James Pringle, rallied to Audubon's cause. Major Glassel of the United States Artillery put "Serjeant Sykes" at Audubon's disposal to help him find the dove. Soon, "with the slowness and carefulness usually employed by a lynx or cougar when searching for prey," Sykes and Audubon were threading through the thorns and mosquitoes of an island scrub forest. Suddenly, Sykes raised his gun and fired. Audubon crawled through the thick underbrush to the spot where the dove had fallen and found Sykes smoothing its feathers. The Key West quail-dove, which Audubon first became aware of in Bachman's study in Charleston, would find its place in *Birds of America* (5:15–16).

The body of the quail-dove was not all that Audubon obtained when Sykes pulled the trigger; Audubon gained something to write about, an adventure to share with his readers. "How I gazed on its resplendent plumage—how I marked the expression of its rich-coloured, large and timid eye, as the poor creature was gasping its last breath." He asked his reader a question: "Did ever an Egyptian pharmacopolist employ more care in embalming the most illustrious of the Pharaohs, than I did in trying to preserve from injury this most beautiful of the woodland cooers!" (5:16).

The Florida Keys yielded Audubon a rich harvest of birdskins and "episodes." He found such exciting new birds as the great white heron, the "largest and most beautiful Heron that has yet been discovered." He experienced a squall so violent that "when at last its frightened blasts have ceased, Nature, weeping and disconsolate, is left bereaved of her beautious offspring" (Audubon 1900, 2:368). He listened while the pilot of the *Lady of the Green Mantle* recounted wading and risking injury by a barracouta that "might at one dart cut off his legs, or some other nice bit, with which he was unwilling to part." He described how a turtle brought aboard the *Marion* demonstrated jaws so powerful it deeply dented a "hammered piece of iron" (2:377).

Early in June the *Marion* tied up at a Charleston wharf and Audubon unloaded the rich harvest from his six-week tour of islands and waters off the tip of Florida. For those Charlestonians who had missed watching five cartloads of natural treasure hauled to Cannonsborough, Bachman prepared a detailed accounting that appeared in the 6 June 1832 edition of *The Courier*. The trove contained shells, corals, boxes of seeds, roots of plants, amphibious animals, mammals, and "upwards of five hundred and fifty birds, principally of the larger species."

Two of the raucous young herons were allowed the run of Bachman's garden. Their wings had been clipped, but they managed to climb high into the garden trees to roost. "They are great at catching butterflies and sphinxes [hawk moths]," Bachman wrote. But as they matured they became fierce, and one of the herons skewered their cat with a single thrust. When they progressed to chasing his children, Bachman had the herons destroyed.

The paintings of Florida birds and plants were stunning. Clearly Audubon and Lehman had perfected their partnership with such drawings as the adult brown pelican and the mangrove, the white-crowned pigeon and with flowers of the gieger-tree, and the gray kingbird framed by crimson blossoms of the Australian corkwood.

Maria Martin studied these paintings with care. By June 1832, she was no longer an amateur in awe of the professionals who instructed her. An intense apprenticeship of eight months had brought her to the point where she could contribute directly to *Birds of America*. Perhaps because she felt herself a working member of Audubon's crew, she innocently asked George Lehman, also on the team, to purchase certain art supplies for her when he returned to Philadelphia. Miss Martin *and* Lehman would hear from Audubon about that (Audubon 1969, 1:196).

Contemplating Audubon's five cartloads of treasure progressing down Pinckney Street, Bachman may have felt that his own discoveries of the spring were paltry and insignificant, but he had not met Audubon empty-handed. Bachman had visited Round O, about thirty miles southwest of Charleston, where Paul H. S. Lee, one of Harriet's brothers-in-law, owned a plantation.

Ten miles from the Lees' place, in a swamp near Parker's Ferry on the Edisto River, Bachman had heard the ringing notes of a bird he did not know. "They resembled the sounds of some extraordinary ventriloquist in such a degree, that I supposed the bird much farther from me than it really was; for after some trouble caused by these fictitious notes, I perceived it near to me, and soon shot it." Bachman collected two additional singing males of the plain, brown, swamp species that Audubon would name "Swainson's Warbler"—Swainson had named a woodpecker after him (Audubon 1967a, 2:84).

Bachman concluded that another bird, a sparrow that he had encountered in April near Parker's Ferry, also had not yet been described. As with Swainson's warbler, his attention was drawn to its clear, strong, whistled notes, a cardinal-like song, which here and there rang out from sandy pine ridges bordering the swamps. "On searching for the same bird in the neighborhood of Charleston, I discovered it breeding in small numbers on the Pine Barrens, about six miles north of this city, where I obtained many specimens of it" (3:113).

Nothing would do but for Bachman and Audubon to go to the pine barrens and listen to the new sparrow. Before riding back to town, "The Hunting Parson" shot one and placed the warm body in the hand of his friend. It was the perfect occasion for Bachman to lecture Audubon on the usefulness of bird song in finding new birds. Though he was no "connoisseur in music," Bachman later recounted, he found no difficulty in recognizing any known American bird from its song. He made it his habit, when looking for new birds, to listen for new songs. It required only close attention and practice. Although Audubon at first expressed doubts about the system, he listened to what Bachman had to say (Bachman 1855c, 11).

A report of an unfamiliar bird in an unlikely setting sent the friends on a wild-goose chase. One of Paul Lee's sons came to the ornithologists to report a pair of flycatchers that he could not identify nesting in the trees on the campus of the College of Charleston. Bachman and Audubon listened politely to the tale, but put little stock in it. A week later young Lee returned to insist that the men come look at the birds. Unfortunately, some boys had destroyed the nest. A "common king bird" (eastern kingbird) flew overhead and the friends jumped to the conclusion that it was this bird that had built the nest. "We jeered our young observer, and returned home" (Audubon 1967a, 1:203).

Audubon and his assistants worked in Charleston for almost a month. He and Lehman painted the black-crowned night-heron, the common egret, and the sparrow that Audubon and Bachman thought was new. The latter would appear in *Birds of America* as Bachman's pinewood-finch; today called Bachman's sparrow (and not, after all, a new species as Bachman thought). In the painting, this obscurely marked "Fringilla" perches on a sprig of the rare fever-tree (*Pinckneya pubens*) of the southern swamps, the specimen obtained from "the beautiful botanic garden of M. Noisette." Faintly penciled on the paper is the date of the painting, "June 25 1832" (Audubon 1966, plate 363).

Probably Bachman's sparrow was the last work that Audubon and Lehman did before they caught a coach for Philadelphia, leaving Henry Ward in Charleston. A position as taxidermist at the Charleston Museum had been arranged by Bachman for Ward so that the young man could support himself while collecting birdskins for Audubon and Bachman.

Enduring the stagecoach ride north, Audubon was reminded of Bachman's claim that one could identify birds simply by listening to their songs. In his 1 July 1832 letter to his friend, he mentioned, "saw *thousands* of *Warbling Bachmani's* as far as the Roanoke when of a sudden this sweet songster gave way" (Audubon 1969, 1:195).

Chapter 6

EUONYMUS AND EAGLES

FTER EIGHT MONTHS in the South that netted Audubon many subscriptions, dozens of new paintings, hundreds of birdskins, and many new friends and subscribers, Philadelphia, a city that harbored deep ambivalence toward Audubon, was bound to be a letdown. In the first place, Lucy and the boys did not meet him there as expected. Then, he was confronted by what amounted to an all-out attack in the April edition of *Louden's Journal,* an important natural history journal published in London (Audubon 1969, 1:195–96). In an article titled "On the Faculty of Scent of the Vulture," Charles Waterton disputed Audubon's claim that American vultures locate carrion by sight rather than by scent. The assault on his credibility shocked and upset Audubon, the more so because he knew that George Ord was behind it. His Philadelphia enemy had made no secret of the alliance he had consummated with Charles Waterton. Under these circumstances Audubon looked forward to staring Ord down at an upcoming meeting of the Philosophical Society, and taking smug satisfaction in laying before the savants of the Quaker City his latest discoveries, evidence of his ornithological eminence. Fate had conspired to strengthen Audubon's credentials. On a field trip near Camden, New Jersey, right under the noses of his rivals, he had collected a startling novelty, the fork-tailed flycatcher of the American tropics (Audubon 1967a, 1:196).

About this time, Audubon got wind of the favor Miss Martin had asked of George Lehman that made Audubon fire him on the spot. Obviously jealous of Lehman because of the friendship that had developed between him and Miss Martin, he commented to Bachman in his 1 July 1832 letter, "I am not angry but rather mortified that your Dear Sweet heart and sister should have commissioned Lehman and not her sincere friend to send her paper colours & & &—She must make this up with me at some future time or other meantime God bless her!" For years after this incident Audubon had nothing to do with Lehman, even going so far as to curtly refuse a requested recommendation.

Sad to say, though there may have been some deeper reason for his treatment of Lehman, Audubon no longer needed him. John Woodhouse was producing bird drawings good enough to publish, and Maria Martin, having completed her apprenticeship in painting botanical subjects, birds, and butterflies, was producing much that Audubon could be proud to use.

Embarrassed and distressed by Audubon's reaction to her innocent transaction with Lehman, Maria Martin penned an apology and followed up by painting industriously. "Maria has drawn for you the Franklinia," Bachman soon reported, "a very pretty red Hibiscus, is preparing to do another of a white color and has also drawn a splendid bignonia. . . . She will not forget her instructor and I am sure will ever do you credit" (Bachman 1929, 178).

For his part, Bachman passed on the news that young Lee had been right when he reported the nesting of exotic flycatchers on the College of Charleston campus. Shortly after Audubon had left for the North, the birds had built another nest, laid a new clutch of eggs, and hatched young. Bachman was notified and promptly identified the family as gray kingbirds, the same species portrayed in one of Audubon's spectacular Key West paintings. Audubon, who had learned from his mentor, claimed that his attention was first drawn to the gray kingbirds of the Florida Keys because their notes were unfamiliar to him (Audubon 1967a, 1:201).

Among Harriet Bachman's relatives, the Lees were particularly close. The young discoverer of the gray kingbirds was a son of Paul Hutson Lee. Paul Lee had married Jane Elizabeth Martin, one of Harriet's sisters. Jane died, and Paul married Lynch Helen Van Rhyn of Holland. Even before the wedding in March 1828, Miss Van Rhyn had become a warm friend of the Bachmans. And on 11 March 1828, almost coinciding with the wedding, John and Harriet Bachman named their eleventh child Lynch Helen.

Lynch Helen Lee welcomed Harriet to Round O. As the years passed and Harriet's health deteriorated, more and more often she resorted to country interludes to restore her. She developed a chronic cough and suffered attacks of severe facial pain, sometimes so intense she could not bear to let anything touch her teeth. When pain overwhelmed her, she would travel to Round O for a few weeks of rest. One of these visits took place in July 1832.

The ride from Charleston to Round O in Bachman's horse-drawn "chair" (gig) consumed the better part of the day. Perhaps the most pleasant hours of the trip were about two-thirds of the way where the road left the barren pine lands, entered Caw Caw Swamp, northeast of the Edisto River, and continued through shady swamps to the river bank at Parker's Ferry. The swamp forest, rich in birds, supported an array of trees—gigantic oaks, black gums, tulip poplars, cypress, and magnolias.

In April 1832, on a similar visit (Audubon 1967a, 3:113), Bachman sorted out the songs of the swamp birds as he rode. The morning reverberated with staccato hooded warblers, buzzing parulas, whistling yellow-throateds, in voice so like the painted buntings, and Bachman's recent discovery, the ventriloquial Swainson's warblers.

Later, on a midsummer morning, Bachman returned to Round O to deliver Harriet to the Lees for another visit. This time, Bachman could hear a different medley of bird sounds in the swamps—the ducklike grunts of white ibis, unducklike whistles of wood ducks, and resentful brawls of great blue herons routed from green-shadowed retreats. For the most part, small songbirds were quiet in July, though every now and then the song of a Carolina wren or a cardinal rang out.

The swamp was cool as usual, the ferry crossing of the clear black waters of the Edisto even cooler. Dense forests shaded the swift and narrow stream, from its headwaters in the sandhills to its mouth at the ocean. Harriet's destination lay only ten miles southwest of Parker's Ferry.

As Bachman had his church to serve, he stayed at Round O just long enough to rest his horse. Near Parker's Ferry, traveling toward Charleston, he glimpsed an active little warbler in the underbrush beside the road, and because he could not identify it, he shot it. "It was an old female that had to all appearance just reared a brood of young" (Audubon 1967a, 2:93).

Even in hand the identity of the tattered old bird was puzzling. Basically, it was yellow with greenish upper parts, a gray bib flecked with black feathers, and a gray crown. Its beak was noticeably long and slightly curved, unusual for a warbler. At home Bachman made a skin of it and began a careful search for its match in his books and birdskin collection. He felt no rush to titillate Audubon with news of the new specimen until he knew its name.

In Philadelphia, Lucy, John Woodhouse, Victor, and Audubon were at last reunited, and for the first time in six years they set off together, this time toward Boston. John Woodhouse, pale after a bout with fever, had dropped his boyish ambition to pilot a Mississippi steamboat. Now he was prepared to learn to draw. Victor brought his experience in the Bakewell financial network to bear on the increasingly complex affairs of *Birds of America,* a cause that would involve Lucy, too.

When he heard that the Audubon family had rallied around *Birds of America,* John Bachman perceived it as an important development. He predicted that the alliance would be seen by subscribers as a guarantee that the work would be finished even if Audubon should die. Subscribers would receive the plates that they had committed themselves to buy. Bachman advised Audubon to mention the arrangement in the preface to the next volume of *Ornithological Biography* (C. Bachman 1888, 107).

The Audubons settled briefly in a Boston boardinghouse—they had no home of their own—and Audubon canvassed what proved to be a lucrative market. He planned a foray to Maine and New Brunswick. The whole family went, and though they found very few new birds, the effort tested their solidarity. For the first time, Lucy got a taste of work in the field.

On returning to Boston, Victor was dispatched to London to supervise the printing and distributing of the prints of *Birds of America.* Audubon stayed put to draw birds, and thanks to his growing fame, some of his models he acquired with minimal effort. Daniel Webster, the great U.S. senator and orator, sent him a pair of rare Labrador ducks. And he purchased a living golden eagle from a trapper for a few dollars (Audubon 1969, 1:200). This magnificent bird, captured in its prime, had had the misfortune to investigate a trap set for foxes in the mountains of New Hampshire and was itself caught. For some time the artist studied the regal postures of the eagle and reluctantly concluded that to draw it properly he must kill it. Anxious not to mar the perfect plumage, Audubon went to great lengths to dispatch it without leaving a mark. He put the captive in a sealed room in which charcoal and sulphur burned. Frequently Audubon stepped out for air, but the eagle survived despite the noxious fumes, and finally Audubon pierced its heart with a steel pin (Herrick 1968, 2:34–35).

The composition of the drawing reflects the violence that attends the lives of golden eagles. In the original painting, the huge bird, wings bent sharply to bring them parallel to its body, triumphantly catapults into the sky with a white hare clutched in its talons, one claw puncturing an eye. In snowy mountains below, a careful climber inches across a fallen tree bridging a deep chasm. It is Audubon. A gun and what appears to be a dead eagle are strapped to his back as he risks life and limb for his cause (Audubon 1966, original drawing for plate 54. Havell omitted the climber in engraving the plate).

While painting the golden eagle, Audubon fell gravely ill. He had spent one night drawing it, and painted for sixty hours before he collapsed in paralysis. Lucy and John thought that he was dying. Audubon himself, treated by some of the best physicians in Boston, was thoroughly frightened. John Bachman shared the crisis via the mail. In his opinion, the illness told Audubon to mend his ways; specifically, Bachman chided his friend "to abandon for a time your sedentary pursuits" (1 April 1833, WCFP).

Audubon bounced back quickly from his illness and left Boston to arrange for the expedition to Labrador. He wrote to Lucy from Eastport that his health had returned and implied that exercise, and a break in snuffing and drinking, which had become chronic, had worked its cure (Audubon 1969, 1:223).

Audubon and Bachman kept in close touch during the residence of the Audubon family in Boston, extending through the fall of 1832 and into the spring of 1833. In Bachman's letter of 20 October 1832, he struck a teasing, almost taunting, chord. On the one hand he told his friend, "I have been studying up my Ornithology in order to be useful to you, and if I am spared I hope to be so. A month in your society would afford me a greater treat than the highest prize in a lottery." On the other hand, he made Audubon's return to Charleston the ransom Audubon would have to pay for possession of Bachman's new birds and Maria's new wildflower paintings. "My sister Maria, has made several drawings, which she thinks of sending you; but I am anxious to retain them for awhile, in hopes that you may be tempted to come for them yourself" (C. Bachman 1888, 102).

Bachman kept rephrasing the message in letter after letter, promising new birds and drawings, but stalling delivery. He tantalized his friend with news of another new sparrow that he had shot and Maria Martin had drawn, and when Audubon begged for the skin and the drawing, Bachman answered, "Your request, that I should send the bird-skins, is a natural one, but it cannot be granted all in a hurry. . . . Have patience, for in good time you shall see all" (104).

Benjamin Strobel sent a box of skins to Charleston, and among other contents Bachman came on a new hummingbird that Strobel himself had struck with a stick from a bush in Key West. By his words, Bachman dangled the new birds just out of Audubon's reach, "So we have now, two Humming Birds." Strobel also mentioned a new pigeon—Bachman added, "but it may all be a mistake; besides, I must always keep something in reserve" (105).

He promised Audubon that he would send information, drawings, and skins when he returned from the annual meeting of the South Carolina Synod in the interior of the state. "Maria has figured for you the 'White Hibiscus,' and, also, a red one, both natives, and beautiful; a Euonymus in seed, in which our Sylvia (the female warbler collected near Parker's Ferry in July) is placed; the white Nondescript Rose, the Gordonica, a Bignonia, &. She is prepared to send them to you—shall she ship them at once to Boston?" Bachman did send a few items, but he held back the specimens and drawings he knew were most important to Audubon (106).

The limited set of Maria Martin drawings, when at last Bachman released it and it reached Boston, satisfied more than Audubon's curiosity. The pace of publishing *Birds of America* had stepped up, and he was pressed to supply Havell with drawings ready for printing. Audubon sorted through the drawings he had on hand, selecting five that worked together as a number, and shipped them to London.

Maria Martin's "Gordonia," or loblolly-bay, was of immediate use. She had painted a clump of the white roselike flowers at top right connected with another at bottom left by a long bare stem on which a bird could be placed. The slender stem was just right for the fork-tailed flycatcher that Audubon had collected in New Jersey. Audubon copied his earlier sketch of the graceful bird directly onto Miss Martin's sheet of flowers. Where the

Fork-tailed Flycatcher. Courtesy of the Thomas Cooper Library, University of South Carolina.

flycatcher's tail crossed some of the Gordonia leaves, green leaves showed through the white (not painted) shafts of the long tail feathers. Besides crediting Maria Martin with painting the flowers, Audubon wrote, "The twig from which the drawing was made was procured from the garden of Mr. Noisette, who liberally afforded me all in his power for establishing my plates" (Audubon 1967a, 1:196–97).

December came and Bachman continued to guard the trove of skins and drawings he had promised to send when he returned to Charleston from the church meeting. Events that had nothing to do with his friendship with Audubon had left him depressed, so much so that despite daily resolutions to write to his friend, the time slipped by and a second letter arrived from Audubon in Boston though the previous one lay unanswered.

The problem weighing so heavily on Bachman was the threat of South Carolina to impose "the hydra-headed 'Nullification'"—the proposition that a federal law could be cancelled if a state deemed it unconstitutional. In this case, it was federal tariffs on manufactured goods that white South-erners felt raised their costs and undercut the price they were paid for cotton, to the benefit of industrial New England. South Carolina threat-ened to nullify the tariffs. Bachman and others in Charleston feared that nullification was a step toward dissolving the Union. The issue troubled him in particular because he felt intense loyalty to the Union, yet he could not bear the thought of disloyalty to South Carolina, his adopted state (C. Bachman 1888, 108–9).

Christmas was less than a week away before Bachman forced himself to write. Principally it was a plea for Audubon's sympathy, for his friend to show "love and charity toward me, by writing me often, although I may not answer you immediately" (108).

Perhaps Christmas diverted Bachman from politics. At last, on 27 De-cember he was able to furnish Audubon with notes on the life histories of the great white heron, Bachman's pinewood finch, and the reddish egret. He also sent some ornithological speculation. "May not the North-ern Marsh Hen, be the Bird which we here call the Fresh Water M. Hen & our Ash coloured one that keeps in the Marsh be peculiar to the South?" (Bachman 1929, 180). This was the opening volley of a discussion that would lead Bachman and Audubon to agree that the king rail and the clapper were different species.

Bachman had collected two sparrows in the salt marsh, one of which he regarded as new. He tried to convince Audubon that a kinglet he had shot and skinned was new because, unlike the other two kinglets, it lacked bright color in its crown. He also pressed Audubon for his opinion of the female "Sylvia," which Maria had portrayed so fetchingly on the twig of the "Euonymus in seed" (180).

Responding to Bachman's call for comment, Audubon suggested that the warbler Bachman had shot in July was nothing more than Wilson's mourning warbler. Bachman believed the mourning warbler was the same species as the common yellowthroat, and certainly was not the same as the female "Sylvia" in question (183). Again Audubon insisted that Bachman send the other skins and drawings said to represent new species so that he could appraise them firsthand.

Not until early February did the good pastor yield the material Audubon wanted. He scratched off a quick message: "On Board of the Barque Chief—Capt Eldridge, I have sent a long promised Box containing Drawings and a few bird skins" (9 February 1833, APSL).

A burden seemed to lift from Bachman's shoulders. He was at his most sentimental in addressing "Old Jostle" in Boston a week later: "I am just thinking had I the wings of your great eagle [the Washington eagles near Cole Island] and could go at the usual rate of a mile a minute, I would just be in time to pounce down upon you all at breakfast time, Old and young Jostle and Lady Jostle—what a treat to shake you all by the hand and look over your drawings. . . . Tell me, friend, when are we to see you in Charleston" (18 February 1833, WCFP).

IN WRITING THAT EAGLES FLY at a mile a minute, Bachman had not just plucked a figure from the air. Ever since Audubon had turned up in Charleston and inspired Bachman to return to his "favorite Subject," suspended when Wilson died, he had been studying ornithology as a science, in particular bird migration. He organized his thoughts into an essay, "The Migration of the Birds of North America," and on 15 March, a Friday, he read his paper before a meeting of the Charleston Philosophical Society (C. Bachman 1888, 117).

As late as the 1830s, many, though not all, naturalists believed that numberless birds wintered under the mud of marshes and ponds. In his journal, Audubon reported seeing huge flocks of tree swallows flying over New Orleans in the spring of 1821. Their spotless plumage, Audubon observed, meant that the birds had not hibernated in the mud, else their snowy breasts would have been stained by it. Bachman shared this interpretation, and in his essay saw no necessity to marshal evidence to prove the point. Rather, he asserted as obvious, "migration is incontrovertible," and went on to address the speeds at which birds migrate and the fundamental question of why they migrate. He limited himself, as a matter of scientific principle, to facts that he had himself had observed (117–24).

"Birds migrate," he postulated, "either to avoid the cold of winter, or to find more abundant food." Well-oiled feathers and thick down insulate them from cold, he reasoned, and hearts that beat so rapidly that "the pulsation can scarcely be counted," sustaining body temperatures "as high as 106 degrees Fahrenheit." On the other hand, birds that depend on active insects for food are more likely than seed-eaters to migrate, he had noticed. Among water birds, those that feed in freshwater lakes and streams subject to frequent freezing are more likely to migrate than those that forage in salt water, which freezes less readily (119–20).

Bachman had seen passenger pigeons that instead of migrating lingered in the North for as long as "beech-nuts and buck-wheat—their favorite food" were not covered by snow. And conversely, "It is only when the forests of the West have failed in their usual supply of mast and berries, that the wild pigeons come among us [in South Carolina] to claim a share of the acorns and berries of our woods, and the refuse grains scattered over our rice fields." He thus concluded that it was to ensure a food supply, and not simply to avoid the cold, that birds migrate (121).

As to the speed of migration, careful observations allowed him to venture an answer. The stomachs of ducks and pigeons killed in spring in "our distant northern settlements [New England]" contained undigested rice, indicating that in a single day they had flown "nine hundred and sixty miles since feeding in the fields of our Southern Plantations"—any longer and the rice would have been digested. Simple arithmetic showed that the well-fed birds had traveled at about forty miles per hour (118, 121).

The migration of birds, Bachman noted toward the end of his paper, "is a wide field open for inquiry and study." Observations he had made in his aviary suggested questions. There he had kept "robins, finches, and orioles, that had been procured when young at the North." With the coming of spring these captives, which had never before migrated, "exhibited, by their constant fluttering, a disposition to escape, and the moment this was effected, they flew off, not to the south or West, but as directly in the line of expected migration, as if guided by a compass" (121).

Here was mystery. How could birds know that the day had come for their return to breeding grounds in New England? How could they determine in which direction they should fly? "The temple of nature, wide and wonderful as it is, stands ever open," Bachman assured his audience, "inviting all to enter and learn lessons which are calculated not only to enlighten the mind, but to improve the heart" (124).

On 17 March, two days after presenting his paper on migration, Bachman hitched his horse to the "chair" (a two-wheeled, single-horse carriage), to transport his ill wife to Round O to spend about a month at the Lee plantation. The ride through the country gave Bachman a chance to ruminate about birds along the way. Several ornithological problems hovered in his mind. He had sent all of the new birds and information that his friend had been so anxious to get, and yet six weeks and several letters later he still had heard nothing from Audubon about them—no acknowledgment that they might be new to science—no indication even that he had received them. Particularly, Bachman yearned for his reaction to the little yellow, gray-breasted, female sylvia he had shot in July.

Bachman lingered for a few days at Round O before hitching up his gig to go home. It was early on Monday morning, 25 March, that he approached the Edisto River at Parker's Ferry where in July he had shot the puzzling sylvia that Audubon now so pointedly ignored. Near the stream "a soft & pleasant note that was new to me" brought Bachman up short. He leaped "out of the chair in a crack" and shot the songster from its perch near the top of one of the tallest tupelos. The singer fell, but its body lodged in a high festoon of Spanish moss (Bachman 1929, 182–83).

Trees in the swamps near Round O towered as high as 163 feet, according to Bachman, and personally climbing to such heights to retrieve a specimen was out of the question. "Goodbye says I & went sorrowing to my chair" (to JJA, 1 April 1833, WCFP). He continued his journey and three miles northeast of Parker's Ferry he reached Caw Caw Swamp. By then his ears must have ached from straining to sort out singing vireos, titmice, and warblers, and especially recently arrived parulas, among the earliest of migrants.

Abruptly "the same sweet note like music from the spheres came over me." This time he did not hurry to shoot. For fifteen minutes he studied the tireless singer. Unlike the female of July, which had "glided" through the underbrush, this male, like the one whose body tangled in the moss earlier that morning, kept high in its tree. Between song bouts it gleaned tender new leaves for insects, occasionally tipping upside down under a branch to forage in the style of a yellow-throated warbler (Bachman 1929, 183).

Bachman fired and the tiny bird dropped lighly to the ground. Its black cap and bib and bright yellow underparts matched the more subdued gray, yellow, and black plumage of the female taken the summer before. Without a doubt they were of the same species. Audubon could not deny that, nor could he any longer insist that the species was already described. In Charleston, Bachman had Maria Martin paint a watercolor of the exquisite male sylvia, and then prepared a study skin from the remains (now in the Smithsonian Museum).

The drawing and the skin had hardly dried when a long letter came from Audubon restating and expanding his opinion that the female collected in July was *not* a new species. Playing devil's advocate perhaps, teasing surely, Bachman tested Audubon's diagnoses of the birds he had sent, the July warbler in particular: "Now take a seat along side of me,— deliberately and patiently go over with me the description & history of this beautiful bird. I have a secret to tell you in your ear, softly my friend, I have the male, it is fairly drawn, it is in full plumage. I have the skin well put up & if Maria's drawing does not suit you, you may draw it over, for the Bird was shot by Jostle the third, and it is now the property of old Jostle and if he cannot swear to it I can" (182).

Within a few days of receiving the new skin and the drawing, Audubon had copied Maria Martin's watercolors of the male and female onto the sheet of *Franklinia* she painted the previous summer. He named the striking new beauty, "Bachman's Swamp Warbler, Helinaia Bachmanii," and used

Bachman's Warbler. Courtesy of the Thomas Cooper Library, University of South Carolina.

the painting to fill out Number 37, one of "Two very beautiful Numbers" he sent to London on 28 April to be engraved and colored by Havell.

Four of the plates of Number 37 (each number consisting of five plates) were a distillation of the first eighteen months of the Bachman-Audubon friendship: plate 182, the ground doves painted as Maria Martin was receiving one of her first drawing lessons; 183, the golden-crowned kinglets on the rare powdery thalia from Noisette's garden; 184, the mangrove hummingbird that Dr. Benjamin Strobel had struck from a bush in Key West; and 185, Bachman's warbler, the bird that with Swainson's warbler had fulfilled Bachman's bold promise to discover new "Sylvias" for his friend.

EMPLOYMENT FOR HENRY WARD in the Charleston Museum should have been advantageous to all concerned, but within a few months the behavior of the young taxidermist became a nagging annoyance to Bachman and Audubon. Neither of the friends should have been surprised. Ward had demonstrated his instability during his earlier travels with Audubon, and although on this expedition he had served credibly, Audubon had felt obliged, before he left for Labrador, to write a cautionary letter to Bachman about Ward's earlier conduct. Bachman responded with a promise to "watch over him with great care" (18 February 1833, WCFP).

However, in actuality, trusting John Bachman waved off the warning. "He has no bad habits—they are only boyish tricks, the result of ignorance," he said. In fact, the pastor seemed to think that with a little polish, Ward might amount to something. The young Englishman wrote wretchedly, for instance, but to remedy this, Bachman required Ward to write to him frequently from the Santee River delta area where he had been dispatched to collect birds. Ward knew little about natural history—Bachman gave him access to his fine library (18 Feburary 1833, WCFP).

Though Ward seldom wrote and did not like to read, there were compensations. He had some good points, Bachman thought. Bachman had the impression that—as a result of Henry's keen eyes and skilled hands, and because Frederick Ward, Henry's older brother, also a taxidermist, had sent Bachman birdskins from Philadelphia—his collection of birdskins was expanding.

Several things changed the pastor's mind about his ward. Bachman realized—maybe he counted—that there were far fewer birdskins in his cabinet than he had believed. Then Ward purchased a horse. Bachman's reaction was that the young man "fools away his money like a boy." The pastor decided to remove Ward from the home of his sister-in-law, Mrs. Strobel, and into his own big house "to guard him from evil" (18 February 1833, WCFP).

Problems concerning Henry Ward and money turned up simultaneously in London. Henry's mother began to harass Victor, claiming that she was due a share of the birdskins that her son collected in America, and now that Henry's contract to travel with Audubon as a bird skinner had been terminated, Audubon should pay Henry's return passage to England. Victor feared that Mrs. Ward might cause trouble unless her demands were settled. He wrote to his mother about it, suggesting she come to terms with the Wards if she could.

Lucy had no idea what to do. She wrote for advice to Audubon, who was then voyaging toward Labrador on the *Ripley,* and to Bachman in Charleston, who was preparing to travel to New York (7 May 1833, HUHL).

In the end, Mrs. Ward's threats amounted to nothing. Lucy's letter caught up with Audubon in Eastport, and he instructed Victor to assure Mrs. Ward that Henry Ward had been promised no skins, that the "ne'er-do-well" had been employed at the Charleston Museum at the behest of Bachman for a salary four times the wages he had been getting, and that he had had letters from the "Dear Boy" acknowledging that Audubon had discharged all obligations to him (Audubon 1969, 1:234). To remove the last doubt that Audubon's obligations had been satisfied, Audubon instructed Bachman to pay Ward off and send him packing (22 September 1833, WCFP).

Ward packed thoroughly. He appropriated money he got from selling one of Audubon's guns and bird's eyes and other articles he looted from the museum, as well as some of the most valuable birdskins in Bachman's collection (4 September 1833, CMBA). Bachman especially regretted the loss of the white-tailed kites Ward had collected on the Santee River. Surprising to Bachman and Audubon, this species had not previously been found breeding on the South Carolina coast. The theft of the skins thus represented a significant loss for ornithology, a loss to Bachman's pocketbook, and a betrayal of his hospitality.

In England in 1834, Audubon kept track of Henry's shenanigans and passed the gossip on to Bachman, who, it must be admitted, seemed as fascinated by the rascal's adventures as anyone. Ward had married, and to raise money had stripped the plumes from the backs of the purloined heron skins and sold them to hatmakers. Then he peddled the mutilated skins to unwary collectors (Audubon 1969, 2:29–30). Knowledge of this unscrupulous behavior should have ended Audubon's patronage, but it did not. Presently Audubon began to correspond with Henry Ward, and by 1835 found it in his heart to warmly recommend that John Children, director of the British Museum, hire the scamp, a generous favor by comparison to the treatment of Lehman, whom Audubon brusquely fired at the conclusion of the Florida voyage and shunned long after (Audubon 1969, 2:94). Perhaps Ward's connection with the Crown and English ornithologists made it seem worthwhile for Audubon to overlook Ward's faults.

Chapter 7

JOHN WOODHOUSE

URING THE SPRING OF 1833, after eighteen months of their absorbing friendship, Bachman and Audubon faced a separation that the swift frigates delivering the mail between the North and the South of the Union could not bridge. Summer was approaching and Audubon resolved not to permit the season to slip by without enriching his portfolio. He arranged to sail to Labrador to investigate a rich fauna of northern water and land birds, taking John with him, but leaving Lucy in Boston to coordinate the publication of *Birds of America* by mail with Victor in London. While organizing his expedition and waiting for summer, Audubon wrote several letters to Bachman asking for information he could use in writing *Ornithological Biography*. One of the queries Bachman found intriguing.

"You asked me a perplexing question with the regard to the change of color in animals," Bachman replied to Audubon, "on these subjects, books contain much that is calculated to mislead." His information, he cautioned his friend, was "merely the result of experience, reflection and experiment." Then he detailed his observations on the molting of such colorful birds as the red-headed woodpecker, the rice bird (bobolink), and the painted bunting (18 February 1833, WCFP).

Audubon's inquiry turned Bachman's thoughts to the Schaghticoke of his youth. Bachman had just entered his eighteenth year when he and George, a family slave who loved nature, began to trap rabbits with the help of a tethered weasel. A stock of captive rabbits and weasels enabled him to observe their molting. Bachman learned that the hairs of these animals do not change from white to brown in spring; instead, as the white hairs are shed, new brown ones replace them. Bachman cited several other conclusions he had reached. "I could say much on this subject did it not look like arrogance," he added modestly (18 February 1833, WCFP).

Two months later, in early April, Bachman addressed a letter to John

Woodhouse informing him that "for the last two months I have been studying rats, shrews and moles." He explained that "our American zoology is very defective." Here was a void in science waiting to be filled. Bachman joked, "Possibly the only way that I shall ride to immortality will be on the back of a mole or rat."

By mid-June Audubon had vanished into the northern wilderness, and the stream of letters between Audubon and Bachman ceased to flow. The annual malaise of summer settled over Charleston and the South Carolina low country. Judges and lawyers locked the courthouses. Silence replaced the music and laughter that had drifted through ballroom and opera house windows. African American listeners on the sidewalks turned their attention elsewhere, and Broad Street slept all but deserted (Bachman 1855c, 13).

To avoid the heat and insects, rich Charlestonians migrated inland, some to the high hills of the Santee one hundred miles from the coast, others all the way to cool Flat Rock in the North Carolina mountains. Summer or no, Bachman's duty was to his church on Archdale Street. He stayed in Charleston, using his quiet hours to study insects. On Maria Martin fell the task of painting Bachman's butterflies, which did not please her, Bachman noticed, but he was her protector and provider, and she served him without complaint.

For the pastor and his sister-in-law, the contrast between the tedium of dog days and the adventures they knew Audubon was enjoying in sub-Arctic Labrador compounded their longing for his company again. Their only hope of hearing about him, and thereby feeling in touch, was the newspapers. Early in September, Bachman read that his old friend Audubon had been heard from "at some islands far north" (to LA, 4 September 1833).

Shortly after that Bachman received a letter from Audubon himself, telling him that the Labrador expedition had been a great success (JB to JJA, 22 September 1833). Audubon had stopped off in Halifax on the way back, had written to his Charleston friend, and soon would be docking in New York. The nub of Bachman's reply was: "This lies nearest my heart. You must pay me a visit this autumn; you must just pay me a visit. Bring, if you can, the wife and son: you shall *all* be welcome—doubly so; but *you* I must see" (C. Bachman 1888, 135).

Another sentence in this letter shows Bachman's interest in mammals intensifying and suggests a competition developing between him and Dr. Richard Harlan, one of Audubon's close Philadelphia friends. Harlan was not only a fellow naturalist who supported Audubon's cause, but he was also a business agent for him, delivering numbers as they appeared and collecting payment for them as they came due. It seems that earlier Audubon had promised the skins to Harlan. But with Harlan in Europe doing research for his book *Fauna Americana*, Audubon switched the promised skins to Bachman instead. Thus Bachman's pen scampered across the page, "A new Rat! a new Bat!—God bless us! I am almost crazy! I am glad that Harlan is off—for now I shall come in for the four-footed beasts" (135).

With a summer of labor behind him, and undecided on the next move to advance the *Birds of America*, Audubon was delighted to come to Cannonsborough. "Let me know candidly," he replied to Bachman, "whether it will be convenient for you to receive us at your house for a few months," though Bachman had already issued the warmest possible of invitations (22 September 1833, WCFP).

Over the years, Audubon had seen relatively little of the twenty-year-old son who boarded the *Ripley* at Eastport and sailed with him for Labrador on 4 June 1833. Between the fall of 1820, when Audubon set off with Joseph Mason to travel down the Mississippi River, and twelve years later the family's reunion in the "little alliance" to publish *Birds of America*, the Bakewells had brought up John Woodhouse Audubon.

First, Lucy Bakewell Audubon had instructed him along with her paying pupils. Then, when John reached puberty, Uncle William Bakewell had taken him in as an apprentice in a Louisville countinghouse. John could not have found a more promising door to success in frontier commerce. The Bakewells were known up and down the Ohio as good businessmen. But John was not an eager pupil. Casual and careless on the job to start with, he appalled Uncle William by leaving the shelter of the family to sign on as a steamboat deckhand. Like father, like son, Bakewell's nephew seemed all too prone to charge off in chase of some dream.

Audubon had sought government help for his expedition to Labrador, and failing that, had financed it himself. In Savannah and Boston, and then New York, new subscriptions and payments on old ones were coming in at a satisfying rate. Delaying the expedition would mean losing a summer of collecting birds, a circumstance that Audubon could not tolerate if he were to paint the northern water birds from life. Consequently, he suspended his sales efforts, chartered the private schooner *Ripley,* commanded by Captain Emery, and sailed on 6 June 1833 for Eastport, Maine. In addition to John Woodhouse and the sailors, Audubon had on board Dr. George Shattuck of Boston, Thomas Lincoln of Dennysville, Maine, Dr. William Ingalls of Boston, and John Collidge, an experienced young sailor (Audubon 1900, 1:345).

The larger than usual crew was necessary because Audubon would spend most of his time painting aboard ship, while collecting and observing birds on the land was left mostly to the others. For the forays from the *Ripley,* he paired his crew according to physical strength and temperament. Young and vigorous John Woodhouse and Thomas Lincoln made a team that Audubon characterized as very venturesome.

By the morning of 14 June, the *Ripley* had anchored in northern waters and was swinging on her lines, heaving and pitching in a hard squall. About half a mile away the Gannett Rocks—the bare peak of a partly submerged mountain—projected from the Gulf of St. Lawrence. Gannets, and other mostly white birds of the open sea, were so numerous on the islet that at first view Audubon took the fluttering birds for snowflakes.

Seamen familiar with the stormy gulf warned him that the ocean was too rough for a landing. Audubon overruled them, "Anxious as we all were, we decided to make the attempt." Armed with guns and clubs, the pilot, two sailors, Tom Lincoln, and John pushed off in the whaleboat (1:360).

For hours, the aging artist waited on the deck of the *Ripley* for the return of the crew. At last, through his spyglass, he caught glimpses of the approaching whaleboat, poised now at the top of a great wave, then lost from sight in a plunge into its trough. As the whaleboat neared the *Ripley,* Audubon detected that Emery's sailors were rowing, and that John stood poised at the helm with an oar, straining to hold the boat on course. Lincoln desperately bailed water that poured over the sides, his bucket no match for the roiling sea. Maneuvering their boat into the lee of the *Ripley,* the men secured a line and leaped aboard. In perfect time with a little hesitation of the waves, they eased the boat on deck (1:360–62).

Indeed, it had been impossible for them to land on the rock, impossible to use their clubs. Instead, they had sheltered behind the island and fired away at the nesting gannets, kittiwakes, and guillemots. The din of the birds muffled the blasts of the guns that had no effect on the colony as a whole. Only when shots found their mark, and maimed birds slid off the cliffs and ledges into the waves, were neighboring birds alarmed. Then they scrambled to take off, kicking a rain of eggs that followed the bodies into the sea. Audubon's hunters fished some of the eggs and bodies from the water to prepare for sale in England (1900, 1:361).

Three weeks into their expedition, the crew awoke to hard rain slanting through thick fog. Audubon could not paint birds under such conditions, with the light so dim and water dripping from the rigging through the open hatch onto his drawing table in the hold. He took the opportunity to go ashore with John and Tom Lincoln, and luck was with him. The weather cleared a bit, the wind rose, and the fog blew away.

In a snug little valley, green with moss and bright with wildflowers that had rushed into bloom with the melting of the snow, the party collected two Canada jays—an adult and an immature. The sun had coaxed ravenous flies and mosquitoes out of the low vegetation, and a few frogs peeped loudly their mating songs.

One of the most wonderful bird songs Audubon had ever heard brought the artist up short. It was "louder, stronger, and far more melodious than that of the Canary bird. . . . So strange, so beautiful was that song that I pronounced the musician, ere it was shot, a new species of Warbler." Unfortunately, the tiny singer dropped into the moss and shrubs of the tundra floor, and search as the hunters would, they could not find it (1:381).

Just as defeat had soon given way to triumph for Bachman in the swamp near Parker's Ferry, so also shortly after Audubon's singer vanished in the Labrador moss, another and different set of sweet and unknown notes "came thrilling on the sense, surpassing in vigour those of any American Finch with which I am acquainted, and forming a song which seemed a compound of those of the Canary and Wood-lark of Europe." Not "music from the spheres," as Bachman described his warbler's song, but a fine performance nevertheless (Audubon 1967a, 3:116).

John and Tom rushed to Audubon's side when he called, and fanned out around the singer. It was shy, ground-loving, and wild, and sang whenever it put a little distance between itself and its stalkers. The chase ended when the bird alighted on a bush within gunshot of Tom Lincoln, and in a moment Audubon was spreading its wings across his palm and stroking its feathers.

The sparrow, though unknown, had been around all along and was not actually uncommon. Its plainness and its stealth had enabled it to avoid previous discovery by such eager ornithologists as Alexander Wilson, George Ord, and even William Cooper of the New York Lyceum, who had befriended, and on occasion snubbed, Audubon over the years. Cooper even had had his hands on the species—for years several specimens had lain unnoticed in his collection of birdskins. But not until Audubon heard the bird singing was it coaxed from anonymity. On the spot, Audubon named it "Tom's Finch, in honour of our friend Lincoln, who was a great favorite among us," and later, in his formal description, he called it "Lincoln's pinewood-finch," thus setting it up (incorrectly) as a sibling species of "Bachman's pinewood-finch." As Audubon himself perceived, the new bird was more closely related to the song sparrow than the pinewoods bird today called Bachman's sparrow (Audubon 1900, 3:116–17).

To cap off the day, Audubon and the boys searched the little valley again and found the body of the morning's singer in the moss. To Audubon's great surprise it was nothing more exotic than a "Ruby-crowned Wren [kinglet]." That Audubon had failed to recognize the song of a bird so common and so tireless a singer, even in winter in the South, showed his need for the bird-song lessons Bachman had given him (1:381). Thrilled by the new sparrow, Audubon left the hunters in the hollow and returned alone to the *Ripley* to paint it against a background of the low flowers that ornamented the little valley—dwarf dogwood, swamp laurel, and white cloudberry.

A month and a half of unrelenting painting and writing later, the fruit of the ubiquitous cloudberry ripened to yellow-red and fed flocks of "Esquimaux [Eskimo] Curlew" that paused as they stormed south across Labrador from Arctic breeding grounds. Audubon reflected on the brief summer—the rush of flowers to bloom, fruit to mature, and birds to hatch, grow up, and fly south. The pace of nature and the pressure on Audubon to paint before the season faded had worn him out (1:423–24).

Part of Audubon's problem was prolonged daily confinement in his improvised studio in the hold of the *Ripley*. No floating boat is without motion. At sea, that motion may be violent. Audubon's drawing table, which doubled for dining, had to be firmly bolted to the floor to keep it from sliding. The secured table then moved as the ship moved, and Audubon found it all but impossible to steady himself. With every wave Audubon tensed to keep from spoiling his work.

He worked as long as there was light, and as the sun, so far north, only rested for a few hours on either side of midnight, the hours of light were long. "At times I felt as if my physical powers would abandon me," Audubon wrote, "my neck, my shoulders, and, more than all, my fingers were almost useless through actual fatigue at drawing" (1:425–26). Still he finished, or nearly finished, twenty-three bird portraits for Robert Havell to engrave and color in London.

One picture was the Eskimo curlew that in recent years has all but vanished from the earth. Audubon's composition for this once-abundant species foreshadows its fate: A live curlew, its tilted head revealing in detail the markings of its crown, gravely inspects a dead companion lying on its back in the moss. Spread wings reveal the pale cinnamon feathers that mark the species.

While Audubon wore himself out painting, John Woodhouse had energy to spare, even after collecting birds all day in the rugged Labrador uplands, skinning them on the *Ripley,* and helping Audubon with the drawing. With his work out of the way, he often spent the luminous evenings playing his violin. A friendship sprang up between him and two young Italian clerks who managed the commercial affairs of the *Wizard,* a Boston-based ship that had anchored nearby. The Italians had been sent to Labrador to buy fish, and had fallen into the habit of coming over in the evenings to sing while John fiddled (1:422–28).

In preparation for leaving port, the crew scraped the hull of the *Ripley,* and Audubon observed that summer's astonishing rush to life had not stopped at the sea's edge. The bottom of the vessel was covered with a luxuriant growth of barnacles and seaweed. Fresh water was brought aboard for the voyage home, and at eleven A.M. on 11 August, the men hoisted sail and put the Labrador harbor behind them. "Seldom in my life,"

Audubon repeated his 1831 appraisal of Florida, "have I left a country with as little regret as I do this" (1:428–29).

After a boisterous day-and-a-half run through choppy waters, the *Ripley* anchored at the picturesque village of St. George, Newfoundland. Birds were plentiful, and Audubon painted while the crew went ashore, slapping blackflies as they replenished their stores with purchases of lobster, salmon, and caribou.

An invitation to attend a village ball was delivered to the *Ripley*. That night, John with his violin, and Tom Lincoln with his flute, played tunes for the dancers. Again old memories visited Audubon, those of nearly twenty years ago when he and the clerk, Pope, played all night to a circle of rapt Indians at Tawatapee Bottom. Now village people laughed and sang and downed rum by the glassful. Strutting young fishermen bowed to ladies who, "in all the rosy fatness produced by an invigorating northern climate," seemed ready to burst their stays. Audubon's spirits lifted and the general merriment enticed him onto the floor with a young woman who had settled beside him (2:429–30).

Not many years before Audubon might have danced out the night with such a partner, but not this night. Despite the gaiety, before eleven P.M. Audubon excused himself and retired to his bunk. The sun was rising when John and Tom, whooping for a skiff to fetch them to the ship, summoned him from a deep sleep (2:430). The voyage of the *Ripley* was about to end.

JOHN WOODHOUSE STEPPED OFF a steamer in Charleston on Saturday, 11 October 1833, and made his way to the house in Cannonsborough, surprising Bachman and his family who thought he would be coming later in the month with his parents. But Bachman quickly took the young man in tow, and the next morning Young Jostle was seated in St. John's Lutheran Church listening to the pastor with the rest of the family.

Bachman had extracted from John the confession that his religious education had been neglected, and had won a promise from him that he would henceforth go to church on Sundays, "provided my father has no hurry work for me to do," John Woodhouse added as a caveat. Bachman coyly cautioned Audubon in his next letter, "Look Sharp, I may have my gown on him before you get among us." As to natural history, he told Audubon how he had organized an ornithology class for John Woodhouse and Maria Martin. On Mondays they studded vultures, on Tuesdays, hawks (15 October 1833, WCFP).

By October of 1833 Bachman had known Audubon for two years, not long in terms of cradle to the grave, but long enough to change Bachman's life. For him, the study of natural history was a social activity as well as an act of science. In Philadelphia, he and his friends had been interested in ornithology, mammalogy, *and* botany.

Earlier in the year, on 15 March 1833, Bachman had given a talk to the Literary and Philosophical Society of Charleston. In it, he looked back to those months when he was a young pastor at St. John's Lutheran Church, just twenty-five years old. He told of how, as a newcomer to Charleston in the spring of 1815, he had discovered a small, dark, previously unknown, rabbit. Because the new mammal lived in freshwater and saltwater marshes, Bachman called it the "marsh rabbit." In the winter of 1816, he added a second new mammal to his South Carolina list, the "Rice Meadow Mouse" (Audubon and Bachman 1989, 72, 396). But then came a hiatus of more than fifteen years during which, for lack of a Charleston companion to share his interests in birds and mammals, Bachman's natural history interests primarily focused on ferns and flowering plants.

His meeting Audubon changed all that. By 1833, Bachman was availing himself of every opportunity to acquire mammal skins and information. He had returned to a question he had studied in his teens—how do some animals change their colors with the seasons. Only a day or two after John Woodhouse arrived in Charleston, Bachman persuaded him to write to Tom Lincoln asking him to serve as a collector and observer of northern mammals, especially weasels, which were well known for their brown coats of summer and white coats of winter. Not only did John comply, but he also followed up when Lincoln proved slow to answer.

John Woodhouse quickly won over Bachman's two older daughters, Maria, sixteen, and Eliza, fourteen. Like her Aunt Maria, who was also charmed by John Woodhouse, Eliza was vivacious. She sang and wrote and kept a scrapbook of poems and drawings. On Tuesday, the third day of John's visit, he painted in her scrapbook a pleasant watercolor of a Carolina wren exploring a tangled honeysuckle vine loaded with berries (Dwight 1965, plate 74).

John also made a pencil sketch of Mary Eliza. She looks up from her notebook page with large, childlike eyes at a handsome adventurer intently studying her. But beyond these moments of intimacy between artist and sitter, it was Maria Bachman who would compel John's lasting attention ("Eliza Bachman's note book," Library Division of the Joseph Downs Manuscript Collection, No. 66×65, Henry Francis Du Pont Winterthur Museum, Wilmington, Delaware).

Disdaining ships and newfangled trains, which showered sparks over the passengers and kept them slapping lest their clothes catch fire, Lucy and John James Audubon clattered into Charleston on 24 October 1833 in the horse-drawn coach from Columbia. Their timing was a little awkward. Ernest Lewis Hazelius, on his way to replace the late John Schwartz at the Theological Seminary that Bachman had founded in the Newberry District of South Carolina in 1831, was due to arrive any day at Cannonsborough (Bost 1963, 322, 324). But Harriet Bachman and Maria Martin found room for the new guests, and Bachman managed to work out a schedule that left time to savor privately in the study with Audubon Labrador triumphs and ornithological insights.

Bachman was willing now to concede to Audubon that the kinglet he had shot in his garden was not new; Bachman himself had begun to doubt its validity as early as the previous March. The small dull bird with no red on its head was only a "ruby-crowned wren," one of hundreds he had collected during his campaign to prove it a new species; indeed, it was the same species that Audubon had thought new on hearing its bold and intricate song in Labrador.

On the other hand, Bachman's uncanny skill in analyzing bird vocalization, coupled with his methodical field work, helped him to convince Audubon that the large, reddish, freshwater rail they had discussed in letters was a different species from the gray, slightly smaller, saltwater rail. But Bachman had checked with various northern museums, and with the possible exception of one skin in Philadelphia, none held a specimen of the bird that they would soon name "king rail" (JB to JJA, 22 September 1833, WCFP).

They also avidly discussed chickadees. Audubon remembered that early in May when he was in Eastport preparing for his Labrador excursion, a Lieutenant Green, whom Audubon called a friend, came to his room. The young officer presented Audubon with a chickadee he had just shot. "The large size of his bird, compared with those met with in the south, instantly struck me," Audubon would write years later (Audubon 1967a, 2:152–53).

Then, apparently, Audubon put Green's chickadee out of his mind. He neglected to preserve the skin or seek other specimens. Although a goal of his expedition was discovery of undescribed birds to paint and publish, he did not note its existence in those of his letters and journals that survive. However, when the "subject of Titmice" came up later in his conversations with Bachman in Charleston, Audubon made it sound as though *he* had brought up the subject, that then Bachman "immediately told me that he for some time had been of the same mind." Thereupon, the two friends went together into the low country woods and "procured some specimens" (2:153).

That summer Bachman also happened to visit black-capped chickadee country. Late in May 1833, at the same time Audubon was loading his gear on the *Ripley* to sail for Labrador, Bachman was lurching by coach through the mountains of New York. His destination was Schaghticoke, where his old mother, her only daughter having died and left her without care, waited for him to take her to Charleston to spend her last days.

Bachman took the opportunity to climb among the Bald Mountains to enjoy the panoramas of his youth. The views were set off by "the beautiful Hudson and Mohawk rivers . . . flowing gently by, as if at my very feet." Nearer at hand, on the mountain tops, the views were filled with the birds of his childhood, and Bachman could savor the "music of a thousand warblers" borne on "the fragrance of flowers." Black-capped chickadees surely were among the numerous birds that flitted among the blossoms (C. Bachman 1888, 79–80).

The friends compared their data in Charleston, analyzing differences between the northern and the southern populations of the chickadees. For a thorough study they needed chickadee skins that they could examine closely. Audubon wrote to "several persons of his acquaintance" asking for skins and soon received chickadee skins from John M. Bethune of Boston, Lieutenant Green, Colonel Theodore Anderson of Baltimore, and others (Audubon 1967a, 153). He explained to Edward Harris that he suspected the northern and southern populations to represent distinct species, and cautioned Harris not to mention this to anyone.

Chickadee skins converged on Cannonsborough, and careful study of them by Audubon and Bachman confirmed that two species existed, one that bred in the North and the other a resident of the South. Surprisingly, until Bachman finally convinced him otherwise, Audubon insisted the larger northern bird, not the southern variety, was the new species. The detection of the Carolina chickadee came in the nick of time regarding the plates of *Birds of America*. Havell was almost ready to distribute the engraving of the original Audubon had painted in Louisiana a decade earlier. Now it was on the verge of being misslabeled as the black-capped chickadee. On 14 January 1834, more than a month after he had returned to Charleston, Audubon wrote to Victor instructing him to revise the name of the chickadee to reflect its southern origin. It became, in *Birds of America*, "The Lesser black headed Titmouse: *Parus Caroliniensis*," later called the Carolina chickadee (Audubon 1967a, 2:152–54).

Audubon might have shared public credit with Bachman for the discovery of the Carolina chickadee, but that he neglected to do so seemed of no concern to Bachman. Having resumed his study of mammals, and publishing about them under his own name, Bachman carefully disclaimed any such interest in birds. "I am sure my old friend, your father," he wrote to John Woodhouse, "will rejoice whenever a new bird can be added to his book, let who will bring it to him, and when I add anything I do so as a pupil and therefore the credit is still all his" (7 April 1833, WCFP).

Subjects less pleasant than new birds were thrashed out as the friends talked before the big fireplace that guarded Bachman's study against the chill of November evenings. In Philadelphia early in October, Audubon had been subjected to a painful indignity, and one not connected with Philadelphia's familiar coterie of snipers. A sheriff bearing an arrest warrant for a debt that dated back to the Kentucky bankruptcy had pounded on his door at Mrs. Newlin's boardinghouse. The issue, Audubon's responsibility for debts run up in operating the mill, was disturbing because it implied that bankruptcy might not have, after all, satisfied Audubon's debts. Scribbled on the writ was a note advising the server to make haste before the defendant skipped town (Philadelphia District Court Appearance Docket, 1 October 1833).

Audubon escaped incarceration in a Philadelphia prison because a rich friend, James Norris, posted his bail. Norris was soon taken off the hook when the suit was transferred to Charleston, where Bachman agreed to act in Audubon's behalf as the case plodded through the courts (JB to JJA, 26 March 1834, Stark Museum of Art, Orange, Texas). Eventually, Bachman paid—with money he had collected for Audubon—a judgment of $630 (JB to JJA, 24 August 1835, WCFP).

Another worrisome charge cropped up in Philadelphia when Audubon read Waterton's latest broadside in *Louden's Journal*. Waterton, an English gentleman, asserted that a woodsman such as Audubon could not possibly have written the literate first volume of *Ornithological Biography*. Waterton even claimed that the real author was William Swainson.

Swainson, out of sorts with almost everybody, contradicted Waterton and confirmed that Audubon was the author. Then he damned both their houses, pronouncing Waterton's style no more correct than that of the wild American.

Waterton's attack, added to his criticism of the vulture lecture, suggested that he was mounting a campaign designed to destroy Audubon's reputation. With Ord supplying the ammunition, Waterton would publish nineteen anti-Audubon polemics before resting, and then only because the world became bored with him. But Ord and Waterton never got enough. A decade after the furor had subsided and Audubon's reputation rested securely on the greatest work on birds ever published, the detractors continued to vent their hatred in letters to one another (Ord to Waterton, 23 August 1843, APSL).

Shortly after their reunion late in 1833, Bachman and Audubon decided to answer some of Waterton's criticism by restaging and extending Audubon's Louisiana experiments on vultures (Audubon 1969, 1:267). Bachman, as an independent and impeccably honest authority, would publish the results, which both men expected would confirm Audubon's earlier work. They postponed the experiment until December.

Meanwhile, Bachman spent a fortnight at Saint Matthew's Parish attending an important meeting of the South Carolina Synod, of which Bachman was president (C. Bachman 1888, 76–78). Audubon felt compelled to "finish" many of his Labrador drawings so they could be sent to London for engraving by Havell. Backgrounds had to be painted and, in some cases, the birds themselves reworked.

Thus began another marathon of painting and writing, as arduous as any Audubon had yet undertaken. Seated at the table in the drawing room with Maria Martin and John Woodhouse, he painted all day. Though John Woodhouse managed at day's end to put his work aside and switch over to music and games with the Bachman girls, Audubon allowed himself no relief.

When daylight failed, he stopped painting and started writing, with Bachman at his side when he was available. Audubon burned candles until he had written an account for at least one bird appearing in the second volume of *Ornithological Biography*. He consolidated field notes and wove in Bachman's perceptive accounts, contributing much to the success of *Birds of America* (Audubon 1969, 1:264).

Fearing that he might not live long enough to complete his work, Audubon's "scribbling" and painting became compulsive, and toward the end of November he broke down. "Weakened & fatigued," he gave up writing at night (1:264). He was rapidly growing old. "So much travel exposure and fatigue do I undergo that the Machine me thinks is wearing out." For ten days he lay in bed, prisoner to a painful case of piles (1:268, 271).

Hard, regular work and his father's encouragement had a good effect on John Woodhouse. After a few weeks in Charleston, the senior Audubon wrote to Victor in London, "John draws sufficiently well for publication" (1:270). He judged that some of John's drawings would appear in the next volume of *Birds of America,* and even suggested that John might exceed his father in "that department" in a month. Audubon's were the eyes of a doting father. While John's drawings had indeed improved, he fell far short of matching his father. To confirm this, he needed only to examine John's rather wooden little sketch of Swainson's warbler perched on a spray of flame azalea rendered by Maria Martin (Audubon 1966, plate 153).

Lucy, too, worked hard for the family in Charleston. Her exemplary handwriting, each letter clear and beautifully traced, was not the least of her contributions. She transcribed and consolidated the Florida and Labrador journals, making the information easily accessible as time drew near to submit the next batch of manuscripts to the printer. Lucy also took it upon herself to instruct the Bachman daughters and "stimulate them to industry" (Audubon 1969, 1:269).

By December, Audubon was on his feet, and John Bachman was home again after the Synod. The time had come to launch the vulture experiments. Earlier in the month, Bachman had written a plan for their project:

"Notes on some experiments made on the Buzzards of Carolina—Cathartes aura & C. atratus."

    1. Is there any truth in the opinion expressed by a person who signs himself Maj. Pillans that when the Buzzards eyes are putout he can by placing them under his wing renew them again.

    2. What food does the Buzzard prefer—fresh or putrid meat.

    3. What are the powers of smell & sight of this Bird—whether is he attracted to his food by sight or by the smell.

    4. The general habits of the Bird. (John Bachman 1834b, 2)

On Monday afternoon, the day before Christmas eve, Edmund Ravenel, Esq. and other learned doctors and teachers of Charleston sorted through their correspondence and found an invitation:

Dear Sir, Desirous of making some experiments on the habits of the Buzzard [vulture] as it respects its powers of smell and sight and anxious that they should be witnessed by naturalists and men of Science; I take the Liberty of inviting you to witness these experiments, during the present week (with the exception of Wednesday) at any hour between 11 & 1 O'clock at the residence of the Revd Jno Bachman Yours with Respect
John J. Audubon (23 December 1833, CMBA).

The experiment had been underway since 16 December. An accidentally killed hare and a snap rat-trap baited to capture vultures had been placed close together in the lower end of the vegetable garden. Bachman stationed himself to watch the soaring vultures crisscrossing the city in search of food. As they drifted effortlessly over his property, he noted how they turned their heads "first one way & then another seeming to look for food." Some flew on, but others banked suddenly, flapped to break their glides, and dropped to the fallow garden near the hare ("Notes on some experiments made on the Buzzards of Carolina—Cathartes aura & C. atratus," CMBA [Bachman 1834b, 2]).

The trap sprung successively on one black and three turkey vultures, but all pulled free—"the Black Vulture evidently was the strongest & extricated himself with greatest ease" (3). To improve chances of catching vultures, bits of fresh meat were placed on the trap. The birds deftly ate the bait without getting caught. On the second day, Bachman added a pheasant killed by a dog, and the vultures put down and fed greedily, seeming to prefer bird flesh to the flesh of mammals. The pastor set more traps and in short order several vultures were caught and locked in an outbuilding.

With these unfortunate birds in hand the friends could address their first objective, the discrediting of Major Pillans's heresy that vultures restore sight to blind eyes by placing their heads under their wings. They perforated an eye of a vulture—"the sight was destroyed." The bird had not recovered its sight when it was examined that night, nor had the eye been restored on 20 December when Bachman next looked at it: "The poor fellow must remain blind in the right eye to prove that Maj. Pillans either from ignorance or design imposed [his farcical theory] on the community" (4).

Proving that vultures liked fresh meat did not require their capture. Anyone could go to the open air market and see close-up how the butchers of Charleston made sport of tossing scraps of flesh to the scavengers waiting on low roofs. The agile vultures snapped the meat out of the air. Should a butcher drop his guard, one would dart in and choke down meat intended for Charleston dining rooms. With this kind of evidence, Bachman and Audubon felt that the premise—that vultures eat fresh meat—was settled, and went on to determine whether the vulture is attracted to his food "by sight or by smell" (2).

Bachman's aviary provided the first bait for the sight or smell experiments. "A European kistel & a red tailed Hawk" were laid in the garden on 20 December. Carrion accumulated when Bachman had delivered to his home "a wheel barrow load of offal . . . containing the lights & intestines of animals." It was dumped under a frame and covered with brush sufficient to hide it, but loose enough to allow air to circulate and disburse the odor, which despite the cool weather, soon asserted itself (5).

The next morning, at least one hundred vultures glided back and forth over the garden, but not one alighted. Not until a bit of viscus was dragged from hiding under the brush and laid in the open did the dusky birds find the garden irresistible. In a few moments they gathered, and in rapid succession five sprung traps—three of these birds were unable to pull free. Meanwhile, others bolted the carrion they had exposed. Though fifty or more shared in the scramble, a few feet from their noses the hidden wheelbarrow of offal that seethed with decay went untouched. Most of the vultures got nothing for their trouble.

Two days before Christmas, the day the medical professors came to witness the experiments, Bachman noted with satisfaction, "The meat is becoming very offensive—and although the Buzzards have not smelt it, the Dogs have" (6).

Audubon came up with a variation on previous tests. On canvas, he sketched the likeness of a dead sheep, its intestines spilling from its ruptured abdomen. Employing the quick bold strokes he had learned while painting potboilers for the English gentry, he finished the bait-painting in less than an hour and propped up the wet canvas in the cold and rainy garden. The first passing vulture braked, dropped down, and walked over. It eyed one side of the canvas and then the reverse, seemed to see nothing that tempted it, and flapped back to a post to study the painting. It waddled back for another try. "Here is positive proof that our vultures are attracted to their food by sight & not by smell," Bachman penned in his notebook (7).

Even when the brush was removed from the rotting meat, a gauzy cloth stretched over it, and bits of fresh meat pinned to the cloth with sticks, the vultures ate the skewered flesh, but seemed oblivious to the odoriferous bait four inches below the cloth.

If not by scent, then how did vultures detect food by sight from great distances? Years of hunting in the low country had taught Bachman that as soon as a deer was butchered the vultures within sight set wings to descend, and others followed. Vultures a little further off, Bachman postulated, saw the descending vultures and realized that food had been found. Quickly the gliding vultures closed in and soon the sky was empty of them.

By the dawn of the new year, 1 January 1834, the vulture experiments essentially had ended. Bachman wrote his report and gave it to the senior Audubon, who mailed it to his son in London instructing him to find a good English publisher, *Louden's Journal* if possible, but *Blackwood's Magazine* would do. The editor of *Louden's Journal* accepted the study for publication, and subsequently Bachman's vulture article was read before several scientific and philosophical societies in Europe and America. Audubon, of course, was pleased: "It is a plain paper, no nonsense, no fudge; but so simple and full of truth that I greatly fear that even the Armour of Waterton will fall to the Earth, and leave the man, a poor worthless Carcass fit (if fresh) for the very Buzzards which he has so deeply abused" (Audubon 1969, 1:277).

Bachman's paper blunted criticism of Audubon's repeated claims that vultures find food by sight rather than smell. And in the long run, the paper laid a foundation for Bachman's international reputation as a careful experimental scientist, though, ironically, it is now generally accepted that vultures, especially turkey vultures, have and use a keen sense of smell in locating carrion.

An unexpected, but welcome, result of the experiment was a subscription to *Birds of America* by William Rees, a visitor to Charleston from the interior of South Carolina. He happened to walk by as Audubon was setting up the disemboweled sheep sketch. Rees signed up for *Birds of America* "at the moment when the Vultures lost their olfactory powers," Audubon said. Rees was a good customer, paying for the first volume on the spot in cash (Herrick 1968, 2:62).

Though the experimenters declared the experiment had ended, and though Bachman had begun to fret about his neighbors' reaction to the wheelbarrow load of carrion scattered behind his fence, he could not resist reaching for a last tidbit of information. He kept the offal simmering until mid-January, all the while closely monitoring dogs, vultures, and other creatures that orbited it. That Bachman's neighbors permitted the experiment to continue was a tribute both to Charleston's tolerance of cultured eccentrics, and to its respect for Bachman as a man of the cloth and science.

The medical professors who had responded to Audubon's invitation satisfied themselves that the experiment was good science and the names of six were affixed to Bachman's published account as witnesses. Some of Charleston's physicians agreed to dissect heads of several unfortunate vultures, and later published their finding that vulture olfactory nerves were not used for finding carrion, the result Bachman had demonstrated, but noted nevertheless, that these nerves were well developed. Audubon, himself, speculated that they might play a yet to be discovered role in the lives of birds (Audubon 1967a, 1:15).

As the Christmas holidays faded into January, Audubon put the finishing touches on the work he had done that winter. He wrote to Havell on 19 January 1834 that he was shipping to London via the brig *Fortitude* three new drawings he had done in Charleston, plus twenty-five Labrador paintings of water birds that he, Maria Martin, and John Woodhouse had "finished" during their marathon in the drawing room. Prudently, he bought four thousand dollars of insurance guaranteeing compensation for this precious cargo should it be lost on its way to Liverpool (Audubon 1969, 2:7, 9).

The next morning Audubon wrote to Harlan, who had completed his European tour, and asked him to publish an extract of "the Buzzard's nose" (Bachman's vulture study) in a friend's "valuable paper." Audubon further suggested that a copy of the article be sent to "John Vaughn to be read before the Philosophical Society of Philadelphia" (20 January 1834, COPP).

At this point, Audubon passed his pen to Bachman to fill the remainder of the sheet with his own concerns. These included asking Dr. Harlan to stop by the "J. of Nat. Science [Academy of Natural Sciences of Philadelphia?]" and correct some slightly out-of-date information on the range of the hare, "Lepus Gracialis," in another of Bachman's papers.

Bachman enthusiastically related his discoveries of mammals to Harlan once Audubon had involved them by the shared letter. One of the most interesting bits of information Bachman had to pass on to Harlan was that he had received "two specimens of a hare from Alabama in size a little less than the L. Virginianus, but so much like our L. Americanus that I know not what to make of it. It keeps only in marshes & is fond of swimming" (20 January 1834, COPP).

Then Bachman, perceiving Harlan as a likely source of zoological specimens for his studies, inquired directly of the physician, "Are you disposed to be a working man in Nat. Hist.? If so how far can you exchange specimens in Quadrupeds and reptiles." Finally Bachman asked, "Can you procure for me an animal you have described as the Arvicola palustris (A. palustris proved to be an invalid name). I wish to compare it with something like it that exists here" (20 January 1834, COPP).

Harlan replied warmly, "I am honored by placing you among the most favored of my correspondents, and feel myself abundantly indebted to you for the interesting facts and valuable hints in your last." He told Bachman that he had taken several extracts of Bachman's letter to the American Philosophical Society at its last meeting, and added, "Your letter attracted much attention, and gave rise to an animated discussion." Harlan even promised, "I shall not fail to profit by your observations in my next edition of the 'Fauna Americana'" (C. Bachman 1888, 136).

The new *Lepus* had come from Alabama, where Bachman's in-laws, the Lees, had moved hoping to get rich by growing cotton. The surprise was that the Lee's hare was aquatic, swimming and diving in the wetlands that edged many southeastern rivers, feeding mostly on the roots of water-loving plants. Bachman later learned that the swamp hare was common in the interior of South Carolina.

This strikingly atypical member of the rabbit family was the second *Lepus* Bachman had discovered, the first being the small rabbit of the Carolina saltwater and freshwater marshes, dark in pelt from nose to tip of tail. It, too, is a lover of wet places, but is not nearly so aquatic as the robust swamp hare.

In a letter encouraging Bachman to publish his discoveries before Harlan beat him to it, Charles Pickering, of the Philadelphia Academy, assured him that "the Academy would be proud to lay before the World such an interesting discovery as you mention." In other words, Bachman should present to the Academy a description of the new hare. Then Pickering had an idea: Bachman might point out the "distinctive characters of our *other* species of Lepus, and thus render it [Bachman's study] a monograph of the American species" (Pickering to JB, 19 January 1836, APSL).

Bachman took the advice. Through 1836 and 1837, his monographs mice, shrews, and squirrels swiftly followed, as well as a provocative paper on molting and seasonal color changes in mammals and birds. "I esteem them [Bachman's studies] as the most important contribution to N. American Mammalogy that has yet appeared," Pickering wrote (25 March 1837, APSL).

As though following a careful plan, Bachman was rapidly accruing a reputation as an authority on American mammals. His correspondence with Philadelphia naturalists expanded and soon included, in addition to Charles Pickering, Dr. Samuel Morton, the new curator of the Philadelphia Academy, and even George Ord! All were supportive, encouraging Bachman with constructive criticism of his writing, making suggestions, and helping him to obtain specimens he needed.

Bachman had launched scientific studies that Harlan had already undertaken himself. As a result, the stage was set for conflict and resentment between two of Audubon's staunchest allies. Mammals were central to *Fauna Americana,* the book Harlan was writing, just as mammals were at the heart of Bachman's expanding field study dating back to his childhood, and revived and intensified by his association with Audubon.

Chapter 8

RELATIONSHIPS

$\mathcal{E}$ARLY IN MARCH 1834, business pressures requiring that the Audubons join Victor in England caused Audubon to defer exploring the prairie, the Rocky Mountains, and the Pacific Coast to collect birds. Instead, he, Lucy, and John Woodhouse bid the Bachmans adieu and boarded a stagecoach for New York. The family spent the night in Fayetteville, North Carolina, 220 miles northeast of Charleston (LA to Bachman family, 9 March 1834, HUHL).

While in Fayetteville, John Woodhouse posted a letter to Maria Bachman in Cannonsborough (9 March 1834, HUHL). It was the first of a busy exchange of love letters between them, threads in a web of relationships developing between the Bachmans and Audubons. Maria Martin's affection for Bachman, Audubon, and John Woodhouse—and them for her—were others. The warp of the fabric was the intense friendship of Bachman and Audubon. But soon, the two families were separated by the stormy Atlantic. Audubon and Bachman expected they would not see one another for at least a year.

Considering it likely that John Woodhouse and Maria Bachman would eventually marry, the question of how the young man would support a family was on the minds of both fathers (JB to LA, 26 August 1835, WCFP). Audubon wrote Bachman that John was hard at work at learning the trade of portrait painter, attracting enough sitters to keep him busy. To show the results of four months of training, John painted a self-portrait and shipped it to Cannonsborough, a token of love for his betrothed and for her parents, and proof of his self-sufficiency (Audubon 1969, 2:73). On his side of the ocean, Bachman saw to the education of his older daughters. With Maria Martin joining the class, they studied botany, drawing, French, and German, a good curriculum for prospective wives of naturalists.

Writing to Audubon on 4 October 1834 (WCFP), apparently with no real news to tell, but eager to fulfill his promise to write regularly, Bachman chose as his theme an analysis of Audubon's behavior. He saw room for improvement: Audubon tended to be dogmatic, he drank too much, he was a poor loser at backgammon, and he went too far with expressing his affection for Maria Martin. Rather than attribute these criticisms to himself, Bachman put the words into the mouths of Lucy, Victor, John Woodhouse, and Audubon himself:

Dialogue in a house in London

OLD JOSTLE: Bless my soul. See what can be the reason that John Bachman never writes me a single line. I am sure he is vexed with me for something.

LUCY: Why my dear you were always contradicting each other. He did not like your drinking grog though he took as much snuff as you and then you would never bear to be told that you could make a mistake in a bird.

YOUNG JOSTLE: Father I think he may be angry because when he criticized your drawings you called him a goose. When he beat you at shooting you said he shut the wrong eye and when he gammoned you you went to bed in a pet.

OLD JOSTLE: Why John that is true. But you know he was no more of a painter than a piano player. As for shooting he was not so bad, but I am equal to him any day and when I get back to America I will lead him such a dance as he will long remember. I don't blame him for shutting the wrong eye because he never could shut the other. In backgammon I confess he could beat me but it is a trifling game and after all he must have grown jealous because our sweetheart thought more of me than him.

VICTOR: As for my part I think you are all mistaken. From what I have heard you were both very free with each other. Like two lovers quarreling today and making up tomorrow. You know father you cannot bear to hear of your faults; he may be in the same way; and I am sure both of you esteem each other as much as ever. The letters may have miscarried as he may have been very busy; be patient and all will yet be explained (the bell rings—a letter).

JOSTLE: God bless me it is from John Bachman himself.

YOUNG JOSTLE: Why father you have kicked over the coffee pot.

NOTE: The letter begins on the same page as follows:

My old Friend,

A line from you would be a pleasant sight just now. It is a long time since I heard the sound of your voice or saw your fine face or looked at your fair hand.

The remainder of the letter told little more than the trivial, everyday affairs of Cannonsborough—Harriet was mending socks; frightened by a cat, two of his daughters were "kicking up a row"; Maria Martin was reading a book on agriculture while explaining to someone how to set a mousetrap; the weather was hot.

So slow were the transatlantic mails that Audubon found himself answering Bachman's letter a full month after Bachman had written it. Not about to acknowledge the personality problems to which Bachman has so slyly alluded, Audubon dismissed Bachman's critique good-naturedly. "We were much amused and gratified at receiving and reading your funny letter of October 4th—It had a famous long passage too [the play within the letter], if this increases its value is certs [certainly] more than doubtful." Audubon went on to swell several pages with requests for ornithological data (Audubon 1969, 2:55).

Nothing was resolved by this remarkable exchange, and with one exception Bachman let his criticisms drop for the time being. The exception was grog. In less than a year, Bachman wrote Lucy a serious letter warning her that Audubon should be "very prudent" because his Philadelphia enemies were "trying to get up a story of his being a drunkard" (26 August 1835, WCFP).

Belying these tensions, and though Audubon did not lay it out as plainly as John Bachman did, his affection for Bachman was real. It showed when he inserted Bachman's name on almost every page of the second volume of *Ornithological Biography,* thus sharing his most jealously guarded treasure, public credit for his work. And when Bachman complained about Audubon's "greasing" him too much, Audubon countered that Bachman might as well cut his [Audubon's] jugular vein as cut off his praise. He promised that in the third volume of *Ornithological Biography* John Bachman would find a sentence about himself for every word he saw in the second volume (Audubon 1969, 2:73).

Audubon's attachment showed how, once he had found the haven of Cannonsborough, he returned to John Bachman whenever possible, as though he could not do without Bachman's support, judgment, and help. Audubon expressed his feelings, too, in a gift.

Before Audubon left England late in the summer of 1831 and proceeded to Charleston and his fateful first meeting with John Bachman, publication of the plates of *Birds of America* had reached a landmark—the hundredth—the completion of volume 1. The prints, which had been accumulating in the portfolios of each subscriber, now could be permanently bound. Through Havell, Audubon located a suitable firm to do the binding.

Audubon selected a set of the first one hundred prints for their crisply printed lines and skillful coloring, and had it specially bound, specifying full, rather than the usual half, "Russia leather." He ordered lavish gold leaf decoration for the binding. Audubon meant to use this book to impress subscribers on his return to America.

One day, during that first happiest month in Charleston with Bachman, Audubon dispatched the special volume to Columbia, where Professor Robert Wilson Gibbs planned to convince officials to subscribe in the name of the state. Gibbs failed to close the sale, and not until Bachman himself lobbied for it did the legislature authorize purchase.

No longer needed in Columbia, "the supurb bound book," as Audubon called it, was sent to Gaston in Savannah to help win subscriptions there. Somewhere along the way, it vanished (C. Bachman 1888, 100–101). Lost for two years, the volume reappeared in March 1834, solving the mystery of its disappearance. It had "in some way got to the *Havana*" (the ship, not the city). But Audubon's Key West friend, Major James M. Glassel, had located it and put it back on track to Charleston. The treasured prints, the opulent binding had come home again. "The great volume . . . I give with all my heart to my valued friends the Bachmans," Audubon wrote in April, "and I shall try to furnish them with the sequel in like binding" (Audubon 1969, 2:16, 21).

In England, with the help of William MacGillivray, Audubon completed the writing and printing of the second volume of *Ornithological Biography* late in 1834 (Audubon 1969, 2:55). MacGillivray, a modest but perceptive critic, considered the writing of volume 2 "more diversified & more satisfactory" than the first. One difference was that much of the second had been written in Charleston under the influence of John Bachman.

Audubon's pressure on Bachman became unrelenting when the artist undertook the writing of volume 3 at year's end. "I must ask you in the most earnest manner," Audubon pled, "to assist all you can and merely enable me to publish no trash, but pure, clean, truths" (2:60). In long letters to Bachman, he listed dozens of birds he wanted to know more about, many rarely observed, and one, Bachman's warbler, heading the list and known to Bachman alone (2:173). For MacGillivray's study of avian anatomy, Audubon urged Bachman to send "the Wind Pipes and Tongues of every species of Water Birds you can in spirits, well Marked with a Ticket on which put the sexes, dates &c—Purple & common Gallinule—Variables.—Anhinga or Snake Bird.—&c—&c—&c" (2:56).

Bachman felt obliged to remind Audubon of the difficulty and expense in obtaining wholesale information and specimens, and to point out that after all, his church had first call on his time. Then, having said his piece, Bachman plodded through Audubon's lists, filling many gaps in the ornithological biographies that would have been left out or reduced to hearsay but for his efforts (JB to JA, no date, CMBA).

As often was the case when Bachman undertook a pressing project, the effort affected his health. He began to suffer from "dyspepsia" (a painful attack of indigestion symptomatic of stress), and when the South Carolina Synod named him their delegate to the National Synod at York, Pennsylvania, he seized the chance to escape his chores for a few weeks, granting his stomach a rest. His daughter, Maria, and his sister-in-law, Maria Martin, went with him.

They booked passage on a steamer as far as Baltimore. There Bachman saw in the *Bucks County Intelligencer* a double-barreled attack on Audubon for his rattlesnake story. George Ord was the assailant. Previously, Ord had struck at Audubon indirectly by feeding material to Waterton. Now, in a newspaper sure to be read in Philadelphia, he was mounting an assault in his own name, quoting Waterton as though the Englishman had given him the material and not vice versa. The editor of the *Bucks County Intelli-*

gencer, Mr. Kelly, fired the second barrel, an attempt to bolster Ord's claim that his attack on Audubon was nothing personal (JB to Kelly, 19 June 1835, APSL).

Scribbling page after page in his hotel room, Bachman prepared a defense, on the surface lighthearted. He poked fun at the fantastic reptile stories in Waterton's book, *Wanderings,* such as Waterton's claim that once he overcame and tied up a boa so large it took three men to carry it and they had to rest ten times along the way. In another, Waterton wrapped his hand in a hat and rammed it down the throat of a ten-foot-long snake, allowed it to coil around his body, and thereupon bore it triumphantly home. Bachman made the case that a spinner of tall tales like Waterton was in no position to criticize a serious ornithologist like Audubon (C. Bachman 1888, 98–99).

Fairness demanded publication of his defense, Bachman proclaimed, and he proposed that should Kelly comply and publish he would be willing to let the game be drawn. Bachman confided to Kelly that over the years he had collected a set of damaging notes and memoranda on Ord and his writing. He hoped that Kelly would not force him to make this dossier public. "I for one (& also I stand alone [Audubon not involved]) would willingly separate the native slanderer [Ord] from the foreign Jesuit [Waterton], and spare his [Ord's] name and his fame."

Bachman urged Kelly to show this letter to Ord, feeling that the threat to make Ord pay in kind for his slander would silence him (19 March 1835, APSL). Kelly complied (C. Bachman 1888, 98–99).

A pleasant forty-mile carriage ride through the rolling Maryland and Pennsylvania countryside took John Bachman and the two Marias to York, Pennsylvania, for the General Synod meeting. Bachman's attention shifted from Audubon's problems to those of his faith: how to enable the South Carolina Synod to keep its ties with the national organization, then strained by feuding over slavery. In a letter to his vestry he pointed out that maintenance of the ties would preserve a facade of national unity that might enable the South Carolina Synod to win guarantees that the General Synod would serve only as an advisory body, "taking no cognizance over the concerns of individual congregations" (Bost 1963, 258).

Bachman addressed the assembly on Sunday evening, the twenty-first of June. He made a strong impression, charming delegates with his courtly manners, his warm personality, the scope of his learning, and his devotion to his church. "He was gay without frivolity, learned without pedantry, and pious without asceticism," one delegate remarked. The performance preceded Bachman's election as president of the Synod, after which he was appointed to a committee to review the National Synod constitution. He left York confident that his goal of maintaining local independence for congregations would prevail (255).

A letter and a volume of Dr. Richard Harlan's book *Fauna Americana* awaited Bachman at his Baltimore hotel. They had been handed to the hotel clerk by a young man who mentioned that he was related to the pastor. The clerk passed this information on to Bachman, and Bachman at once surmised that the messenger was a son of Jacob Martin and Elizabeth Pennington, for whose love Jacob Martin had deserted his family.

That night Bachman sat down to write to Harlan explaining the complications of the Martin-Bachman family, which prevented him from entering Philadelphia. "Strange enough," he mused, "that you should have entrusted my letter to one of their bastard sons, whom my family can never consent to see." At that moment Bachman's writing was interrupted. The hotel clerk came in and made clear that the young man was not Maria Martin's half-brother after all, but a *bona fide* (but no name given) Bachman cousin (29 June 1835, COPP).

The moment had come for Bachman to consider his situation before completing his note to Harlan. Several of Bachman's letters to Audubon had suggested an ambivalence in Bachman's and Harlan's relationship. Barely a year after Bachman and Audubon had met, Audubon wrote that Bachman should "try to make an apology to Dr. Harlan" for a "long silence." The reason for Bachman's silence (probably failure to answer letters) the pastor chose not to discuss (18 February 1833, WCFP), but his references to Harlan in letters to Audubon typically were brief and noncommittal, and left little doubt that Bachman frowned on Harlan's science. He found faint praise for *Fauna Americana*—"I've just seen Harlan's work," he wrote. "It is a republication of his old matters contained in the journals. I confess myself a little disappointed" (22 January 1836, WCFP).

Despite the sudden restoration of legitimacy to Harlan's messenger,

Bachman and both Marias elected not to enter Philadelphia. Instead the trio from Charleston turned inland to the mountains.

AT FIRST LIGHT one cool July morning near Salt Sulphur Spring in West Virginia, Bachman had the satisfaction of spying several small brown birds that slipped nervously from a hole in a limb of a fallen oak. He had already identified them. On hearing a song strange to him when he first arrived, he had shot one, and had found to his delight that the singer was a Bewick's wren, the species that Audubon had discovered fourteen years earlier in Louisiana. As almost nothing but the drawing that Audubon made at the time was known about this wren, Bachman set about to record its life history (Audubon 1967a, 2:120–21).

Bachman had been lucky to hear the song. By July, bird songs were few in the mountains, and Bachman rode through woods that lay silent except for the "occasional 'cank'" of the white-breasted nuthatch. The quiet mountains made him sad—but Bachman noted the birds and mammals he saw or heard, and when he returned to Charleston after several weeks, he forwarded the information to Audubon (24 August 1835, WCFP).

Back in Charleston, Bachman remarked that his dyspepsia had responded well to his month in the mountains, though he still struggled with depression. On the other hand, the Virginia springs had not helped his daughter Maria, and Bachman—who had twice almost died from severe hemorrhages—must have suspected that she suffered from consumption.

One morning Bachman found on his desk a letter that John had addressed to Maria Bachman. Bachman surmised that the letter was left there for him to read. John's morose "complaining of his hard lot in being obliged to wait so long" suggested to the worried pastor the source of his daughter's poor health, "the idea that John was discontented and unhappy" (26 August 1835, WCFP).

Replying indirectly, Bachman wrote to Lucy wishing that John's letters "might always be cheerful. Let him look a little more on the bright side of the picture. Maria's health will be all the better for it and all will yet be well" (26 August 1835, WCFP).

Delay after delay conspired to keep John in England. Ironically, the cause of the prolonged separation was the quickening publication of *Birds of America.* Havell had added more colorists to his staff, speeding up production. Audubon was hard put to provide new drawings fast enough. From British museums he obtained dozens of skins of American birds he had not yet painted, and devoted months to drawing them. Interspersed with painting sessions were writing binges that propelled Audubon and MacGillivray through more than one thousand new pages of *Ornithological Biography.* In a surge of optimism, Audubon forecast completing the *Birds of America* project late in 1837, four years earlier than he had once expected (Audubon 1969, 2:109). Sheer momentum created tasks that postponed the family's return to America.

Eventually the day dawned when England seemed to have exhausted her supply of new subscribers and new birds to paint, but at that point chance intervened with a new delay. Fire had gutted New York. Buildings were reduced to charred bricks and ashes, including Nicholas Berthoud's warehouse, where Audubon had stored "bedding, sheets, implements of Drawing . . . and our Guns." The guns were the critical loss. Difficult to replace, Audubon was not prepared to mount his next expedition without them (2:117).

Several months passed while a master English gunsmith filled Audubon's order for new rifles. Because John and Victor had run out of tasks to keep them busy, they traveled to France to tour the land of Audubon's childhood, and to Italy, that favorite of English travelers.

At last, early in the summer of 1836, John could write to Maria Bachman that they soon would be together again. Lucy and Victor would remain in London to supervise printmaking and other business, while John and his father sailed about the first of August for New York on the *Gladiator,* a sturdy new packet well tested by four Atlantic crossings. Maria responded with "strong observations" on hearing that John and his father would commit themselves to such a voyage at the height of the hurricane season (2:121–22).

The Bachmans, Maria Bachman in particular, rejoiced when they heard that the *Gladiator* had docked in New York after a routine thirty-three-day voyage. Maria's happiness at being once more on the same side of the ocean as John Woodhouse was tempered, however, by the knowledge that her father and Maria Martin had posted a letter to New York informing the

Audubons that "we cannot see you for several weeks to come." A siege of rheumatism had almost incapacitated the pastor, but the compelling reason for postponing the Audubons' visit was a cholera epidemic that had swept through the North and the West of the United States, had reached South Carolina, and now neared the gates of Charleston (C. Bachman 1888, 137).

Disappointed, Audubon responded with a sad little letter describing the euphoria he had felt at "once more reaching our dear Shor," then lamenting how sharply his mood had spiraled into depression when told that he would have to wait a while before traveling south. "You cannot imagine how hard We both feel it, that we cannot go to Charleston at once, where we know we both could and would enjoy ourselves a thousand times [more there] than anywhere else in America!" Nor was Audubon's "sorrowful Mood" lightened by a chilling item he read in a New York newspaper in September, 1836—the cholera had reached Charleston (Audubon 1969, 2:131).

Cholera, when it struck, was swift to infect and often fatal. Some victims fell ill only a few hours after exposure. The symptoms were headache, lassitude, loss of appetite, and low fever. Several days might pass before a second stage appeared with violent vomiting and diarrhea, an unquenchable thirst and hiccuping, and painful cramps that spread from limbs to trunk, involving all of the larger muscles. The terminal stage lasted from a few hours to a few days. Blood circulation would slow and body temperature would drop as low as eighty-five degrees, except in the belly of the victim, where the cholera flamed at 106 degrees. The dying stared with sunken eyes, their skin wrinkled and parched, but almost to the last breath, their minds clear (Thomas 1981, 280–81).

Charleston harbored recent memories of the disease. In November 1832, a particularly virulent strain had broken out among Irish immigrants on a ship nearing the city. Docking at Charleston would have exposed the population to disaster, so vessel was purposely run aground at isolated Cole Island. Wave after wave lifted the ship and pounded the hull on the hard sand bottom, threatening to break her to pieces. More than fifty passengers died in the next few days. Their bodies were shoveled under sand dunes where a year earlier Bachman and Audubon had stood in the clean promise of a November dawn, awed by the whispering wings of thousands of curlews (C. Bachman 1888, 107–8).

As the cholera of 1836 infiltrated the city, the tense population relaxed a bit when it seemed that this strain was mild. Some observers even doubted that it was the dreaded "Asian cholera" as reported. Astute John Bachman flatly disagreed with that optimistic thought: "The state of collapse [from Asian cholera] can scarcely be mistaken; and those who have died have, nearly all, fallen into this state before death" (140).

Bachman's explanation for the relative mildness of this epidemic was that the disease had been attenuated as it stormed the North and West on its way to South Carolina. With more than a hint of hubris, he opined that the cholera in Charleston was confined mostly to the slaves and "the irregular whites," and that "as yet, not a respectable, temperate white, that I know of, has died" (139).

In the week that followed, Bachman learned that this cholera was no respecter of social standing or skin color. Weak, chastened, and propped in his study chair "with your three large Books of Engravings near me," he recanted to Audubon (141): The first stages of his cholera, he knew now, were mild, but a relapse had brought a frightening coldness to his limbs. As sometimes happens to cholera patients at the moment when life dims and flickers, his temperature rose alarmingly (142).

That was the crisis. His temperature dropped and a quick recovery followed. Moreover, the disease left an unexpected blessing. "Hitherto I had been obliged to limp and use a cane, and now I walk without one, and feel no pain, so you may set it down that Cholera cures Rheumatism" (142). Throughout the epidemic, Bachman studied the medical literature on cholera intently, so intently he claimed that he had become a quack himself, qualified to evaluate the published opinions of Audubon's friend, Dr. Harlan, whose "reports I found most sensible and his writings have raised him, in my estimation, as a Physician of excellent judgement" (139–40). But Bachman's praise applied only to Harlan's medical qualifications.

For Bachman, the year of 1836 began with a disturbing incident. He had shipped a box containing specimens of the genus *Lepus* (rabbits and hares) to Charles Pickering, Corresponding Secretary of the American Philosophical Society. Twelve days later, the box had not been delivered and Pickering feared it had been lost. On top of that, Pickering suspected that Harlan might publish a description of the genus *Lepus* before Bachman could get to it. "Previous to Dr. Harlan's departure for Europe," Pickering wrote to Bachman, "he [Harlan] read before the Academy a letter on the new *Lepus,* understood to be *private,* and no communication was ever offered to the Academy" (Pickering to JB, 19 January 1836, APSL).

Cholera having played out in Charleston, Bachman ended the embargo on his friends stranded in New York. Soon, Bachman wrote, "the old ship and the tight little schooner may sail boldly into port, without lying at Quarantine. In other words, you and young John may, ere long, come and feast your appetites on specimens of tough beefsteaks, dry rice and hominy [grits]" (C. Bachman 1888, 142).

The epidemic was a blessing in disguise for Audubon. Forced to delay his reunion with the Bachmans, he decided to go to Philadelphia. A letter from Ed Harris had tipped him off that a haul of birdskins from the Rocky Mountains had arrived there. They had been collected by John Kirk Townsend, an ornithologist who had traveled with the Scottish botanist Thomas Nuttall. Nuttall had immigrated to Philadelphia about the same time as Alexander Wilson, and then had become director of the Harvard herbarium in Boston.

Townsend's collection included new birds, and many others that though known Audubon had not yet drawn. If Audubon could get possession of those skins he would have seized the fruits of a Pacific Coast visit without the time and expense of traveling across the continent. "As I cannot withstand the desire to examine the *rara avis* at Phila, I will go there on Monday morning," Audubon wrote to Bachman on 10 September 1836 (Audubon 1969, 2:130).

Many of the Townsend skins, however, were in custody of Philadelphia's Academy of Natural Science, and Philadelphia had never been kind to Audubon. Would he be allowed to draw and publish the new birds? "I have some doubts whether these Gents will allow me to do so," Audubon wrote. The doubts were well founded. Audubon was greeted with the indifference that had typified his earlier Philadelphia receptions. Allowed to look at the birds, he was refused permission to paint them. The excuse, a reasonable one, was that the collector of the skins, young Dr. Townsend, was the only person who could release them, and Townsend was not expected back from the West for several years (2:131).

Fortunately though, news that Townsend's companion, Thomas Nuttall, was unexpectedly on his way to Boston, reached Philadelphia, and wasting no time, Audubon arrived in Boston on the heels of the Harvard botanist. Nuttall, whom Audubon knew from previous visits to Boston, was pleased to turn over several of the coveted birds, four of them new species, including the handsome band-tailed pigeon and specimens of a striking new dogwood as well. Nuttall assured Audubon that the fruit of the western dogwood was a staple item in the pigeon's diet (2:133).

The botanist, of course, could have made the dogwood known to science himself, yet he bestowed that privilege on Audubon. This generous favor ensured that the most spectacular botanical discovery of Nuttall's career would be named *nuttalli,* and all but guaranteed, considering the beauty and rarity of the doves, that they would be illustrated life-size and presented to the world in the most talked about natural history book of the age (Fries 1973, 99).

On Audubon's way to Charleston, he was cheered by a gift of "some very rare Bird Skins" from William Cooper of New York. Edward Harris also provided skins Audubon needed. And Philadelphia's Titian Peale handed over skins of a new rail with half a dozen young he had collected nearby. The most exciting development was the Philadelphia Academy's willingness at last to sell to him ninety-three of the western birdskins for the bargain price of $184 (Audubon 1969, 2:135).

"Such beauties! Such rarities! Such novelties!" Audubon gloated, attributing his success to being thought of as "a-a-a—" he was stuttering with mock modesty, but managed to get it said—"a Great Naturalist!!!" More likely than Audubon's reputation, however, the reason for Philadelphia's thaw was Edward Harris's intercession with Dr. Samuel Morton, the newly installed curator of the Academy (2:136).

Audubon and his younger son reached Cannonsborough on 16 November 1836. The western birdskins Audubon brought to Charleston needed to be drawn promptly for several reasons, not the least to minimize delay printing *Birds of America.* Acquisition of these skins had suddenly and unexpectedly extended Audubon's reach into territories he knew that probably he would never explore in person. *Birds of America* now spanned the continent, Atlantic to Pacific, a grand accomplishment. On the other hand, the very richness of Nuttall's collection posed problems. Audubon was faced with the time-consuming chore of painting lifelike birds from museum specimens. With much help from Maria Martin, some assistance from John Woodhouse, and the use of the drawing room in Bachman's big house, Audubon was equal to the task.

Painting at his best, Audubon drew a fine likeness of the band-tailed pigeons, the softness of their feathers and the subtlety of their patterns bearing the mark of a master hand. Maria Martin drew the western dogwood the doves perch upon (Audubon 1966, plate 144). Despite the necessity that she paint from pressed plant specimens, Maria Martin captured the grace of a living tree and the luxuriance of its blossoms. The blooms consist not of large petals but of six white, pointed bracts surrounding inconspicuous clusters of tiny yellow flowers. Her drawing achieved the goal of the collector of the specimens, to document not only the leaves and blooms but also buds and fruit as well, a compression of stages unlikely in nature.

Up to this point, Audubon had sold *Birds of America* to subscribers with the promise that they need buy only four hundred plates to complete the set. Exacting English subscribers, in particular, were likely to balk at paying for an unexpectedly large, and proportionally expensive, final volume. Attempting to hold the collection to four hundred plates—ultimately they numbered 435—Audubon placed several bird species on one page with consequent sacrifice of artistic quality and natural history content. For example, within the bounds of one of the plates he squeezed ten woodpeckers representing five species (Audubon 1966, plate 333).

Creating a satisfying composition here was all but impossible. And under no natural circumstance would these widely dispersed species appear and crowd together in the same tree. In the original drawing, however, Maria Martin compensated to some extent. Her meticulously rendered lichen-crusted branches, splintered wood, and time-worn bark supplied such fine details as to create the illusion of living space; the ten woodpeckers seem at home (Fries 1973, 107–8).

Havell's hand-colored engravings, unfortunately, did not quite preserve the textural richness of Maria's branches. As a result, the numerous woodpeckers seem crowded (Audubon 1966, 333). The California sycamore on which five members of the crow family perch (Scrub jay, Steller's jay, yellow-billed magpie, and two Clark's nutcrackers) translated more successfully than the birds into engraving. Thomas Nuttall no doubt supplied the botanical material that Maria Martin painted, and also he provided the centerpiece of the drawing, a yellow-billed magpie. Audubon again rewarded Nuttall by naming the magpie *Pica nuttalli* in his honor.

Throughout December, Audubon, Maria Martin, and John Woodhouse labored on the windfall collection, painting more than seventy birds and many backgrounds. Never having seen most of the birds alive, the artists often were unfamiliar with their postures and environments. Some of the backgrounds by John Woodhouse lack detail to the point of obscurity, and in some paintings, Maria Martin was obliged to resort to pairing western birds with eastern plants, or no plants at all. But such compromises were unavoidable if Audubon were to finish his monumental project on time. Nearly fifty-two years old, Audubon complained of exhaustion and depression, and worried that he would not live to complete his work. Once again he had committed himself to an exhausting schedule.

With the western birds safely on paper, and tracings made and put away at Cannonsborough so that John and Victor, "with the *prime* assistance of John Bachman" (Audubon 1969, 2:143), could restore the paintings and complete the project should anything happen to the originals or to himself, Audubon turned his energy toward organizing an expedition to the "Mexican Gulph." The cutter promised by Washington friends had yet to cross the bar into Charleston harbor. With every spare man-of-war diverted to the campaign against the Seminoles in Florida, Audubon concluded that success in securing space on a naval vessel was unlikely, and instead decided to travel overland to Mobile, perhaps to obtain marine transportation there (2:140).

Ed Harris, who had agreed to accompany Audubon to the gulf, had met Bachman briefly and had struck up a friendship with him. Impressed, Bachman had informed Audubon, "I have taken a great fancy to Edward Harris, could you not bring him with you, and let him join our old fashioned party?" (C. Bachman 1888, 142).

Harris arrived on 6 February 1837, and an outing to Liberty Hall was promptly arranged for him to be treated to a Carolina version of a weekend at the country estate of a titled Englishman. Slaves Sambo, March, and others put the deer-stands (blinds) in order, and then stationed mounted hunters along trails and roads where the deer were most likely to cross. The hounds were loosed in the forest to track the deer, and eventually many of the hunters got shots as pursued game bounded within range of their guns.

Amid much riding, whooping, and yelping, five deer were brought down, including a stately buck shot by "the tall, refined, cultured gentleman," Edward Harris. It was Harris's first kill. Tradition mandated that Harris be "bloodied," that is, his face smeared with the hot blood spilled when the buck's throat was slashed immediately after it fell (C. Bachman 1888, 145–46).

The sport might have continued through the weekend, but the closing ceremony was held on Friday night in deference to Bachman, who had to return to his study in time to prepare for Sunday services. Forewarned, each hunter had written a verse about his companions to sing to the tune of "a time-honored Southern Ditty." John Woodhouse, minstrel by acclamation, stepped up in front of the all-male gathering, tucked his violin under his chin, rapped with the bow, and led the singing.

Written in the dialect of the slaves, the humor was unsparing. Laughter and applause built to the penultimate verse in which John, soon to take a bride, was rallied for his youth and inexperience with a double entendre by John Bachman.

> Young Jostle, he mount on "mossa" big hoss,
> And he look so fine, we took him for Boss,
> But soon he began to ride more sideway than
> straddle,
> And to beg for a sheep-skin to put on the
> saddle.
> Chorus—Clare de kitchen, ole folk, young folk,
> Old Virginny, nebber tire.

(147)

The pastor was saved for last, and John got even. Bachman's passion for rats was parodied, in particular his tireless pursuit of the elusive, never-before-to-be-described short-tailed rat. John Woodhouse was referring to the "Rice Meadow-Mouse" (Audubon and Bachman 1989, 394), focus of the on-going dispute between Bachman and Dr. Richard Harlan. At the song's end, with a grossly exaggerated bow, John tipped his bow to an object strung up over the door—the body of a short-tailed rat, the short tail not a design of nature, but a creation of John's clippers (394).

IN MID-FEBRUARY 1837, as Audubon, John Woodhouse, and Harris boarded the train for Augusta and beyond, Bachman was fretting for an answer to a letter he had written to Dr. Samuel Morton asking for help. "I had half finished a monograph on the Genus Mus with some new species," he lamented. "Your friend the Dr [Harlan] broke in upon me & by carrying off a lamb scattered the flock." Harlan, Bachman complained, had published the Rice Meadow-Mouse ("Stillman's journal, vol. xxxi"), claiming he had based his description on a specimen previously unnoted in the Academy collection (17 February 1837, APSL). Bachman had intended for his description of this rodent to be a keynote in the monograph on the genus *Mus* he was preparing for publication. Now Harlan had published first, and the pastor's efforts seemed wasted.

In an earlier exchange with Bachman, Harlan had insisted that the rice rat was a well-known common species. After Bachman pointed out the characteristics that set his rat off from all known species, Harlan dissected Bachman's specimen to obtain details of its skull and teeth. In the process, the specimen was mutilated.

As Harlan also had read Bachman's unpublished manuscript describing his rice rat and other quadrupeds, Bachman commented to Morton, "He who takes my shoes, will make no bones in taking my stockings also." The pastor assured Dr. Morton that "had Dr Harlan asked me for a specimen stating his intention to describe the animal I would have sent him the drawing [by Maria Martin] which is just now staring me in the face, & a history of one of the most singular of all its species—I have studied it many years. Instead of that we have a name and meagre description & a very doubtful godfather" (17 February 1837, APSL).

In correspondence with Morton and Pickering, Bachman agreed that hereafter he would send drafts of his monographs, and the specimens on which they were based, to the Academy in Philadelphia. Pickering read

Bachman's manuscripts aloud to colleagues at the next meeting of the Academy and identified the author. Assuring Bachman that his work was safe from further piracy, Pickering announced that he considered Bachman's studies "the most valuable contribution that has ever been made to our [American] mammalia" (25 March 1837, APSL).

Bachman related these developments to Audubon, informing him of receiving "a letter from Philadelphia" warning him of "foul play in the magazine" regarding a plot to preempt his description of "new species of Quadrupeds." He told Audubon how their Philadelphia friends advised him to publish immediately and "defeat the cunning one." Bachman did not name Harlan as the cunning one, but Audubon could not have questioned at whom the finger pointed (8 April 1837, WCFP).

Less than a week after Ed Harris had his face daubed in blood, Harris, Audubon, and John Woodhouse boarded the train for Augusta, Georgia, the first leg of an overland trip to Mobile and then to New Orleans. Audubon decided that he had waited long enough. He would, if he could arrange it, board a vessel to explore the Gulf Coast, but, if not, he would wait no longer for government guarantee of transportation. He was anxious to get underway. Adventure, as well as the thrill of finding new birds to advance production of *Birds of America,* drew him on (Audubon 1969, 2:140).

Left behind in Charleston, Bachman also felt the pull that had taken Audubon away, and remarked in a letter that reached Audubon in New Orleans, that if his congregation had been willing for John Woodhouse to fill St. John's pulpit for a few weeks, he would have joined the expedition. "Then both of us would be at home"—John with the woman he loved, Maria Bachman, and Bachman with Audubon and Harris (8 April 1837, WCFP).

But the intense activity of the past few weeks had wearied Bachman, and he felt both regret and relief when Audubon, Harris, and John departed. "There is a strange monotony always after you have left us. Glad to get clear of you for a while but still now and then a new subject of inquiry will arise and I say to myself I should have no objection to have a little argument over the speckled duck" (8 April 1837, WCFP).

If only the tensions that had infiltrated their relationship were confined to speckled ducks. Bachman's irritation over Audubon's drinking was nearing a flash point. When at last a government ship was made available in

New Orleans and Audubon boarded her, he needled Bachman in a letter, "There is no Grog on board of the Campbell!!—What do you say to that?" (Audubon 1969, 2:157).

Bachman responded that just as the man who invented sleep should be blessed, in his opinion the man who invented grog should be cursed. He had cut "a parson's acquaintance the other day for smelling too strong of the creature," and he warned Audubon in phrases he muted with humor that he was "in the habit of doing so by all of my friends." Then he turned lightly to memories of Liberty Hall—the short-tailed rat, the Jersey man with his specs and whiskers (Edward Harris), the old man after wood-peckers (Audubon), and sore Young Jostle with his sheepskin (8 April 1837, WCFP).

In addition, Bachman nagged Audubon about their competition for Maria Martin's attention. She had been an intimate of Bachman's family for twenty-one years, and he depended on her as household manager, assis-tant naturalist, companion, amanuensis, teacher, and artist. With his wife chronically ill and often absent from the home while recuperating at the country house of a relative, where would he have been without Maria? On the other hand, Maria was devoted to Audubon and his cause.

" 'Our sweetheart,' has scarcely found time to let me give her a kiss since my return [from Savannah on church business]—I am afraid she feels ne-glected since you are gone," Bachman teased (15 March 1837, WCFP). A few days later, he played a variation of the theme, "Our sweetheart, bless her, is sitting beside me good-naturedly like a kitten longside of the old puss. She sends as many loves and kisses as she can spare from me—not very many I guess" (8 April 1837, WCFP).

In the autumn, the playful repartee erupted into a sharp exchange. Bach-man, who read the letters Audubon wrote to Maria Martin as freely as he read those addressed to himself, complained about overly intimate phrases Audubon employed in letters to her. Audubon countered definitively, "As to my 'regular built Love letters' to our sweet heart, I cannot think what you have to do with them—and I can assure you that I will continue to speak to her, to Kiss her, and to Love her as far as she may permit me to do without ever troubling myself as regards your thoughts on the subject" (Audubon 1969, 2:180).

A conflict arose in Bachman's travel schedule in April when he felt obliged to attend the Lutheran General Synod in Philadelphia in June 1837, just when his friends were to return from the Gulf Coast. He regretted having to leave at such an inopportune time, but reminded Audubon that his church came before "Ornithology, or even Matrimony." The particular case of matrimony had been on Bachman's mind at least since 28 February 1833, before he had met John Woodhouse. On that day he had mentioned in a letter to Audubon's younger son that he could "tie a knot that no *Jack-knife* can sever." The knot, he seemed to imply, would unite John Woodhouse in marriage with his daughter Maria (C. Bachman 1888, 128).

Bachman was elected to a second consecutive term as president of the Synod, the maximum allowed. In addition to the business of his church, Bachman enjoyed communing with such friends as Benjamin Kurtz, the aging editor of the *Lutheran Observer*. Kurtz, like Bachman, was "an American Lutheran," a product of the Age of Enlightenment and the frontier. Unlike some of the fundamentalists of their faith, both men believed that the Bible was subject to interpretation.

Bachman enjoyed his reunion with the city of his youth. Besides the fine eating places, he took pleasure in trees and shrubs luxuriantly green despite a chilly May. All over Philadelphia the scent of hyacinths sweetened the air, and tulips lifted swelling buds above the cool earth. Otherwise, plants were so backward that Bachman elected not to take time to visit the gardens, not even Bartram's garden, where more than thirty years earlier he had become a friend of Alexander Wilson.

Philadelphia's libraries provided natural history books Bachman rarely consulted, as, for the most part, they were unavailable in Charleston. In the "Philosophical Hall," he sat in Benjamin Franklin's chair and mused, "If knowledge could be communicated in this short way, by touch or sympathy, what a world of Philosophers Franklin's old chair would have produced!" His visits with Thomas Nuttall, Titian Peale, and Charles Pickering, colleagues with whom he had discussed mammals by letter, provided an opportunity to talk about his quadruped studies (C. Bachman 1888, 155–56). But he made no mention of Harlan.

Audubon, Harris, and John Woodhouse entered Charleston on 9 June 1837 after a long and trying overland journey from New Orleans. Bachman returned from Philadelphia just in time to greet them.

Soon after his arrival and reunion with his friends, Bachman, Audubon, and Harris read and discussed—surely with great satisfaction—a letter from George Ord. Bachman had submitted a paper, "Changes of Color in Birds and Quadrupeds," to the American Philosophical Society, and a committee consisting of Nuttall, Titian Peale, and Ord had been assigned to review it. The essential point that Bachman made was that birds and mammals change color by way of a molt, that hair and feathers already in place do not change color as others had assumed. In the paper, Bachman rowed Ord, Wilson, and—in the spirit of fairness—Audubon, "up Salt River" for publishing secondhand observations to the contrary (26 May 1837, HUHL).

Ord grasped at once that Bachman was right and he was wrong. Nuttall was out of town, so Ord spoke for himself and Peale in notifying Bachman that the Society would be pleased to publish his fine study. Ord heaped the acceptance letter with humility, alternately excusing and apologizing and explaining that Wilson's errors were the result of misplaced trust. Ord said Wilson had been grossly misinformed about the molting of the cowbird by Dr. Potter, whose account was "as impudent a fabrication as ever was palmed off on the public." About his own errors, Ord groveled, "Nothing in the course of my natural history pursuits, has given me more mortification than that silly paper" about dunlins and other molting birds, lamenting that hardly had the paper left his hands than he made observations which proved his position "totally in error." His blunder exposed, he prepared to publish a retraction of his "abominable Paper, which, like the ghost of Banqo to Macbeth, haunts me at every turn" (26 May 1837, HUHL).

At that point, however, Bachman's stinging refutation had arrived in Philadelphia and it was too late for Ord to retract. "Your paper, Reverend Sir, is truly a valuable contribution to Science; and I am persuaded that the lovers of Ornithology, as well as physiologists, will read it with no ordinary attention." Ord's summary comment captured Bachman's credo as a scientist: "You have taken the proper course, Reverend Sir; you listen to all, but you examine for yourself; and report the result only of your own investigations" (26 May 1837, HUHL).

Bachman had predicted this humiliation of Ord in a letter he wrote to Audubon on 8 April 1837. "I have arraigned friend Ord before the Bar and just want to show him that here are some things in Heaven and Earth that are not dreamt of in his philosophy," he explained. "I have long wished to have a lick at him and have given the gentle hint which he at last will understand that 'a knowledge of our own liability to error should teach one not to condemn unsparingly the faults of others'" (26 May 1837, HUHL).

The friends had little time to gloat. For the last time, the focus of Audubon's great work *Birds of America* was shifting from collecting birds in the wilderness to publishing the results. To support his family, the faster Audubon took charge of publications in England the better.

John Woodhouse Audubon and Maria Rebecca Bachman were married by John Bachman in mid-June. Bride, groom, and father-of-the-groom departed Charleston on the heels of the ceremony. Farewells were tearful, parting embraces strong and emotional. By the second of July, Audubon was resting at the home of Edward Harris in New Jersey. He had accompanied the newlyweds on their journey north, and had seen them off at Philadelphia for a ten-day trip to Niagara Falls (Audubon 1969, 160–62).

"Never in my Whole Life have I enjoyed travelling so much as I have with My beloved Daughter—Everything has been new to her senses," Audubon wrote to Maria's parents. "Hills and Dales—Trees & Fruits, Bridges, Rail Cars, and Highly fashionable Circles have been danced before her alternately like so many novelties of Nature and the World" (Audubon 1969, 2:162).

The only social event that Audubon felt worthy of note was their visit to the home of Dr. Harlan, who "feels very sore at J.B. not having called upon him." But Harlan and his wife harbored no grudges, according to Audubon. They were "very Kind" to the bride and entertained her with a "grand Ride to the Water Works Hospitals &c" (2:163). Hovering on the fringes of a honeymoon, Audubon savored every moment of it. But the honeymoon was almost over. Passage for Audubon, John, and Maria had already been booked for an Atlantic crossing on the *England,* with departure set for 16 July 1837.

Just before boarding the *England* Audubon reported, "Our Dear Children returned from Niagara a few days ago quite well and as Happy as if Angels in heaven. My Sweet Maria becomes dearer to me every moment, and my heart swells with joy as I see her approaching me to Kiss me as she would Kiss her dearest of Friends. God bless her!" (2:169).

He was ecstatic, and for reasons besides the vicarious honeymoon. Most of the drawings and observations necessary to complete the *Birds of America* were now in hand. Though the Union was in an economic depression, Audubon had managed to sell sufficient subscriptions to finance his last trip to England. And when, in a year, he would return to America, he believed he would have money "to purchase a Place somewhere in our Country!" Audubon had come to the point where he was, in the words of his friend and in-law, Nicholas Berthoud, "the happiest of Men—Free of debts, and having *available funds* and *Talents!*" (2:169).

Chapter 9

ACROSS THE ATLANTIC

$\mathcal{A}$s BIRD SKINNERS, both Audubon and Bachman were familiar
with the powder down of birds, particularly conspicuous in herons, where
it is concentrated in certain areas along the feather tracts. Audubon expressed his notions on the subject to Bachman in a letter of 31 October
1837. Many times, Audubon had it on the tip of his tongue to tell his theory,
only to lose it in the torrent of ideas that tumbled between two friends. "I
have for sometime past thought that the Cottony substance, attached to
the breasts and rumps of Herons was capable of becoming *luminous* under
certain circumstances, as during dark nights &c—when by the assistance
of these Magic Lanterns being lighted at the will of the birds, as it is in
certain insects; they may be enabled to detect the quarry, which otherwise
would pass by unheeded!" (Audubon 1969, 2:187).

The notion was enchanting. No one, as far as Audubon knew, claimed
to have seen luminous feathers, but he could picture it. A formation of
herons motionless in the dark wait for fish to swim within range. Suddenly
a heron glows and stabs a victim in the dark water. Before the heron swallows its meal, it snuffs its magic lanterns. Through the night the swamp
glitters as the herons gorge.

Reading about the process in a letter Bachman received months after
Audubon had reached England to conclude his work on *Birds of America*
and *Ornithological Biography,* gave Bachman's flagging spirits a lift. Audubon asked him to check out his idea in some swamp or rice field on some
moonless night, and hurry, before his book went to the printer and it was
too late to use the information. He warned Bachman not to reveal the
theory until its validity was settled one way or another, lest some rival
steal credit by publishing first (2:188).

As Audubon noted, the fact that some animals can produce light is well known. Several insects, notably fireflies and glowworms, flash rhythmically in the dark. And anyone who has sailed a southern sea, or taken a nocturnal dip in a warm ocean, has seen the swirling waters brighten with millions of tiny, coldly glowing marine creatures. In the deeps, a society of fish and other animals live out sunless lives courting, attracting prey, and confusing predators by means of strategically placed, many-colored, biological lamps that blink, gleam, or fade as required.

And the truth is, powder-down feathers grow continuously and are never molted. Dust is released as the down feathers emerge from the skin and break from their sheaths. Powder down in some birds imparts a metallic sheen to some of its feathers. No zoologist examining birdskins could fail to notice and to wonder about the function of powder down, yet the best that ornithologists have been able to offer is a theory that it helps to waterproof plumage (Welty 1979, 29, 32).

Perhaps a moment of reflection and a bemused smile were all Bachman gave the twinkling herons. Dozens of other requests for information were flooding in from Audubon, and physically Bachman was not up to nocturnal heron-watching. Sadly, exhaustion had forced him to suspend his studies of mammals, which, as monograph had followed monograph into print, had become a veritable survey of the mammals of North America.

Hardly had Audubon and John swept into Charleston in June of 1837, and John married and carried off Bachman and Harriet's first-born daughter, than the pastor's left leg and arm became numb and weak, and he surrendered to a great lassitude. The least effort sent him to bed. So profound was his weariness, he doubted he would recover from it and said as much in a letter to Audubon. "This winter—if I am alive, I shall use much exercise on horseback, which agrees well with me although walking does not" (2 October 1837, CMBA).

And then he softened the grim "if I am alive" with a bit of humor. He had cleaned "John's large Gun" and was astonished at its precision when he tried it out on a target. At one hundred yards it could bring down a turkey or a deer every time. " 'Tis true the Gun is heavy to carry for an invalid," he commented, "but the poor horse has to bear the burden & this when I am in the country is always a borrowed one, so it will cost me no oats" (2 October 1837, CMBA).

When Bachman felt strong enough, he exchanged letters with anyone he thought would help Audubon, and as a result, he obtained many of the birds preserved in rum that Audubon and MacGillivray wanted to examine for their internal organs. About this time, adding to Bachman's depression, he had to report to Audubon at the end of a long letter the loss of one of their Charleston compeers, Dr. Edward Leitner, a botanist who had borrowed Bachman's gun to collect Florida birds for Audubon and had been killed by Seminoles (10 March 1838, WCFP).

Bachman's health deteriorated further in the spring. "The left arm and leg," he wrote to Audubon, "continue very much benumbed" (10 March 1838, WCFP). He became so handicapped that the vestry employed an assistant pastor to take over Bachman's duties, and Bachman, freed from those responsibilities, elected once more to test the restorative power of an ocean voyage, this one coupled with an extended land tour of Europe. The choice he made of the first stopover took account of word the family had received from London. Maria Audubon would soon deliver a child. "Bye bye [by the way], old man," Bachman wrote to Audubon, "I am told we are soon to be, in hieroglyphic language, (⚲ ⚲ ⚲)—comprenez-vous Grandpapa" (16 April 1838, WCFP). The stick-figures represented Audubon and Bachman and their grandchild to be.

Bachman's short letter included several paragraphs of gossip and an assurance that Audubon had been shipped "a barrel containing flamingos" in rum. It also contained a response to Audubon's query of what project he should undertake after the last volume of *Birds of America* was published. "What you will do next, I know not," Bachman wrote. Then, almost as an afterthought—"I doubt whether the giving of our quadrupeds would be profitable although it would certainly be serviceable to science" (16 April 1838, WCFP).

Having decided to tour Europe, Bachman chose a voyage advertised in the *Charleston Courier* on 21 May 1838: "For Liverpool. The fine fast sailing Charleston built ship CHICORA, E. L. Halsey Master."

CHRISTOPHER HAPPOLDT, an engaging lad of fourteen, whom Bachman had selected to be his companion on the journey, no doubt also read this notice with interest. The bright youngster dreaded "the tedium of a sea voyage," and before boarding the *Chicora* committed himself to keeping a journal. The journal, he thought, might "afford some gratification to my Parents," and he could use it for comparison with any later trip he might make to Europe. He committed himself to the task on boarding the *Chicora* on 5 June 1838, "I have resolved therefore to keep a record of the daily occurrences on the passage, of my thoughts & actions" (Happoldt 1960, 119).

When Christopher and Bachman climbed on deck they were confronted by sailors so drunk and quarrelsome that Captain Halsey locked them up in the forecastle. Then it developed that guards in Charleston had arrested the first mate following a "drunken frolick." Halsey went to town to search for the sailor, and failing to find him, hired another mate. Rough as any of his men, Halsey knew well their ways, and handled them accordingly.

The departure of the *Chicora,* delayed for two days by a calm, caused Halsey to engage the steamer *South Carolina* to tow his ship into open water. Once at sea, a breeze sprang up and the *Chicora,* awakening to her element, skimmed over the waves, making Christopher seasick (119).

Thereafter, Christopher reported, the sailors had time to repent their sins. At noon for three Sundays they were summoned to the deck, lined up on benches, and heard out sermons Bachman preached successively on the parable of the prodigal son, Peter's denial of his lord and master, and the rising of Lazarus from the dead.

Presumably coached by Bachman, the boy became interested in the birds of the open ocean, noting the "Razor-billed Auks" that rose on the waves and dipped into the troughs, the fluttering petrels, and the "schreeming" Arctic terns. Christopher was the ideal companion for the ailing pastor, and the boy's tendency to noisy nightmares proved to be a minor annoyance compared to the lift he must have given Bachman's spirits, as daily the *Chicora* multiplied the miles between the travelers and worries back in Charleston. Bachman and Christopher stepped onto the docks of Liverpool late on Sunday, 1 July 1838, with Bachman rested and strengthened by the voyage.

The pastor and his charge took the coach to Oxford where a letter from John Woodhouse awaited Bachman in the Roebuck Hotel. Lucy Green Audubon had come into the world while they were sailing, and Bachman had become a grandfather. John Woodhouse also revealed that Audubon had gone to Edinburgh to work with MacGillivray on the fourth volume of *Ornithological Biography;* thus Audubon would not be in London when Bachman and Christopher arrived there.

The travelers visited with Arthur Hugh Clough the next day, a nineteen-year-old poet who had spent his childhood in Charleston where his father, an English cotton merchant, had immigrated. Clough attended Oxford as holder of the Balliol scholarship (Balliol is a college of Oxford University). He escorted Bachman and Christopher to "the principal Universities & chapels & Libraries & picture Gallery."

Late in the afternoon Bachman and Christopher boarded the train to London, arriving there about eight P.M. Forewarned by Audubon's letters that Lucy was not in the best of spirits, Bachman had some inkling of the climate behind the door at 4 Wimpole Street. The knocker was tied up and Bachman had to pound for admittance. After a while the door was opened and they entered, then more time passed before a meal was produced. Christopher noted that he and Bachman were received "with great kindness." Nevertheless, the hungry pair were made to understand that dinner at Lucy Audubon's house was served at five o'clock (134, 140).

Lucy Audubon had lived a hard life in America. Deaths of two infant daughters, financial crises, endless servant problems, and long separations from her husband wore her down, and she drifted in and out of the condition Victorian physicians called hysteria. In his absence, Audubon had tried to soothe and calm Lucy with almost every letter to her. On 13 November 1831, writing in Charleston, he urged, "Do take great care of thy Dear Self and of thy intellect!" Again on 29 March 1832, he told of his success in selling *Birds of America* in Savannah, and reassured her, "This will ease my Lucy's mind I am quite sure."

But Audubon also confided to Bachman in a letter of 14 August 1837 (Audubon 1969, 2:175), written shortly after he and the newlyweds reached London, that Lucy was not very well, that the arrival of himself and the newlyweds had produced a "great revolution in her nervous system." The pressure did not soon let up. The oblivious bride, Maria, wrote to Cannons-borough that her lucky stars dazzled above her. "I am now surrounded by many who use all their endeavours to make me happy and comfortable" (MA to Mrs. John M. Davis, 24 October 1837, CMBA).

A physician was called, and "after a while all was gayety and Happiness at our house in Wimpole Street." The cure that had brought Lucy such high spirits did not last, however, and her symptoms became all the more alarming. Just before Christmas 1837, Audubon wrote to Charleston that Lucy was confined to her room, and frequently to her bed as well (Audubon 1969, 2:192–93).

But Lucy seemed well enough on 6 July 1838, the first day of Bachman and Christopher's visit. She escorted the boy to a tailor and had him measured for a suit. Later, John Woodhouse took over Christopher and led him on a walk in St. James Park, from which one could see the "royal Palace." Christopher was impressed by the size of the palace panes, some of them "12 feet in height & 6 in breadth" (Happoldt 1960, 134).

Bachman remained in London for three days. He went to see the House of Commons on the first day, and the next, a Saturday, he hurried through his agenda. He managed to do some sight-seeing with Christopher in the morning and then visit Dr. Benjamin Phillips, the Audubon family doctor. Dr. Phillips, one of the most respected medical men in London, assured the pastor that he was suffering from nothing more serious than indigestion, and prescribed whiskey water when needed.

After calling briefly on his daughter and his newborn, first-born grandchild, Bachman boarded the nine P.M. steamer to Edinburgh. Lucy, John and Maria, and Christopher were left to their own devices in London.

Bachman assisted Audubon, Victor, and MacGillivray with the text of *Ornithological Biography*. Three weeks at Audubon's side passed all too quickly, and when Bachman departed, Audubon penned a passage for the introduction of his book that defined Bachman's visit: "The days which we enjoyed together were few, but delightful; and when at the end of a fortnight my friend left us, I felt as if almost alone, and in the wilderness."

The pastor returned to Wimpole Street on 28 July, just ahead of Victor. A crisis was brewing. Lucy's illness, which overcame her the day Maria Audubon moved into her home, flared again during the days Bachman and her husband worked together in Edinburgh. Nobody explained the situation to Christopher, but he picked up enough to know that Victor had returned to Wimpole Street "to settle the point, whether Mr. John [Woodhouse] should go over to America, or to France" (141).

The overriding reason for Victor's return to London was the necessity to relieve the pressures of the crowded household on Lucy. Bachman decided that it was time for him and Christopher to move on to Europe, but John had no plans to find housing for himself, his wife, and his daughter. On the first of August, the Audubons at Wimpole Street arrived at a joint decision. As Christopher understood it, he and Bachman would embark for Europe, and John, Maria, and their baby would tour France for a couple of months, and then "all go to America early in the spring" (141–42).

Lucy put her part of the plan into effect immediately. She abruptly announced that she would give up the Wimpole Street house and within the week join Audubon in Edinburgh. In effect, Bachman and the others were given seven days to vacate Wimpole Street.

Bachman took full advantage of Lucy's week of grace. Pausing only to christen his granddaughter, he worked long hours almost every day in the Zoological Department of the British Museum and the Museum of the Zoological Society. As an authority on American mammals, he quickly secured access to those institutions and glibly identified skins in their collections that he had only recently described in his monographs. He struck up a friendship with George R. Waterhouse, curator of the Zoological Society, who bestowed on Bachman the privilege of describing several unnamed mammals Bachman ferreted from the museum's collection cabinets.

A week was not enough for Bachman to complete his survey of the Society's treasure. As the 8 August deadline for vacating the house on Wimpole Street approached, he was still deeply immersed. Audubon was in Edinburgh preoccupied with birds, rightly so, but Bachman's attention was on mammals. It was clear to him that no one could write authoritatively about American mammals without study of the collections in the London museums. Their doors had swung wide—nothing could deter Bachman from entering.

On the eve of the Lucy's deadline Christopher suffered one of his nightmares. "I kicked & jumped most tremendously last night, until Mr. Bachman was obliged to pinch me, but the more he pinched, the more I kicked, and he could not awake me so he let me alone until I laid still." While Bachman went to the museum as usual the next morning, and worked until five in the afternoon, Christopher remained at home to help the Audubons and to pack his baggage and Bachman's (145–46).

That night everyone vacated 4 Wimpole Street, the Audubons off to Edinburgh, and Christopher and Bachman to a rooming house at 7 Leicester Square, conveniently near the museums, where nine days later Bachman finally was satiated. Some nights he did not set aside his papers until an hour after midnight. But Bachman did not neglect Christopher—by day he took him sight-seeing.

Mercifully, on 14 August, Bachman's almost nonstop study ceased. Young Happoldt went sight-seeing in London in the morning, and in the afternoon he made the final financial arrangements for their tour of the Continent. On his way home in the omnibus, after conducting the necessary transactions with Mr. Stolkdenfelt, their London banker, he "had a very unpleasant seat opposite to a drunken woman, who kept opening her mouth, which smelt very strong after rum" (150). Christopher eagerly left the omnibus, reached home, and pitched in with Bachman for the final packing. They were committed to board the steamboat *Britannica* by midnight. Bachman, however, was scheduled to attend an important meeting of the Zoological Society. He left Christopher at Leicester Square to finish the job on his own.

Christopher may not have been told what compelled Bachman to attend the meeting at the eleventh hour, though it was perhaps the most important affair of Bachman's tour. When the members of the Society arrived, they found a table bedecked with a series of skins of the squirrel genus *Sciurus,* "including with one or two exceptions, all which are known to inhabit North America." *Six* were new species. In due course, Bachman read his manuscript to his English peers, the document replete with formal descriptions, habits, and other squirrel data (Yarrell 1838).

After Bachman's performance, George Waterhouse presented "a new species of Hare from the collection made for the society of the Late Mr. Douglas and proposed to characterize it under the name of *Lepus Bachmani,*" an honor, indeed. Prompt publication of Bachman's *Sciurus* study in the proceedings of the Society ensured that problems such as he had experienced with Harlan and the short-tailed rat would not repeat themselves with the squirrels (Yarrell 1838).

THE NORTH SEA WAS TURBULENT on the 15th and 16th of August, and the journey plodding. Confined on the slow German steamer, Christopher suffered from acute *mal de mere*. Once ashore, however, the Charleston tourists set off for a pleasant and productive jaunt across the Continent.

In Berlin, clerics and naturalists welcomed Bachman as a compatriot. Martin Heinrich Lichtenstein, director of the Zoological Museum of the University of Berlin, was particularly kind and opened the collection to the American. He also entertained Bachman and Christopher at home. Bachman's fluency in German, a skill he had mastered during his twenty-three years in Charleston, was a key to this warm reception. Christopher tried to follow suit, but was embarrassed when his hosts corrected his pronunciation of German words with gentle amusement. The young man undertook daily study sessions in the language of his forefathers and soon intricate German words and phrases began to work their way into both his conversations and his journal.

After an inspection of a German school, which Bachman pronounced fine enough to serve as a model for the schools of America, they set off to the west, meandering the breadth of the German kingdoms by *schnellpost* (mail coach), pausing at such cities as Dresden, Prague, Carlsbad, and Munich.

During their journey, Bachman and Christopher frequently changed coaches. Some were so ponderous Bachman could walk beside them, studying the roadside plants just as he had on the banks of the Erie Canal beside the *Albany* more than a decade earlier. His illness out of mind, he and Christopher made their way to Switzerland, the land of Bachman's ancestors. There he marveled at the Alps and placid Lake Constance, and noted with pleased surprise a lone "European 'Stormy Petrel'" fluttering over the lake, seemingly as at home in the alpine water as those he and Christopher had seen sporting in the mid-Atlantic (C. Bachman 1888, 170).

A meeting of the Society of Naturalists and Physicians of Germany at Freyburg was an unexpected bonus of their tour of Europe. Timing their travels perfectly, Bachman and Christopher again crossed the German border in a coach crowded with naturalists. They arrived in Freyburg on the eve of the convention. More than six hundred delegates attended a short introductory session on the morning of 19 September. They then assembled in a great hall for a dinner that lasted three hours. Meat was devoured, toasts guzzled, speeches made. The food was excellent, though the

Americans thought the eating of it entirely too prolonged. For Bachman, the real feast at Freyberg was intellectual (Happoldt 1960, 175–76).

Charles Bonaparte, for whom Audubon had mixed feelings, dropped by Bachman's room one evening and talked late into the night. As usual, Bonaparte fished for information about new species of American birds he wanted to include in his *American Ornithology; or, The Natural History of Birds Inhabiting the United States, Not Given by Wilson*. Bachman watched his tongue, betraying nothing that Audubon had not already disclosed to the Prince of Canino. Bachman was not intimidated by Bonaparte's royal trappings. A revolutionist American-style, Bachman had earlier turned down an audience with the ruler of Prussia, commenting that he "would not have it said that he ran after a King" (159).

As the only American scientist at the Freyburg convention, Bachman was invited to speak on "the progress and present state of Natural Science in the United States" (C. Bachman 1888, 172). When he finished his short talk delivered in German—he planned to provide a longer written account later—officials on the podium crowded round to congratulate him. The sharp-eyed adolescent at Bachman's elbow observed that his mentor was "kissed by several of the headmen—some with long m[ustaches]," which Christopher did not much like. "The Germans have a very ugly habit of kissing one another, & it is a laughable sight, to behold two fat men, hugging, & rubbing their long [mustaches] in each other's mouths" (177).

Unfortunately, the cost of attending the convention was that Bachman and Christopher fell behind on their travel schedule. They left too hurriedly for Bachman to prepare a written account of his message for the delegates. In the last minutes before departure, he managed to finish an informal letter, including important information he had not covered in his talk.

His message was direct. The day had passed when all new mammals, birds, reptiles, fish, insects, and plants discovered in America would be described and published in Europe. At that very moment thirty new mammals—some of his own discovery, he could have added—were "in the course of publication." Bachman called attention to the works of Wilson and Audubon. Works of the latter, for those who wished to subscribe, were obtainable from England. Europe also could look to the journals of the philosophical societies of Philadelphia and New York for much that was new in American science, and to Stillman's journal for the latest in mineralogy. For botany they should consult the works of "Torry of New York, and Nuttall of Phila." (JB to Society of Naturalists and Physicians of Germany, Zoology Department, 21 September 1838, CMBA).

Seven weeks remained before Bachman and Christopher would sail from Liverpool for Charleston on the *America*. The grand landscapes of the Rhine and the glories of Paris remained to be seen. Paris diverted John Bachman. He and Christopher lingered there until, to Bachman's dismay, his illness returned and French physicians bluntly told him he had no chance to recover.

Crossing the English Channel in a small steamer was more unpleasant than the bad crossing of August. Christopher, who had been reading the travel writing of Mrs. Frances Trollope, had become a skilled recorder of the ways and character of people he met along the way. He wrote a vivid sketch of how their little boat shipped some water at every wave. "I at first made light of it, but it was not long before I & Mr. Bachman also were dreadfully seasick; the cabin was strewd with Ladies & gentlemen, & the gentlemen forgot all their politeness,—they laid themselves in the births, & allowed the ladies to lay on the floor" (Happoldt 1960, 200).

In London again, Bachman summoned strength for ten days more of museum research, choosing to omit going to Edinburgh, where his daughter was nursing her baby, now almost four months old. He contented himself with an exchange of letters with Audubon. Audubon complained that he could not see why Bachman would not visit Liverpool by way of Edinburgh "and give us another hearty shake of the hand ere you return to the 'Mother country!' "

In his last letter before Bachman left England, Audubon wrote, "We are all well just now, the Babe is grown very fat and lively, and my beloved Wife is certainly much better than she was last year." He rarely referred to Lucy's condition without pronouncing her "better" (Audubon 1969, 2:209).

John Bachman and Christopher Happoldt sailed from Liverpool on the *America* on 11 November 1838, and docked in Charleston on 27 December 1838 (Happoldt 1960, 214). Christopher was "not long in reaching home," and soon Bachman, too, embraced his loved ones again. After seven anxious months, his family saw at once that his European trip had not improved his health. Bachman had lost seventeen pounds, and his other symptoms were, if anything, more alarming than before he left. His doctors ordered complete rest. Though many interesting-looking letters from fellow naturalists had accumulated in his absence, Bachman contented himself with the addresses and postmarks for a while.

On 5 March, he felt strong enough to read his letters from Thomas Brewer, a Boston zoologist. He then could not resist acknowledging receipt of them, though the writing had to be "by stealth," lest Maria Martin catch him breaking doctor's orders. John Bachman knew the value of friends, particularly those who might help him with his study of the quadrupeds. While tramping over Europe he had taken the trouble to collect bird eggs along the way for Brewer. In his note to Brewer, Bachman promised that as soon as he was able he would pack the eggs and send them to him. He told Brewer, too, that he probably would be traveling north in the summer and might visit him for a few days. Bachman was free to travel. Because of his continued illness, St. John's had retained an assistant pastor (5 March 1839, CMBA).

Escaping the debilitating Charleston summer would serve several purposes. Bachman was outgoing president of the General Synod, which convened during the summers of odd-numbered years. Though it was not mandatory that he attend the assembly in Philadelphia, he wanted to work once more to prevent the issue of abolition from splitting the American Lutheran church. There were other items on Bachman's agenda, as well, including a visit to Victor in New York.

When Bachman reached New York toward the end of June, he moved into the boardinghouse with Victor and commuted to the Synod in Philadelphia in his successful campaigned to blunt the abolition controversy. The issue would not reemerge in the Lutheran hierarchy for nearly twenty years.

Chapter 10

THE STORM IN CHARLESTON

ℬIRDS OF AMERICA rushed toward completion in England, and by the closing days of 1838 little remained for Victor Audubon to contribute to his father's cause there. He began to think of preceding the rest of the family to New York, and then of striking south to Cannonsborough. During John Woodhouse and Maria Bachman's four-year engagement, and after their marriage in 1837, Victor must have heard much about Mary Eliza, the second Bachman daughter.

Maria Audubon thought it likely Victor would visit Charleston when he returned to New York and she wrote to Aunt Maria to prepare her for the possibility. Young Maria declared, Victor Audubon "likes to have *two pitchers of water* and at *least three towels always* in his room." She further advised that Victor "takes gin or something of the kind at his meals, and prefers his *coffee very strong* with plenty of boiled milk and little sugar" and did not care for foods flavored with rose water (MA to MM, January 5 1839, Collection of Miss Georgiana Grimball, Charleston).

Only twenty, Eliza knew French and German, had studied botany, sang, and played the guitar. And she was more sprightly than her sister Maria, John's somewhat grave and dutiful wife. Victor, for his part, was nearly thirty and had courted several women, most recently singer Adelaide Kemble, younger sister of actress Fanny Kemble, who had chanced on an American tour to meet and admire his father (Ford 1988, 301).

Victor's goals and his loyalties were in conflict. For his first eleven years, save a brief period when the Audubons lived in a cabin of their own in Henderson, Victor bounced from relative to relative. After Audubon left the family and sailed for England in 1826, Lucy's prosperous brothers took Victor in as a countinghouse apprentice. His bent for numbers made him useful in Uncle Thomas's Ohio River establishments, and when his parents reunited and formed the "little alliance" to complete *Birds of America*, Victor was sent to London to supervise production and distribution of the prints while his father remained behind to search out new birds and subscribers.

As the well-heeled son of a celebrity, Victor mixed easily with England's elite. Rich American travelers sought him out. Young Henry De Rham, scion of a powerful New York financier and diplomat, commissioned him to paint an oil of black cocks, ritually hunted by English aristocrats, and De Rahm followed up by subscribing to *Birds of America*. While John Woodhouse and John James Audubon were scouring America, in England De Rham invited Victor and Lucy to extravagant parties.

His father's return to London preempted Victor's role in the family endeavor. Still, he served the "little alliance" by standing ready to take over in the event that his visibly aging father died, a possibility that preoccupied the family, especially Audubon himself, who was working as much as eighteen hours a day. With little to do, Victor developed a fondness for leisurely seashore vacations. At last, in January 1839, he sailed for New York on the *Great Western* and docked in mid-February (*Charleston Courier,* 23 February 1839). He had business to conduct in America and preparations to make for the return of the rest of the family.

The Bachmans had no inkling that Victor would knock on their door early in the morning of 5 April 1839 (MM to EA, 24 April 1840, CMBA). Victor had traveled from New York to Wilmington and there boarded the steam packet *North Carolina* for Charleston (*Charleston Mercury,* 6 April 1839). Obviously aware that he had come to meet Eliza, the Bachmans made arrangements for him to sleep at the house of Mrs. Mary E. Davis, several blocks away. Mrs. Davis, a widow, was a longtime family friend and in effect a grandmother to the Bachman children (VA to Mrs. Mary E. Davis, 29 July 1939, CMBA).

Charleston is most beautiful in April. In the garden, Bachman's magnolia towered over sweet-scented jessamine vines. There were roses, and crepe myrtle, and lilies to cap the romantic setting. And besides Eliza, Victor had the whole Bachman family to get to know. Even so, Victor found time for work. On 3 May 1839, for instance, he wrote to "the Columbia College

[University of South Carolina]" concerning $505 due on the latest numbers of *Birds of America,* delivered per the subscription Bachman had secured for Audubon in 1831 (Ridge 1985, 70).

During those brief weeks in Charleston, Victor's life changed course. He and Eliza fell in love, and Eliza promised to marry him. Toward the middle of May, Victor departed, but instead of sailing to New York, he took a coach through the mountains of Virginia, where he dallied for about a month, relaxing at the sulphur springs.

In his own good time, Victor reached New York and moved into Mrs. Waldron's boardinghouse, and when Bachman turned up, Victor took him in. Both anxiously awaited the overdue *Toronto,* a sailing vessel then becalmed just offshore. John, Maria, expecting her second child in about three months, and "Lu Lu," their first baby, were aboard. Eliza had insisted they leave England in summer to avoid the fall hurricane season (JB to JJA, 5 July 1839, CMBA).

The steamers plying the Atlantic with great regularity by 1839 were not subject to some of the constraints of sailing vessels. Calm or no, rumbling and smoking they rounded Sandy Hook and thrashed through the harbor. One of these ships brought a letter from Audubon to Victor that combined business and family affairs, including several requests for help to be passed on to Bachman. Most important, Audubon wanted Bachman to prepare "a more particular list" than the one Bachman already had provided. Earlier in the year Audubon had made his decision to publish *The Quadrupeds* and without consulting Bachman had embarked on the necessary preliminary steps.

That Audubon had jumped the gun made Bachman "shockingly nervous." He had no access in New York to the books he needed to compose the list Audubon wanted. The books he would have consulted had he been in Charleston were in his own library—"Richardsons Fauna—Harlan—Godman—Catesby—D'Azara—Louis & Clarke—Lang expedition—Trans. Zool Society—The Works of Lichtenstein & of Ehrenbach of Dresden"—all unfortunately now out of his reach (5 July 1839, CMBA).

Bachman advised Audubon to prepare the list himself, and gave him other advice as well: "It would be wise for you to study the skulls & teeth [in the British museums] a little—you take these things by intuition."

He admonished his friend to "leave nothing in England that you may be obliged to send for hereafter." Specifically, Bachman suggested that before Audubon departed he draw the rare mammals likely to be found in English collections, including "the Sable, the Fisher, the common martin & the rascally grizzly bear" (5 July 1839, CMBA).

Though Audubon and Bachman were working together on the *Quadrupeds*, details of agreement between Audubon and Bachman had yet to be struck. Bachman revealed to Audubon that he had been discussing the project with several of his American colleagues. "I promised Harris & others that I would give a full synopsis of American Quadrupeds—I have done no more [until now] than make pretty full notes—These and all the information I have to give are at your service." The important requirement was that "the Book must be original & credible—no compilation & no humbug" Bachman insisted. "I am not often far out of the way in predictions & I assure you it will, if managed with your usual zeal and the boys' industry & attention to the commercial part, be the most profitable speculation into which you have ever entered" (5 July 1839, CMBA).

Without Bachman's involvement, Audubon might not have dared to attempt the work on mammal prints they gave the ponderous title *The Viviparous Quadrupeds of North America,* a title they usually shortened to *Quadrupeds* in correspondence and conversation. But with Bachman's cooperation, Audubon, worried about getting old, began work without further ado.

In mid-September Bachman was astonished to learn that Audubon had already distributed a public announcement of plans to publish not only *The Quadrupeds* but also a small edition of *Birds of America.* It unsettled Bachman that without warning him, Audubon would make public so conspicuous and ambitious a commitment. "But are you not a little fast in issuing your prospectus in regard to the *Birds* & *Quadrupeds,* without having a No. of the Works, by which the public could judge of their merits?" he asked (13 September 1839, CMBA).

If Bachman thought that he had satisfied Audubon's dependence on his counsel, a letter he received in October dispelled the notion. Old Jostle continued to prod for favors, yet without disclosing his own ideas. "About the quadrupeds, I can say nothing til you see fit to enlighten me in regard to your plans," Bachman firmly asserted. "Beyond the information you have given me of your intentions to publish them, I am left as much in the dark about the matter as our friend, George Ord."

The reason for Audubon's reticence—Bachman did not need to be told—was not secrecy; it was that Audubon had no plans. His slate was blank except for advice he had coaxed piecemeal from Bachman. "About the size of the work—the probable price—the kind of engraving—the place of publication—whether it is to come out in numbers or volumes— I as yet know nothing," Bachman complained. He cajoled Audubon with mild sarcasm, "Perhaps when you are more at leisure you may find an hour to say something on the subject" (17 October 1839, WCFP).

In mid-July the *Toronto* finally reached New York, and John, Maria, and their baby settled into rooms in Mrs. Waldron's boardinghouse. News of the young family's safe crossing of the Atlantic reached Cannonsborough and inspired old Mrs. Martin to give her daughter, Maria, and her grand-child, Harriet Bachman, funds for a trip to New York to see Harriet Audu-bon, her new great-grandchild. Eliza Bachman stayed in Cannonsborough to look after the house, her grandmother, and the other children, bitterly disappointing Victor. He worried about the behavior of Eliza's brothers, William Kunhardt and Samuel Wilson, ages nine and ten. True, Mrs. Martin was at home, but Eliza could not expect the old lady, now confined to bed, to help discipline the active boys (MM to Mrs. Davis, 26 July 1839, CMBA).

For the first time since 1827, when Maria had nursed Bachman through the terrible fever he contracted in upstate New York, Maria Martin found herself residing in Mrs. Waldron's Broadway boardinghouse again. Broad-way was more noisy than ever, and Maria disliked the din and bustle of large cities all the more. "It is almost impossible to converse unless you bawl out in the highest key," she observed. Victor and John had read some letters to the rest of the family, and in order to hear their voices, Maria Martin and her kin had to close the windows to deaden the din from the street. "It almost sets me crazy," said Maria in her letter, "and noth-ing would tempt me to live in such a situation!" (to Mrs. Davis, 23 July 1839, CMBA).

But the distractions of a noisy boardinghouse were a "slight inconve-nience of travelling" compared to Maria's satisfaction at seeing with her own eyes that her niece had a good marriage. Right down the street John Woodhouse was setting up a portrait studio, an encouraging move toward independence. "Lu Lu," as they called their lively and healthy, year-old daughter, had begun to walk, and Aunt Maria had no doubt that soon the child would be talking.

Lu Lu's mother, on the other hand, was herself having trouble walking. Expecting her second child, and with her legs painfully swollen, she disappointed her aunt who wanted "Ria" with her at all times. Aunt Maria even had to forego shopping, despite the wider choices and lower prices that made big city stores so tempting (MM to Mrs. Davis, 23 July 1839, CMBA). Maria Audubon did manage to accompany her aunt and mother on a cruise up the Hudson to West Point, where they called on Dr. and Mrs. Adams, old Cannonsborough neighbors. Though Harriet Bachman, escorted by Victor, had decided to join her husband in Philadelphia the next day, Mrs. Adams did her best to convince Maria Martin to linger a while at West Point. Maria Martin declined, promising to visit on her next trip north.

The truth was, she could not bring herself to part with her niece, Maria Audubon, and Lu Lu. Maria Martin dallied with them for a week in New York before she could bear to take the train to Philadelphia, the first leg of her return to Charleston.

IN CHARLESTON, in November of 1839, Eliza Bachman suddenly began to cough bright red blood. This symptom of consumption so terrified the Bachman family that they sent word to the Audubons that the survival of Victor's fiancée was in doubt. The Audubons decided that Victor should go to her at once and he boarded a packet that put him in Charleston in five days. By the time he arrived, the attack had subsided and Eliza seemed out of danger. Greatly relieved, Maria Martin contended that as the episode was unprecedented, and had run its course, perhaps it would never be repeated (Audubon 1969, 2:222–23). She suggested in a letter to Lucy that Victor might spend the winter in Charleston.

Lucy Audubon however concluded that Maria Martin's optimism was only self-deception inspired by her desire to keep Eliza in Charleston as long as she could. To the contrary, Lucy contended, Eliza should be brought at once to New York where the Audubons had recently rented a warm house on White Street, and where expert doctors were available.

Lucy and Audubon pleaded with Victor not to stay in Charleston as she and Audubon could not do without him. The winding down of *Birds of America,* the gearing up of the miniature edition of the same, and laying the groundwork for *The Quadrupeds,* which would involve much travel, was too great a load for Victor to expect Audubon to bear alone. And John could not fill the gap. Still striving to establish himself as a portrait painter in New York, he was too preoccupied to look after his mother, his wife, and his daughters while his father traveled seeking subscriptions.

This was enough for Audubon to remind Victor that he had been assigned the task of editing and publishing the "Small Work" on birds. Addressing his older son, Audubon pointed out that the decision on whether to return to New York was up to his own "good sense and reflective powers." Obviously, Audubon's letter left Victor with little choice in the matter (2:224).

On 4 December, barely a week after Victor reached Eliza's bedside in Cannonsborough, they were married. For a second time under his own roof John Bachman had united in marriage one of his daughters with one of Audubon's sons. On the heels of the ceremony, to the acute distress of the Bachmans, Victor and his consumptive bride boarded a ship to New York.

Audubon was delighted by the addition of Eliza to his family. He wrote to Bachman from Boston where he was testing the water for sales of the "small edition" and *The Quadrupeds,* "I wish to congratulate you as I congratulate myself on the happy event which has taken place under your roof last Wednesday last; when, you acquired a second son and Valuable friend, and myself a beloved and most Welcome second Daughter to my heart's wishes" (2:226).

Bachman could not be consoled. Admitting to Audubon that his daughters "have good husbands who will take care of them," he countered, "To me I feel it to be a very great loss." He was glad that he was compelled to be absent from Cannonsborough for two weeks "preaching incessantly twice a day," without time to dwell on the departure of a second daughter (24 December 1839, CMBA).

On Christmas Eve, in a nearly empty house, Bachman settled himself to make his feelings clear to Audubon. Except for Jane and Catherine, who remained at home, his family had scattered for the holidays. He was so lonely his "dispepsia" gave him "strong warning of another social visit." He made no attempt to hide his feelings. "Your congratulations about this double union in our families are alright & proper no doubt—nor ought I to be so selfish as to wish to retain my children around me, when their happiness requires a removal, but somehow the event which gives you so much pleasure had a contrary effect on me, & I have these two occasions looked forward to these happy events, very much as a man does to a funeral" (24 December 1839, CMBA).

The new year, the new decade—both seemed to Audubon full of promise on the frozen morning of 2 January 1840. His "Little Work" was succeeding beyond all expectations, 160 subscribers resulted from his trip to New England alone. He had obtained fifteen subscriptions for *The Quadrupeds*, which in reality was barely further along than a few remarks passed between Bachman and himself.

Though the weather was bitter cold, inside the house at 86 White Street in New York "Miss Lucy" scooted over carpets and between legs. In a few months, "Miss Harriet" would join her on the floor. The "younger ones"—John, Maria, Victor, and Eliza—were "a loving," by which Audubon implied to Bachman a steady supply of Audubon-Bachman grandchildren to come (Audubon 1969, 2:231).

"My Hair are gray, and I am growing old, but what of this?" Audubon mused. "My spirits are as enthusiastical as ever, my legs fully able to carry my body for some Ten Years to come." He foresaw no problems with producing *The Quadrupeds*. Within two years the illustrations should be ready, he thought. Another year and the descriptions and habits of the mammals would be written and printed. A glorious vision! "Only think of the quadrupeds of America being presented to the World of Science, by Audubon and Bachman; the latter one of the very best of D.D.'s [Doctor of Divinity] and the former the only American F.R.S.L. [Fellow Royal Society of London]." As soon as the winter of 1840 would release its grip, Audubon expected to set the project into motion. He would join Bachman in Charleston "and express a few words about our quadrupeds Mss 'en passant' " (2:229, 230).

He and his sons would then collect mammals in the wilds, and he and his "Sweetheart" would paint them in the drawing room. The first "number," a set of five prints, would be out, he believed, "by the 1st. of May Next!" (2:230–31).

With a few reservations, John Bachman indulged himself in Audubon's dream of restoring the happy past by working together again. All along he had been certain that the need to begin work on *The Quadrupeds* would bring Audubon back to Charleston in the spring. "You cannot do without me in this business," he wrote to Audubon on Christmas Eve, 1839, "I know well enough so you will have to pay me a visit soon" (24 December 1839, CMBA).

"Here you come," Bachman summoned a vision of Audubon under his roof once more, following him to the basement study. Once settled in their chairs, Bachman would turn to a "faithful servant" and say, "Shut—shut the door, old Tom—tie up the knocker—& tell any lie you please—!" Alone with his friend, he would look him in the face, "& now for the yarns—aye, & the quadrupeds too" (13 January 1840, CMBA).

Beyond the fantasy, however, Bachman saw a less rosy picture. He doubted that the painting of the quadrupeds would move as rapidly as Audubon expected. "Don't flatter your self that this Book is child's play—the birds are a mere trifle compared to this." Moreover, "About this partnership in *The Quadrupeds,* we will talk about it when we meet." He assured his friend that he would not be embarrassed to let his name stand beside Audubon's. In fact, Bachman believed that his own reputation would boost *Quadrupeds* sales. But he asked no share of the profits—his portion would go to Audubon's sons. As Bachman put it, "I am also anxious to do something for the benefit of John & Victor, which alas in addition to the treasure they have already is all I can do for them whilst my head is warm" (15 January 1840, CMBA).

Bachman was troubled about the health of his daughter, Maria Audubon. Word from New York brought an account of her "sore mouth, its lasting so long & her weakness continuing" (EB to Mrs. Davis, 21 January 1840, CMBA). He thought that "a change of climate might be indicated," and he had one in mind. "Will not Maria come [to Cannonsborough] in the spring—This lovely climate is a cure for sore mouths & sore hearts" (to JJA, 13 January 1840, CMBA).

The Audubon contingent did not wait until spring to travel. In mid-February Audubon informed the Bachmans that, though he would spend a week in Baltimore, "Maria, Miss Lucy Johny and myself are all here in pretty comfortable health, and all bound Southerly!" (1969, 2:231). Four-

and-a-half-month-old Harriet—Little Dud—had stayed behind in New York in Lucy's care.

Audubon was, however, forced to delay his trip south. He had sold three hundred copies of the small edition of *Birds of America* so quickly in Baltimore that he had to return to New York to have a new supply printed. During his wait for the printer to deliver the books, he picked up a pair of traveling companions, Victor's friend, Henry Casmier De Rahm, Jr., and an English acquaintance, Mr. Craycroft. These two, like Audubon, were attracted by Charleston's spring and the budding social season (EA to Jane Bachman, 22 March 1840, CMBA).

The plodding southward migration of the Audubons must have sounded like a wonderful diversion to Eliza, again left behind and lonely, this time in New York. A visit to Charleston would have been the perfect antidote to her miserable first northern winter. Nursing a cough, and under the hands of the expert New York doctors, she had repeatedly endured applications of an ointment that, she confided by letter to her southern kin, "brought out little pustules over my chest and although this remedy is quite disagreeable I think I have been greatly benefited by it and I hope in a few weeks to be as well as ever." By nature, though, Eliza was cheerful. "Take care of your hearts," she warned, teasing her teenage sisters, Jane, Harriet, and the strikingly beautiful Julia about the handsome young men her father-in-law was escorting toward their city (EA to Jane Bachman, 22 March 1840, CMBA).

John Bachman campaigned for candor in all things, and in particular he wanted realistic reports on the health of absent loved ones. "A concealment of facts only awakens suspicion in the minds of our friends & eventually leads very frequently to deeper and more poignant sorrow than if the whole truth had been once revealed & the mind been gradually prepared for the event." Even so, he was unprepared when Maria Audubon, accompanied by John and Miss Lucy, reached his home and he saw "the ravages which disease had made on her poor frame" (JB to VA, 8 May 1840, CMBA).

John Woodhouse, on the other hand, seemed honestly blind to his wife's serious illness. He continuously claimed her on the mend, within a few weeks of complete recovery. While awaiting that recovery, he busied himself with painting a picture of deer for Dr. Charles Desel. Despite John's denial, however, Bachman regarded him one of the most attentive of husbands, "the best of nurses I have ever known" (C. Bachman 1888, 185).

Bachman clung to the hope that by breathing her native air Maria Audubon might yet rally, but the promise of spring was fleeting. Looking back, he sadly concluded that, after all, kind days and gentle nights had had no effect on the illness. Maria's health had been "for months on the decline" (184).

This was the grim situation that greeted Audubon when he joined the Bachmans on 21 April. The reunion Bachman promised was not to be had. Tall, austere Old Tom was unavailable to make the fire, to settle the friends in the study, bow, withdraw, and latch the door. He had other, more pressing, duties.

Maria Martin explained their domestic situation in a letter to Eliza. Responding to Eliza's earlier claim that Lucy Audubon was more sorely tried by hired servants than the Bachmans were tested by managing a dozen or so slaves, Maria assured her that neither she, her sister Harriet, nor her niece Jane had a moment to spare for visiting and other amusement (EA to Jane Bachman, 22 March 1840, CMBA). Old Tom had to work in the kitchen because the cook, Nancy, was pregnant, a condition that made her "lie by for three or four months at least." And besides indisposed slaves, Aunt Maria elaborated, the Bachmans were burdened by "a parcel of noisy little blacks about the premises to annoy us" (MM to EA, 24 April 1840, CMBA).

In truth, Maria Martin was under such stress as might have undone a less determined person. Only once had she gone to church since John and Maria Audubon had come from New York, and as long as Rebecca Solars Martin, Miss Martin's bedridden mother, survived, Maria Martin could not expect to be free. On her fell the responsibility of nursing the old lady, who was "in such a helpless condition" that she required almost constant care (MM to EA, 24 April 1840, CMBA).

Maria Audubon's Charleston doctors decided that the pure air of Aiken, a town about one hundred miles west of Charleston and a few miles east of Augusta, Georgia, might help her. She, John Woodhouse, and Jane—the latter in the role of nurse—boarded the train for what seemed, to John Bachman at least, a journey of last resort.

John Audubon's glowing reports from Aiken, touting progress and plans for his wife to walk short distances every day, failed to reassure Bachman. Just the opposite. Disturbed by John's pertinacious optimism, Bachman boarded the next train to Aiken to assess his daughter's condition in person. As he feared, she had lost ground and begged to go home.

Leaving Maria at the home of Aiken friends, Bachman went to Charleston, recruited Dr. Horlbeck, and returned to Aiken. There he and the doctor had a railroad car fitted with a bed for Maria. Speeding through the countryside between fifteen and twenty miles per hour, the train reached Charleston in less than a day (JB to VA, 8 May 1840, CMBA).

Terribly weak, Maria Audubon was so emaciated that when taken into the house at Cannonsborough, it pained Audubon to face her, actually Maria Audubon had handled the journey better than anyone save John expected. Once at home, though, heroic medical efforts failed to slow the decline. Bled by her doctors ten to twenty times a day, her pain was dulled by an anodyne, almost surely laudanum, a standard pain killer available on demand from most pharmacies. Under the drug's influence, the fever surged back and the doctors prescribed another sequence of bleeding, pain, and anodyne.

Weak and agitated, she always wanted to be doing something, to knit, to move from her bed to a chair, and be moved back—all the while desperately hungry. But no stock of food could keep pace with the craving of a body sapped by bleeding and a disease out of control. Even John Woodhouse lost his optimism and became pitifully distressed, "requiring all our sympathy," Bachman said (to VA, 8 May 1840, CMBA).

Torrential rains swept over the city. Bachman's strength was tested. "I have had philosophy & I hoped religion to stay me under other calamities," he wrote to Victor, "but now I am bewildered & unhappy" (10 May 1840, CMBA).

Audubon had been drinking from the start of this visit, sometimes waiting until after dinner—the midday meal in Charleston—and sometimes commencing earlier. When Audubon drank, Bachman noted, he became "garrulous—dictatorial & profane." This so disturbed Bachman that he would retreat to his front bedroom and lock the door behind him. The day after a binge, Audubon could not recall the rows he had instigated or the foul language that had so offended his friend. Among the women of the house, Maria Martin, who loved Audubon, was especially distressed and "shed many a tear on that account" (JB to VA, 25 June 1840, WCFP).

Audubon planned to canvass Savannah, Augusta, and Columbia for subscriptions to the "Little Work," but though he was miserable in Charleston, he could not bring himself to leave, feeling it his duty, he claimed, to see his son and daughter-in-law through their crisis. Occasionally, Audubon left the house and went into town. There he barely recognized the friends he encountered, rejecting them in effect, though knowing that his return to Cannonsborough would only feed his misery. Some of Audubon's Charleston friends—Doctors Elias Horlbeck, Samuel Wilson, and Eli Geddings—saw his distress and tried to lift his spirits. This exposed them to Audubon's drinking, which they ascribed to idleness and urged Bachman to send Audubon on his way.

But Bachman could not bring himself to order the friend he loved from his home. He asked John Woodhouse to convey the message, and when John Woodhouse did, Audubon brushed it off, insisting that he wait out Maria Audubon's illness (JB to VA, 25 June 1840, WCFP).

Of course light now and again penetrated the gloom of the spring of 1840. Lu Lu attached herself to Grandfather Bachman, calling everyone else in the house, "bad child," even Harriet Bachman, her grandmother. Just before Grandfather Audubon appeared on the scene, the child had a painful bout of teething, but by the time Audubon and his companions arrived—as usual so early in the morning no one was up to let them in—Miss Lucy was "quite well and full of fun and frolic." Watching through the study window, the grandfathers shared "the delight of Little Lu Lu" (JWA to VA, 25 February 1840, Stark Museum of Art, Orange, Texas). Maria Martin pronounced the obvious—Lu Lu was in danger of being spoiled (MM to EA, 24 April 1840, CMBA).

The exploits of Henry C. De Rahm, Jr., and Craycroft, Audubon's young friends and travel companions, provided some diversion from the family's anxiety over Maria's health. Though Bachman regretted having to do it, he had taken Audubon's advice and engaged a hotel room for the two bachelors, rather than try to squeeze them into his home. After a few days, when the Bachmans had time to catch their breaths over Audubon's arrival, they invited De Rahm and Craycroft in for a "social evening." The

New Yorker and the Englishman were already well into a conquest of Charleston society. Hardly had they stored their things in their hotel room than a Mr. Trapman invited them to a gala affair, his son's wedding party, which they attended the next night. Mr. Trapman was a friend of Henry De Rahm, a New York banker.

Maria Martin wrote a letter to Eliza, in New York, detailing activities at Cannonsborough, including the progress of De Rahm and Craycroft. "We were very much pleased with them, and particularly so with Mr De Rahm who appears to be remarkably amiable and agreeable." Eliza was told that some Charleston gentlemen planned to give the visitors sport in the country, and Maria Martin predicted that they would "receive great attention as they are likely to get into a circle where strangers are always entertained" (24 April 1840, CMBA).

Apart from the social whirl, young De Rahm seemed increasingly caught up in the study of natural history. He pleased Audubon with plans to buy a substantial number of the birdskins Audubon had stored in New York. The possibility of a profitable sale, and Audubon's plan to draw some of the skins, stirred Audubon to warn Victor not to send them to England as they had planned, but to "see that they are free from insects" (Audubon 1969, 2:268).

The sale was never consummated. Within a few days, De Rahm came down with yellow fever and Mr. Trapman had De Rahm moved from the hotel into his home. De Rahm died less than twenty-four hours later, requiring Bachman and Audubon to reach beyond their own heartaches and attend the funeral in St. Philip's, the oldest Episcopal church in Charleston. The body was deposited in a vault. A church record was inscribed: "Church fee 20 / Minister Mr. Gordon / No pall—full service."

Henry Casmer De Rahm, Jr., was the younger of his father's sons, both of whom died in early manhood. "How melancholy to his family," Bachman inserted in a letter to Victor already burdened with dismal reports, "I pity them from my whole heart" (10 May 1840, CMBA).

Audubon had his fill of sorrow and tension. He revealed in an addendum to Bachman's letter that while he was quite well physically, he worried about his ill daughter-in-law. Maria Audubon's cough had worsened, and she suffered an "attack of the head" that all expected to recur. But she clung to life. Sorry for himself, Audubon wished that he "had not come South this Year" (10 May 1840, CMBA).

Heavy rains again pelted the city. On 28 May the *Southern Mercury* reported, "Our streets are full of water, and if it continues we shall have to charter some canoes to navigate them."

Then came an offhand remark by Bachman to the morose diners at his table. Bachman thought it a trifle. In reference to a letter John and his father had written about Maria Audubon, he said, "I place no confidence either in his [Audubon's] or John's statements—he representing her worse than she was & John always better—meaning that one was too sanguine & the other too desponding" (JB to VA, 25 June 1840, WCFP).

Drinking, Audubon countered that Bachman was just as bad. He told how a few days earlier Maria Martin had come from the sick room with a message, and on hearing it, Bachman had jumped up and gasped, "My God, Maria is dead!" (JB to VA, 25 June 1840, WCFP).

Bachman denied he had done so. He had *heard* Maria speak, he admitted, but had not parted his own lips. Audubon, Bachman asserted, would not have guessed his thoughts had not he overheard him telling Maria Martin how badly she had frightened him. Audubon rejected that explanation and Bachman's composure snapped, "He had taken too much whiskey & I was angry." Bachman lashed out that Audubon must have lost his brains! Audubon's answer was the scrape of his chair. He arose, steadied, and walked out to seek Dr. Wilson and enlist him to his side of the argument (JB to VA, 25 June 1840, WCFP).

During the few days that Audubon remained as Bachman's guest, he "indulged no more to excess." As after Audubon's outburst years before in Louisiana, when Mrs. Pirrie ordered him and Jo Mason out of her house, Audubon's behavior became exquisitely correct, his conversation with Bachman restricted to the minimum skirting rudeness.

On 6 June 1840, the visit the best of friends had anticipated so eagerly came to an end. Bachman wrote the obligatory report to Victor that Maria Audubon was no better. Then Audubon added to Bachman's page that despite his previous resolve to stay at John's side for as long as John's wife lay ill in Charleston, he had changed his mind and would leave that afternoon on the steamboat to Wilmington (WCFP).

Audubon addressed Victor as his accountant rather than as his son. Stiffly business-like, Audubon sketched the itinerary for his journey, itemized the moneys that had been paid him in Charleston, how much was still owed, and which numbers of the "Small Work" should be sent where and when—not a personal word in half a page of writing. He concluded, as always, with, "God bless you all, Yours ever faithfully, John J. Audubon" (6 June 1840, WCFP).

Audubon had planned to stop at Richmond, Washington, and Baltimore to resume the quest for subscribers to the "Little Work," but his heart was not in it. In less than a week he covered the miles between Charleston and New York.

On his father's arrival at home on 12 June, Victor sensed that something was wrong beyond the stress and sorrow attending Maria Audubon's illness. Perhaps Victor became uneasy when Audubon could not, or would not, give a coherent account of the months in Charleston. His father was uncharacteristically subdued, unaccountably loathe even to mention Bachman. After brooding for a week, Victor felt he must write Cannonsborough for an explanation (25 June 1840, WCFP).

Replying, Bachman traced a passionate, no-humbug account of the family spiral into darkness, and having told the facts as he saw them, he laid down the law:

> whilst on all occasions my house is open to your father, whilst he uses liquor in moderation, I cannot consent to welcome [him] here under such habits such as myself & family were recently made the painful mistress of. I have written this with reluctance & regret. I am willing to admit that I am hasty—I am willing to take all the blame on myself provided this miserable habit is abandoned. I wish to save him from degradation. I am willing to do anything & every thing to effect it. His name & memory are very dear to me, therefore have I taken this stand. (25 June 1840, WCFP)

The wounded friendship survived. Too much had been invested for it to fail. Audubon and Bachman had been friends for eight years and five months. They shared mutual friends and enemies, and the hopes and fears of two young families. They pooled their efforts in behalf of one great endeavor, and were on the verge of launching another. The silence of the weeks of summer between them would lift by the end of autumn, and together the friends would resume work in earnest on *The Quadrupeds*.

In years to come, Bachman would always be warmly received in Audubon's home, and repeatedly Bachman invited Audubon to his home in Charleston. But happenstance, preoccupation with *The Quadrupeds*, Audubon's failing mind, and the lingering pain of the spring of 1840 all conspired against Audubon's acceptance of Bachman's entreaties. Never again did he rap at dawn on Bachman's door to rouse the servants and be ushered to the cluttered study for just one more talk about the speckled duck.

BY AUGUST 1840, Audubon's spirits had revived enough for him to resume selling the "Little Work." Complaining of weariness, he crisscrossed New England in creaky, crowded coaches. Business was fair at Plymouth; accommodations good. Locally abundant passenger pigeons were served for dinner at the inn (Audubon 1929b, 6).

On 22 September, hoping for news from home, he checked for letters at the Boston post office. "I was handed one.—The seal was black.—My heart heaved dreadfully for I thought of both my beloved Wife and my beloved Maria.—I scarcely dared to break the seal, but it was done. I read—and now our Beloved Child is no more." Maria Audubon had died in Charleston on 15 September, and been buried in the shadow of St. John's Lutheran Church (25). She had lived for twenty-three years, nine months, and twelve days.

Shortly after the death of her niece, Maria Martin gathered her things to accompany John and Lu Lu to New York. She and John chose to travel by ship, the quickest and the easiest way with a two-year-old. Maria Martin needed the rest a ship would offer. Late into the nights of summer she had nursed her dying niece. Maria Martin's sleep habits had been shattered and she suffered from severe headaches. Often she lay listening as the chimes of the clock rang out the small hours past midnight.

In the house on White Street, as she transferred her services from one ill niece to another, Maria Martin found Eliza Audubon "sadly changed." Charleston's climate having failed to help the young Maria, the family chose to send Eliza to Cuba. They booked passage on a steamboat to New

Orleans on 20 October, paying an exorbitant fare (JB to VA, MM, and EB, 27 October 1840, CMBA). Victor planned to sell subscriptions to the "Small Work" in the vicinity of New Orleans, and from there to sail to Cuba. Bachman took heart at the Cuba decision. He credited his recovery from his second lung hemorrhage, at an age almost exactly the same as Eliza's now, to a cruise to Jamaica (27 October 1840, CMBA).

Reports of cholera in Cuba stirred misgivings among the three pilgrims, but a prudent delay in New Orleans might allow the epidemic to play out. While they waited, Maria Martin received brotherly guidance from Bachman on how to spend her time in New Orleans. For the sake of *The Quadrupeds*, Bachman wished that Maria Martin had learned to skin squirrels, as he had heard of several species that might be obtainable from the New Orleans market. "If Victor was good for any thing beyond accounts & painting he might have spunk enough to attend to this," he observed disparagingly. And while admitting that Maria had a "considerable share of prudence," Bachman cautioned her about "the temptations of New Orleans—fandango balls &c." Though he had scorned Victor's talents as a naturalist, he had confidence in him as a chaperon. "Always ask Victor," he advised, "where it is most prudent to go" (27 October 1840, CMBA).

Victor tried to sell subscriptions, traveling as far from New Orleans as Mobile, but without success. He, Eliza, and Maria dawdled without accomplishment for almost a month before they traveled on to Havana, where they rented a house on an outlying coffee plantation.

Avenues edged by tall smooth trunks of royal palms stretched from the house in three directions across an exotic landscape that Victor enjoyed painting. Nearby beaches offered striking tropical shells for Eliza and Maria Martin to select among. They enjoyed perpetually blooming flowers, and admired the colorful handmade costumes that the local women wore. They had joined a society of exiles, including such familiar faces as that of Dr. George F. Wurdemann of Charleston for whom Wurdemann's heron (a variety of the great blue heron) was named. All of these people had been drawn to this lush island by hope of a cure (to Mrs. Davis, 24 January 1841, CMBA).

Had Eliza been offered a choice, she would have gone to Cannonsborough for her convalescence, but she accepted the Audubons' insistence that she and Victor return to Minnie's Land, and took comfort in Victor's tender concern for her. In a letter to Jane, the oldest of her surviving sisters, she revealed that her husband had promised to stop by Charleston on their voyage to New York. Then, fearing that her plans might inspire undue family optimism about her illness, she cautioned Jane not to allow her letter to give false hope. When they met again, she assured Jane, she would still show signs of her disease. With every breath she was reminded that she was far from well, "and yet when I see the many invalids who come flocking to this Island, in the very last stages of disease," she wrote, "I feel grateful that I have had kind friends to remove me in time and perhaps prolong my life for years" (to Bachman siblings, 14 March 1841, CMBA).

In a few weeks, Victor and Aunt Maria lost confidence in Cuba as a health spa, and sailed to Charleston where they lingered for an unhappy week. On 8 May, with Jane relieving Maria Martin as nurse, they boarded the *Calhoun* for New York. Before the sad little group took leave, Doctors Geddings and Horlbeck told the family to prepare themselves for Eliza's death in less than a month, warning that she might not even survive the voyage north (JB to JJA, 8 May 1841, CMBA).

Eliza's departure devastated Bachman. As the *Calhoun* was clearing the harbor he made sure that Audubon and Lucy knew how he felt, "We have yielded to a sad and bitter necessity in parting from her, under these circumstances. Mrs. B. has a return of tic doloreaux, and is confined to her bed" (to JJA, 8 May 1841, CMBA). Eliza survived the voyage. Three weeks after leaving Charleston, she died in New York at 2 A.M., 25 May 1841. She was twenty-two (C. Bachman 1888, 196).

So deep was Audubon's sorrow—he had called Eliza "Rosie" after the pale half-sister he loved so much and left behind in France—as soon as dawn brought light into his studio he turned to his brushes for solace. The subject was a baby cottontail attended by its parents. At the bottom of the paper he explained, "I drew this Hare during one of the days of deepest sorrow I have felt in my life, and my only solace was derived from my Labour" (Ford 1951, 49, 139).

Chapter 11

THE QUADRUPEDS

*T*HE GRAY RABBIT, or eastern cottontail, subject of the painting to which Audubon turned for consolation on hearing of the death of Maria Audubon, demonstrates that Audubon was painting for *The Quadrupeds* in May of 1841. The beautifully executed animals in the original watercolor still measured up to the high standard that Audubon established in his paintings for the *Birds* (Audubon 1966, 49). As the eastern cottontail is among the most common, most easily observed, and most familiar of North American mammals, Audubon knew them intimately. Small enough to kill and pose with wires and nails on a squared board (as he posed the birds), he arranged three of them in a plausible, animated composition. He omitted the background, leaving it for later, perhaps an assignment for Maria Martin, or John, or Victor, contenting himself that morning to daub in a few pale shadows suggesting a surface for the animals to stand on.

Changes made in the cottontail composition when it was printed typify some of the problems that plagued the publishing of *The Quadrupeds* throughout. The male, scissored from the paper, was placed above the other rabbits. Now, although the baby and the female still cast shadows on the ground of an expanded landscape, probably painted by John Woodhouse, the male, severed from his shadow, hangs in the air. A few sprigs of grass added to the print arise from behind the female, but cross in front of the male, confusing the viewer. Either the male is a very large rabbit in the background, or despite the evidence of the grass, he floats directly above his family (139).

With some marvelous exceptions—the Canada lynx, the Virginia opossum, the thirteen-striped ground squirrel, the Norway rats with cantaloupes, and there are more—the plates for *The Quadrupeds* fall short of those in *Birds of America*, though Audubon's craftsmanship, honed by passion and struggle between 1820 and 1839, stayed with him even after his mind had begun to dim. When it came to mammals that he had never seen in the wild, or that were too large for him to pose on the squared board, the spark often eluded him. More frequently, as time passed, composing, painting, and supplying backgrounds for *The Quadrupeds* revolved to John Woodhouse, Victor, or Maria Martin.

In a frenzy of painting reminiscent of his best years, during the grief of 1841, Audubon completed some of the loveliest paintings of *The Quadrupeds*. The angry words spoken at Bachman's dining table fading from memory, he painted both the "Rocky Mountain Squirrels" and a family of beavers. In August, he could write to a fellow naturalist, "I am now closely engaged in conjunction with my friend the Revd. John Bachman of Charleston, S.C., in the preparing of a work on the viviparous quadrupeds of North America, and I have already drawn about one hundred figures of them, including thirty-six species" (Herrick 1968, 2:229). By "one hundred figures" Audubon meant one hundred individual mammals, several often grouped in one composition.

Audubon and Bachman had arrived at an understanding of the details of their partnership. Audubon took responsibility for illustrating *The Quadrupeds*, though he would call on Maria Martin for contributions. For purposes of credits, Audubon and Bachman were co-authors, but Bachman assumed responsibility for the text. The Audubons bore the expenses of preparing, producing, and selling the work, and received the profits.

By taking responsibility for writing the text, Bachman seized the opportunity to make important contributions to science in a field in which he had already become the preeminent American (C. Bachman 1888, 279). He told Audubon, "The books we have [about American mammals] are really worse than nothing." Without making bones about it, he assured Audubon that in the two years since he began writing *The Quadrupeds*, he had been trying to unravel "the confused mess into which our quadrupeds have been thrown." Not inclined to exaggerate, Bachman boldly stated, "I know more of our quadrupeds than anyone else." And he did (22 November 1841, WCFP).

Bachman laid out the dimensions of his task for Audubon's edification. About 190 true American species had been described and provided with scientific names, a score of which had been described by Bachman himself. Another twenty-three had been described, but Bachman doubted their validity as species (JB to JJA, 5 August 1841, CMBA). Additional species surely awaited discovery. Bachman set up a network among friends in South Carolina and other states to provide him with living and dead specimens, and usually, after examining the specimens, he shipped their skins to the Audubons to be drawn.

Bachman himself collected mammals in the wild, venturing as far from Charleston as Augusta, Georgia, where with much effort, he caught a "pouched rat" (pocket gopher) by its foot in a rat trap (JB to JJA, 7 December 1841, CMBA). Bachman wondered why this mammal was found "on the very banks of the Savannah River, on the western side," yet no traces of it had been seen east of the river in South Carolina (Audubon and Bachman 1989, 406).

In April 1842, the Audubons moved into the house they built on twenty-three acres on the Hudson River near New York City. It was the first home of their own since the cabin they had lived in briefly in Henderson, about thirty years earlier. Audubon named the estate Minnie's Land, "Minnie" being the Scottish diminutive for Lucy. The Audubons planted fruit trees and put in a garden, and Victor and John Woodhouse discovered the pleasures of sailing and netting sturgeon on the Hudson. From where he sat working in the house, Audubon could "peep at the window," and see across the water the Palisades framed between trunks of many trees (Herrick 1968, 2:245, 246).

One day, on shaking the hand of a visitor to the new house and exchanging a few words, Audubon commented, "How I wonder that men can consent to swelter and fret their lives away amid those hot bricks and pestilent vapors [of cities], when the woods and fields are all so near?" (2:238). The visitor, a writer, reported Audubon hard at work, painting life-size mammals fourteen hours a day, "master pieces in their way, surpassing if that be possible, in fidelity and brilliance, all that he has done before" (2:235, 236). It would seem that Audubon's career would never end.

He retained, in 1842, sufficient wit and strength for a midsummer sales tour through Philadelphia, Baltimore, Washington, and Richmond, taking with him the first four lithographs that J. T. Bowen of Philadelphia had printed for him to use in selling subscriptions to *The Quadrupeds*. Audubon showed prints of the bobcat, woodchuck, eastern wood rat, and red squirrel at the capital, and "astonished the Natives" (Audubon 1929b, 67).

Audubon was amused by the way the government officials he called on interpreted his pictures. The pair of wood rats with two young scrambling on a pine branch were taken for squirrels. The red squirrels were called flying squirrels, and his woodchucks either beavers or musk rats. Only the bobcat was recognized for the cat it was, and Audubon made a mental note to set up and draw the remaining quadrupeds carefully to ensure that "the World Knows 'What's What!'"

Prints in hand, he also campaigned for government support for his long-anticipated, long-delayed, expedition to the West, and obtained ringing endorsements from Massachusetts senator Daniel Webster, and from the president, John Tyler. These endorsements made likely the cooperation of the army should Audubon mount another expedition.

The acquaintance Audubon struck up in Washington with Pierre Chouteau proved almost as important to his cause as his meetings with government officials. In the course of several lengthy conferences, Chouteau, the son of a wealthy fur trader, "told me many strange things about our Government and his own affairs." Later, in the spring of 1843, Audubon and several companions would be entertained by the Chouteau family in St. Louis, before he and his men traveled up the Missouri on a Chouteau shallow-draft steamboat (67–68, 73, 75).

No sooner had Audubon returned to Minnie's Land from his trip to Washington, D.C., and other cities, than he pushed off again to find subscribers in the "East," winding through Connecticut and Massachusetts. Clearly age, alcohol, and illness were taking a toll on Audubon who, by comparison to earlier days, tired easily. Routinely collecting and observing mammals in the field, as Bachman would have him do, seemed beyond his strength. On the brink of exhaustion by day's end, he retired by 8 P.M. to some rented bed, chronically fretting to his journal about the scarcity of grog in the East. "All the Houses here are purely Temperance houses," he complained (Audubon 1929b, 87).

At intervals, though, his enthusiasm came to the surface. On 16 August 1842, while visiting his friends the Pages in New Bedford, it was their guest, Mary Eliza Dana, "a well informed and most worthy Lady," who inspired him. He danced with her on the eighteenth. On the twentieth he wrote in his journal, "We walked together admiring the moon now full. Returned home. We enjoyed this superb evening, talking Dancing etc. until nearly 11 o'clock when I went to bed." That same evening he had had the pleasure of conversing with Miss Green, another "delightful young lady" visiting the Pages (93, 96–97).

In Canada, Audubon resumed the trying task of soliciting subscriptions and information for *The Quadrupeds,* and his languor returned. He was only fifty-seven, but he claimed to be years older, preferring, it would seem, to be viewed as a grand old man rather than a man old before his time. Worn and weary in Montreal, he called on Dr. Douglass, and as he left, he heard the doctor predict to another guest that Audubon never would live to finish *The Quadrupeds.* "A glorious Prophecy!" Audubon sardonically pronounced to his journal (115).

After fifteen years of managing the business of publishing *Birds of America,* selling subscriptions was second nature to Audubon. It was his field work on behalf of *The Quadrupeds* that fell short. He made no incursions into the woods and meadows for the observations necessary to write the life histories of *The Quadrupeds.* Despite Bachman's pleading, he did not set the traps he had brought along to catch the small mammals. Instead of going into the wild himself, Audubon sought out trappers and purchased the skins they had collected. He visited a Canadian zoo, where he saw "a beautiful marmot alive of a dark gray color, which I can have if I choose," but he dawdled, and when he went to claim it, he was told that the marmot had escaped (134).

With winter closing in, the weary artist meandered back to cozy Minnie's Land and his thoughts once more turned to the foray into the West that he had been contemplating for more than twenty years. The West, with its Great Plains and Rocky Mountains and Pacific Ocean, always danced just out of reach. Now, with the help of the Chouteaus, "this grand and Last Journey, I intend to make as a Naturalist" (Herrick 1968, 2:250) seemed accessible, and before the snows stopped blowing he had recruited his crew: his tested friend, Edward Harris; John Bell, recommended by John Bachman; Lewis Squires, a youthful, tough, and willing neighbor; and young Isaac Sprague, an artist Audubon had encountered in New England. Except for Squires, who served as secretary and general assistant, all these men would be immortalized by Audubon who named for them new bird species they had discovered while on the expedition.

Bachman longed to join the crew gathering around Audubon. Each time he had seen Audubon off on an adventure he had toyed with the idea of going along, and obviously, given Audubon's age and health, this adventure would be his last chance. Bachman believed that, besides the fun of doing science in the field, his own contributions to the success of the expedition could be pivotal. At his friend's side, he could personally collect the small mammals so likely to be overlooked and so vital to the success of *The Quadrupeds;* he could harvest the scientific information that he insisted was there to be taken. "You must hammer away at the squirrels and set traps for the mice," Bachman wheedled Audubon, "Aye, my friend, you must turn mousecatcher. Remember they run about at night" (15 January 1843, WCFP).

As both men probably expected, Bachman stayed put in Charleston, repeating what he had said from the beginning of their friendship, that his church came first. "If I were not tied down to duty, I would go along and we would astonish the quadrupeds," he assured Audubon. Having committed himself not to go, he wanly reminded his friend, "You can scarcely go wrong in collecting everything you can lay your hands on" (15 January 1843, WCFP).

Because it was impossible for Bachman to go with Audubon, Bachman appealed to Audubon to come to Charleston. Head to head in the study, Bachman insisted he could go further toward educating Audubon—which mammals to watch for, how to catch them—than in dozens of letters, no matter how passionately written. Even that hope failed. Audubon countered that he had no time for Charleston; his pressing need was to paint quadrupeds up to the last minute at Minnie's Land in order to ensure that others could shoulder completion of the work should his strength fail and he be interred beneath the prairie sod.

Vicariously at Audubon's side on the prairie, Bachman's pen let slip the hope that his friend would take advantage of the opportunity to collect prairie birds, seeds, plants, and reptiles as well as quadrupeds. At the same moment, Bachman realized that by bringing up birds, the focus of Audubon's life, he might have justified Audubon's neglect of mammals. Bachman returned to the main point. Nothing should be permitted to interfere with "looking for quadrupeds and knowing all about them." Surely Audubon could agree to that (12 March 1843, WCFP).

Audubon, Harris, and the young men Audubon had recruited, reached St. Louis in March 1843, but then had to wait for two months before the ice that blocked the upper reaches of the Missouri broke up. Audubon took advantage of the stopover to observe, write, and post to Charleston a long and interesting account of the behavior of pocket gophers. At the end of April, Audubon's men packed their supplies on the Chouteau's shallow-draft trading steamer, a modest vessel bearing the right name for a last expedition—*Omega* (22 April 1843, CMBA).

As for Bachman, he regretted that he could not devote all of his time to collecting and studying South Carolina mammals. Faced with the obligation to give an "anniversary address" in the interior of the state, he complained, "I am constantly taken off Nolens Volens [willing or unwilling] from the quadrupeds which beyond my profession is the only thing I mean to care about for the next three years if my life is spared so long" (15 January 1843, WCFP). Victor wrote Bachman urging him not to falter. Especially in Audubon's absence it was necessary that the publishing of the plates continue.

With the completion of each number subscribers paid for that installment, creating a cash flow necessary for the family's support. By June of 1843 only two numbers (plates 1–10) had been published, but Bachman had prepared names for six more mammals for Victor's attention (14 June 1843, CMBA).

Victor would have preferred to name the mammals himself, without waiting for Bachman to act, but it soon became evident that Victor was not familiar enough with the scientific literature to accomplish this task. First, the mammal had to be correctly identified, and second, if it proved that the mammal was yet unknown, a proper scientific description, a Latin name, and the name of the author and date of publication had to be provided.

Even Bachman ran into difficulties. "Charleston is a poor place for scientific Books," he wrote to Victor (5 August 1843), and those books that were available were expensive. Bachman implied that the books required to complete *The Quadrupeds* text might run to thousands of dollars in purchase costs. When only short passages were required, Victor or John Woodhouse could copy them, but how were the Audubons to decide in Bachman's absence which passages to copy? Then again, some of the references were in languages other than English and had to be translated.

Feeling pressed, Bachman became brusque in his calls for materials he felt he had to have to continue. He wrote to Audubon on 29 November 1843, pointing out an obvious error in the newly published plate of the snowshoe hare. Bachman insisted that one of the hares obviously was a common female cottontail (gray rabbit). Audubon defended his mistake, lamely claiming that the hare's youth accounted for its small size. He promised to correct any wrong impressions by printing "young" before "female" when additional copies of the plate were run off (10 December 1843, HUHL).

Half a continent of forested mountains and sparsely settled plains lay between the friends, making delivery of letters problematic, though in June 1843 the pastor did unfold a short note from Audubon datelined "Fort Lewis," an installation located at the juncture of the Yellowstone and Missouri rivers. The note was Bachman's only contact with Audubon during the summer and early fall. He could only imagine the wonderful mammals Audubon and his men were collecting in this far country, and the fascinating observations they were making.

Actually, news of a sort did reach Bachman that summer. The messenger was a Charleston newspaper carrying a letter widely published in the eastern states. The writer, using Audubon's name, declared he was on his way home and boasted that among other western mavels, he was bearing a "cangaroo kind of an animal as big as a camel" to his Charleston friend, John Bachman.

Bachman saw the story as a joke. He read it, dismissed it, and went on to urge Audubon to let him know what the expedition had accomplished. "But any how you must have many things rare & some things new," he wrote, and moved on to "O how I long to Tumble over your skins; Talk of Turtle soup & all other delicacies they are trifles compared to such a treat" (1 November 1843, CMBA).

In Philadelphia, George Ord read the article, or one like it, and thought it interesting enough to send an extract to Charles Waterton, his English cohort. "Have you seen the account of Audubon's wonderful discovery of a new genus of Quadrupeds? As it has gone the rounds of our periodical press, I presume it must have got into your papers, ever awake to the marvels of the world." Ord identified the writer of the "cangaroo" story as "some wag," rejecting the "Audubon" by-line. Perhaps Ord was on the right track. The joke may well have sprung from the mind of one of the younger members of the expedition.

"Audubon," whether John James or some other fun-loving sport, claimed that he had encountered a pair of enormous animals on the prairie, each weighing upward of six hundred pounds. The behemoths were playing, fighting, or sitting on their hind legs. Their front legs were short, like kangaroos', but armed with sharp claws. Nine feet and four inches tall, they bore short, deerlike antlers on their small heads. But their sheeplike tails were scarcely a foot long, a departure from the "cangaroo" model. A twelve-inch-wide ring of flesh circling their waists produced a high quality oil, and even more surprising, their dark brown coats, according to the writer, were of the most beautiful fur that he had ever beheld.

Attracted to the scene by the frighteningly loud animals, Audubon's friends shot one *Ke-ko-ka-ki,* as the Native Americans supposedly called it. The survivor fled, bouncing high above the grass.

The writer, presumed to be Audubon, ended his piece with an assessment: "I think without doubt, in point of usefulness and value, I may pride my self in surpassing most of my compeers, in thus bringing so great a discovery to light."

Ord's evaluation was different. He pronounced the composition "what is vulgarly termed a hoax" (Ord to Waterton, 23 August 1843, APSL).

On 5 November 1843, Audubon returned to Minnie's Land. The next day Victor handed him Bachman's passionate request that he bring the quadruped skins to Charleston right away so that they could study them together. Worn out, with only one night under his roof after an absence of nine months, Audubon declined the invitation and suggested that Bachman come to Minnie's Land.

"How can I come to you Friend?" Bachman asked in response to Audubon's letter of 10 October, which Bachman had just received. "Your animals require an examination of three months," Bachman pointed out that he could not be spared from his church to examine them even for a single Sunday. For the time being, a journey to Minnie's Land was quite out of the question. Almost as though Audubon were a child, Bachman chided, "I am quite sure that you will soon be here with all your treasures & we will discuss these matters as men ought to do who are in earnest" (1 November 1843, CMBA).

To mollify Bachman, Audubon sent him a short summary of his journey. He had gained twenty-two pounds, though Harris had lost weight. He had secured "no less than 14 New Skins of Birds." He admitted that unfortunately, "the variety of quadrupeds is small in the Country we visited, and I fear that I have not more than 3 or 4 new ones." He asserted, nevertheless, that he and his companions had collected most of the larger mammals, had written much, had taken samples, and had made "minute measurements of *every thing.*" Audubon believed that the "Cargo of skins," which had been shipped to New York, would arrive within a week (12 November 1843, HUHL). For all practical purposes, this sketchy account was as far as the Audubons would go in supplying the information and specimens Bachman demanded.

Bachman's frustration showed in his reply that nothing that Audubon had accomplished on the plains had been revealed to him, "having never received his [Audubon's] journal & not twenty lines on the subject." Because of this neglect, beginning late in 1844, and lasting for nearly a year, Bachman suffered "hopeless despair," and gave up working on *The Quadrupeds,* in part to ease his misery, and in part to force Victor to yield the information Bachman had to have to sustain proper publication of *The Quadrupeds* plates (Herrick 1968, 2:269–70).

A measure of Bachman's despair arose from his loss of direct communication with Audubon. By then almost all of the Minnie's Land letters came from Victor, whose lack of interest in the writing of *The Quadrupeds* showed all too clearly in Victor's neglecting to send books and other reference documents Bachman requested. The writing of *The Quadrupeds* text had veered off-track and had been all but abandoned in New York. Convinced that a survey of the mammals of North America was needed for the sake of science, Bachman was also confident that he was the person best qualified to write it. But as the winter of 1845 approached, it became clear to Bachman that his own refusal to supply Victor with the scientific names for *The Quadrupeds* had failed to force Victor to send him the other data vital to the project.

Bachman rallied, left Charleston accompanied by his twenty-one-year-old daughter, Julia, and took a brief tour of Albany, Baltimore, Philadelphia, Washington, and New York. In various museums Bachman reviewed mammal skins and consulted with authorities. At Minnie's Land, Bachman obtained Victor's "solemn promise" of help. At last—Bachman allowed himself to believe—he would be given the data, books, mammal skins, and even Audubon's Missouri River journals (Herrick 1968, 2:270).

Julia Bachman seemed oblivious to the wrangling over *The Quadrupeds,* and thoroughly enjoyed her visit to Minnie's Land, only a mile or so from Broadway. She had a chance to flirt with the young men of the Audubon social circle and to observe the latest fashions. "You should see the Ladies in Broadway," she wrote to her sister Lynch in Cannonsborough, "all dressed off in the most splendid style. They seem to turn up their noses at every thing but Silks or Satins." These trend-setters were the most extravagant and at the same time "the most tasteless set of people" Julia had ever seen. "Oh dear," she exclaimed, "I have no patience with them" (3 October 1845, CMBA).

Bachman might have lingered in Minnie's Land wrestling what information he could from the Audubons, and he could have visited Ed Harris at Morestown, where he would have heard a frank account of the accomplishments of Audubon's prairie expedition, had he not been obliged to hurry back to Charleston "on account of the indisposition of my poor wife." By the time he reached home at the end of October, however, Harriet's health had improved, and for the time being she was free from facial pain (JB to JJA, 31 October 1845, CMBA).

Two months later, Victor and his father had disappointed Bachman again and he desperately turned to Edward Harris for help. "I find that the Audubons are not aware of what is wanted in the publications of *The Quadrupeds,*" Bachman wrote on Christmas Eve of 1845, pleading with Harris to intervene on his behalf, "You can be of service to me, to the Audubons

& the cause of science." He itemized his complaints: "They have not sent me one single book out of a list of 100 I gave them and only 6 lines copied from a book after having written for them for 4 years." He wrote that for *The Quadrupeds*—"Tell it not in Gath, he [Audubon] never collected or sent me one skin from New York to Louisiana along the whole of the Atlantic States" (Herrick 1968, 2:269). Bachman believed that Audubon's enemies in Philadelphia would be as comforted by this evidence of Audubon's decline as were the people of Gath by the deaths of Saul and Jonathan in battle (Samuel 1:20).

As for Victor, Bachman's son-in-law had ignored his October promise to make amends. Bachman had received no books with which to describe new quadruped species, and "what is a sin qua non to me," no specimens. He begged Harris to pass a message to Audubon, "Now I do not like to make any threats, but if my reasonable requests are not complied with I have it in my mind not to write another line at the end of the first volume" (Herrick 1968, 2:269–70).

Harris, who lived an hour or so by train from Minnie's Land, and had been Audubon's constant companion during the nine-month expedition to the prairie, probably understood the Audubon family's situation better than Bachman. Harris was too close a friend not to notice the limitations of Audubon's sons—Victor's limited knowledge of natural history and John Woodhouse's disabling bouts of depression. Harris had been at Audubon's side when his friend plunged into such lethargy on the return voyage down the Missouri that he seemed lost in another world, his conversations "impulsive and fragmentary" (2:257). What Harris had and Bachman did not was on-the-scene knowledge of how shockingly short of expectations the expedition had fallen.

Harris probably passed on to Victor word of Bachman's distress over the Audubons' failure to cooperate with him. At any rate, between Christmas and New Year's Day, Victor encountered in New York Dr. J. C. Faber, a member of Bachman's church about to depart New York for Charleston. Victor wrote his father-in-law a quick note to accompany a twelve-page list of data Bachman had been seeking.

"I have been, and am now, very busy," Victor scribbled, "but I cannot let the opportunity afforded by Dr. Faber, pass without writing a few lines to you" (27 December 1845, WCFP). Victor's bundle arrived in Charleston on 3 January 1846. Bachman was doubly gratified. On the day that it arrived, he acknowledged receipt of Victor's list and pointedly commented that he had also applied elsewhere [for books and other matter] and had received a large bundle of "most excellent notes" from that unnamed source.

By unrelenting effort Bachman wrote the text for volume 1 of *The Quadrupeds of North America* in about five months. Committed to completing one species every three days, he entered his study at four A.M., took time out for breakfast, and then wrote until three P.M., the traditional dinner hour in Charleston.

Nothing went smoothly. The first mammal treated, the bobcat, presented a problem. It belonged, Bachman decided, to the genus *Lynx*, established by the eccentric naturalist Rafinesque in an article in the *American Monthly Magazine*. Bachman wrote asking Victor to send him a copy of the magazine at once. Victor ignored him. As 1846 drew to a close with Audubon no longer able to work and John in Texas collecting and drawing mammals, Victor felt it paramount that he devote his time to the women and children of the Audubon compound. Nothing was mailed to Bachman.

The Christmas season of 1845 had weighed heavily on Bachman. His wife's health was in relentless decline. His great friendship with Audubon was in disarray. And his master work, *The Quadrupeds,* was maddeningly neglected in Minnie's Land, perhaps stillborn. The flow of information from the Audubons slowed to a trickle, and when they tried to work on their own, the resulting mistakes, he wrote to Victor, were "terrible owing to the want of knowledge [resulting from] your never looking at books." Bachman concluded that he could expect "no literary and scientific aid" from them in publishing the work (17 January 1846, WCFP).

He minced no words with the Audubons, pressing Victor to accept that painful truth, and proposing that they substitute Bachman's knowledge in these matters for their ignorance. Even in the modest capacity of furnishing specimens and books the Audubons disappointed him. "My letters are either not answered at all or they are not answered with the necessary precision," he chided, finding such conduct incomprehensible (17 January 1846, WCFP).

Troubling, too, was Audubon's reaction to Bachman's criticisms of a few of the mammal paintings. When Bachman noted that Audubon had failed to show the features that set the species apart, Audubon countered, "I cannot help copying nature" (17 January 1846, WCFP). Bachman knew better and was ready with specifics and analysis. Similar flaws to those of the mammal paintings had been avoided in painting the *Birds* because Audubon, in the main, had used as models birds that he, himself, had killed and wired. The Richardson's ground squirrel, *au contraire,* had a hairless tail because the collector had let the hairs fall out of the skin that Audubon copied. "That tremendous scrotum" of the woolly squirrel of California, the very squirrel that Victor and Audubon had wrongly renamed *Scurius longipilis* (Audubon and Bachman 1989, 95), "was not given to it by its creator whose works are natural but was stuffed out of character by Bell" (JB to VA, 17 January 1846, WCFP).

Bachman vividly vented his complaints in a two-thousand-word letter to Victor dated 17 January 1846. This outpouring was not simply an indictment of sloppy work and the burden it imposed on Bachman in his struggle to maintain scientific standards and to protect Audubon's reputation; it was fueled by a flood of anger in Bachman that had crested in the months since the conclusion of the Missouri River expedition. "If you had not my poor services at your elbow would you not make a fine kettle of fish of the *Quadrupeds.* Who in America could you get to aid you? You ought never to have commenced the work when you did—I urged your Father to study—to make drawings and to wait [until he was better prepared to launch the project]. So you had better make good use of me whilst you have me for I am now perfectly convinced that you cannot move a step by yourselves" (17 January 1846, WCFP).

Audubon had slipped beyond the cut of Bachman's anger and the burden of his demands. When the call came from Charleston for the ranges of the mammals described in the first volume, Audubon wrote what came to mind, and if nothing came, he innocently scratched on his paper "know nothing," and posted it to his co-author.

Bachman, unable to accept that Audubon's mind was failing, saw such comments as evidence, not of diminished capacity, but of raw negligence. "I am very sorry that for the tenth time I have been again misunderstood. I wrote for the western range of the species," he harangued Victor, "& he has not as I can see given that of any one, besides the whole affair was written so hastily & without looking at the species that I am very sorry to say I cannot make use of a single line—no not of a single species." Citing examples, Bachman lay bare the worthlessness of the list. Opposite the meadow vole, Audubon had penned another "Know Nothing." Bachman scathingly commented, "If you know nothing then I pity you all, for it is the most abundant species you have under your noses" (JB to VA, February 18, 1846, CMBA).

No longer the fiery friend of yesterday, Audubon meekly conceded, "I will at once write another list of the Geo. ranges of the quadrupeds for the first volume of letter press." And though he put more effort into it, the second list was of little more use than the first (JJA to JB, 25 February [incorrectly transcribed as "July"] 1846, HUHL).

Forgetting his earlier stand, Audubon surrendered the Missouri River journal, so long sheltered from Bachman's flinty eyes and uncompromising pen. Now, in innocence, Audubon could hardly wait for his friend to give his opinion of the journal.

Bachman obliged—"very interesting"—and allowed one line of sincere praise: "The narratives however are particularly spirited—often amusing & instructive." The body of Bachman's critique was a lament over lost opportunity and misspent effort (6 March 1846, CMBA).

Thrusts of racial humor sharpened Bachman's attack. Audubon had written factually how the beautiful eighteen-year-old Native American, Natawista (who eventually married Alexander Culbertson, the Fort Union post agent), had eaten the warm brains of a bison that had been killed for Audubon, in the process ruining the skull as a specimen for study. Bachman retorted, urging Audubon: "I wish you would write to Culbertson, & find out some way of getting—not his princess, brain eating–horse straddling squaw for I suspect neither of us would like to be bothered with such a specimen from the black foot country—but for 1. The Skunk—better than the black foot princess . . . ; 2. Hares in winter colours . . . 3. The rabbit that led you so many chases" (6 March 1846, CMBA).

Bachman was gratified to learn from reading Audubon's journal that his friend had dropped his long-held view of the Native American as a noble savage: "It just occurs to me that you will not quarrel with me any more about William Penn & the noble generous race of Indians. Why friend from your description they must be the most blood thirsty, lazy, lying, thieving, murdering carrion eating, lousy set of rascals that ever disgraced this habitable globe the wolf & grizly bear are civilized gentlemen compared to them" (6 March 1846, CMBA).

Audubon meekly conceded, "No matter about W*am* Penn, Let the Dead rest, and as to my accounts of the Indians unfair, it is true as if you had seen them yourself, and written I have no doubt in the Same Grain about them." Audubon missed the point. Bachman had defended neither Penn nor the Native Americans (12 March 1846, HUHL).

In mid-March, barely four months after Bachman began actively writing the text of volume 1 of *The Quadrupeds of North America,* he sent the completed manuscript to Victor (22 March 1846, CMBA). Before the year was out it had been published and had won praise as the finest work yet produced on American mammals.

The years of stress, frustration, and sorrow that lay between Maria Audubon's death and the publication of volume 1 of *The Quadrupeds of North America* were tempered for Bachman by a few interludes of unalloyed satisfaction. In January, when the material from the Missouri River expedition at last began to arrive in Charleston, Bachman plucked from a box of skins one that gladdened his heart. He shared his pleasure with Victor. "It is true blue—a good species no doubt—a species new to the United States—I cannot say that it has never been described for I do not know what recent species have been procured from California & Mexico. I think however the world as yet knows nothing about it."

"What a treasure," Bachman mused as he examined the skin and reconstructed the circumstance of its collection. It had been killed by a rifle ball, the body severely abraded either while stuffed in a saddle bag or slung by its neck on the saddle skirts. It had been competently skinned, but "most rascally stuffed." Unfortunately, the tip of its tail had broken off, but Bachman could tell that not more than an inch had been lost, enough remaining for him to see that the tail was black-tipped.

No "history" had accompanied the skin Bachman pondered, but it had been stuffed with "a species of plant that exists on the north fork of the Platt River"—a clue to its origin. "It was not a cat," Bachman felt certain.

He thought it more like the "Masked Glutton [weasel] of Griffiths—but not that species" (JB to VA, 23 January 1846, CMBA).

It was, in fact, a black-footed ferret, obtained from fur traders by J. B. Bell, the taxidermist Bachman had nominated for the expedition. Bachman had no way of knowing then that this mammal depended almost exclusively on prairie dogs for survival and that with the impending destruction of the prairie dog towns as the grassy prairies were converted to farms and ranches, it would become perhaps the rarest mammal of North America, all but eliminated from the wild.

John Woodhouse eventually painted the ferret for *The Quadrupeds,* one of his most appealing studies. The little beast gazes hungrily at the eggs of some ground-nesting bird. Unfortunately, the skin was lost after John painted it, as were many precious specimens held in Minnie's Land during the years of Audubon's decline, and rumors spread in the scientific community that Bachman and Audubon had faked the new species to increase sales of their book. Almost coincidental with Bachman's death in 1874, additional ferret specimens came into the hands of naturalists, vindicating the authors of *The Quadrupeds.*

Chapter 12

TRIALS

HE SUCCESS OF VOLUME I of *The Quadrupeds of North America* did not immediately increase pressure on Bachman to supply additional texts for the remaining volumes, but even if it had, Bachman could not have responded at once. In the spring of 1847, Harriet Bachman, racked by coughing, diarrhea, and agonizing seizures of tic douloureux, obviously had not long to suffer. Since the year of her marriage, 1816, she had given birth to fourteen babies and had been ill almost constantly, frequently spending weeks or months recuperating out-of-town in the homes of relatives. She had lost five children in infancy and had seen two adult daughters die of consumption, which was now consuming her.

Through it all, she remained optimistic, by faith coming to terms with pain and sorrow. "I have suffered so long and so severely," she wrote to a daughter who herself needed encouragement; "from experience I have learned to be content and satisfied with my lot come what will. I view it all as coming from a kind providence intended for some wise purpose, and that it is our duty to submit, always hoping that some remedy will be sent us" (to Jane Bachman, 24 May 1846, CMBA).

Harriet's faith prevailed. Believing in the efficacy of a popular placebo for tic douloureux, she spent her final three months relatively pain-free. As John Bachman wrote to Minnie's Land, "We are at last indebted to the Electro-galvanic battery for the first signs of improvement."

Harriet's appetite revived and she gained a little weight, eating at the table with the rest of the family. She was able to take rides around town (to VA, 22 March 1846, CMBA). One Sunday in June she attended both services at St. John's. The next Sunday she dressed for church, but settled for a moment in a chair to catch her breath and dozed off. Tiptoeing through the narrow front door, the family left her sleeping, and when she woke to a still and empty house, a rueful little thought amused her, "I shall have quite a laugh on me when they return" (HB to Harriet Haskell, 21 June 1846, CMBA).

She used the solitude of that Sunday morning to write to her daughter, Harriet Haskell, who a month or so earlier had given birth in this same house to the Bachman's first grandson, John Bachman Haskell. The letter was upbeat, full of happy gossip. She signed off, "Kiss little Bachman a thousand times for me" (21 June 1846, CMBA).

Bachman became increasingly concerned about Harriet's health and decided that perhaps she would be helped if the two of them sailed to New York. He went so far to select a stateroom on the *Carolina,* a ship that had just tied up in Charleston. Before they could leave, however, Harriet suffered an acute attack of tic douloureux and died at seven P.M., 15 July 1846, slipping away "as quietly as an infant falls asleep," Bachman wrote. "God's will be done!" (C. Bachman 1888, 218–19).

Enervated by her death, Bachman struggled through proofreading the sheets of volume 1 sent to him by Victor almost as fast as the printer pulled them from his press. All his life Bachman had tried to limit the hours he devoted to grief, and it was not getting easier. "I am now living for others—& more especially for my children," he wrote. He confessed to Victor a powerful urge to withdraw. "When they [the children] are all once placed together at Totness," with his daughter, Harriet Haskell, and her family, "I shall keep possession of my solitary house in Town where I am most happy when I am alone" (2 August 1846, CMBA).

John Woodhouse had returned from an unsuccessful collecting trip to Texas and had at once sailed to England to paint from skins of mammals not available in American collections. Soon the transatlantic steamships were delivering his paintings to Victor. Prints of them were struck in Philadelphia and relayed to Charleston. Momentarily cheered by improvement he saw in John's work, Bachman concluded that if the young man kept it up he would rival his father in his "palmiest days." In particular, Bachman admired John's knack of taking a ragtag museum skin and restoring it on paper to something that approached the living animal (JB to VA, 21 January 1847, WCFP).

At the same time, John's casual approach to natural history, manifested by an infuriating refusal to send information about the skins he painted in London, offset Bachman's satisfaction with the drawings. "Is it not a shame—a disgrace—a sin," Bachman lashed out in a letter to Victor, "that John should be so mizerable careless as not to send us the names," from the labels attached to the skins. "All my writing & scolding will do no good." John's aversion to writing, even copying something so brief as a label, bordered on phobia (14 December 1846, CMBA).

Among other trials overtaking Bachman were disabling injuries inflicted by dogs. The first occurred early in December 1846, when the pastor was attacked by "a rascally Dog that flew from a yard in Town" and lacerated his leg. Infection set in. Damage to tendons left his foot stiff and an injury to nerves left it always cold. His doctor ordered him to bed. Though Bachman cheated some—he hobbled around the house when Maria Martin was out of sight—for the most part he remained flat on his back, longing to take up some task to divert his thoughts from troubles (JB to VA, 8 December 1846, CMBA).

The Sunday after Christmas found him alone in his study "with a rousing fire burning & a scorching plaster on [my] foot." Deserted by his churchgoing family, he was free to write without being scolded. "Friend Victor— I am now disposed to go to work on the [text of the] 2nd vol. I want information on many species—cant you write to those who know something about their habits. Many species in this vol are not known to me from personal observation. Your Fathers Journals contain information about some species that should all be collected & properly arranged." Bachman had repeatedly begged Victor to send him reference books, and Victor, of course, did not send them (21 December 1846, CMBA).

Audubon himself was no longer up to copying and arranging data, and Bachman at last seemed to acknowledge Audubon's limitations. In his next letter to Victor, Bachman addressed an affectionate postscript to Audubon, wording it as though his old friend were a child interested in nothing more substantial than snippets about friends, family, weather, and the birds in Bachman's aviary. To describe his own health for Audubon, Bachman called up the saying: "The man recovered from the bite; the dog it was that died" (21 January 1847, WCFP).

Meanwhile, Bachman found a way other than classifying mammals and writing text to further the progress of *The Quadrupeds*. War had broken out with Mexico over the annexation of Texas, and hundreds of hot-blooded Carolina men converged on Charleston to volunteer. Some, like Benjamin Strobel, the journalist and physician who had befriended Audubon at Key West, were old acquaintances or relatives of Bachman—both in Strobel's case. Bachman gave the departing soldiers lists of mammal skins he needed, and specified monetary rewards for skins of each species. By arrangement with their unit quartermasters, the soldiers would be paid in Mexico on presentation of the skins (JB to VA, 14 December 1846, CMBA).

A "sad cold" rendered Bachman "*hors de combat*" for a week in April (to VA, 26 April 1847, CMBA), and in June an inflammation led his doctor to patch both of his eyes. He pressed Maria Martin into service as secretary and dictated letters to Victor that could not be put off. Once more he pleaded for information and specimens that would enable him to begin the text for the next volume of *The Quadrupeds*. He thought that printing could start by November or December 1847, if only Victor would bestir himself (19 June 1847 CMBA). "I sometimes wish that you Victor were not so good natured," he wrote, "nay—that I could work you up into a fury of passion—then I might have a chance of blowing at you in return & tell you that we are doing nothing—nothing to advance science in the great book" (18 November 1847, CMBA).

In the summer of 1847, Julia, the beauty of the family, the daughter who so loved to go to parties on Sullivan's Island that Bachman worried that she might forget she was the daughter of a pastor, fell ill. It was decided that she should spend the summer at the Virginia springs, where hot baths, a cool climate, and the absence of biting insects might bring relief. A hospital industry had sprung up in the Virginia mountains to accommodate the thousands of consumptives who came hoping for remission or, unlikely, a cure.

John Bachman, Julia, and her younger sister, Lynch—to help with the nursing—journeyed north by coach through steamy pine woods and swamps, and then through the no less stifling low hills of the piedmont. During the first weeks of the slow journey Julia could sit up, but as the trip continued she weakened and had to lie on the seat, propped with pillows. More than once the travelers interrupted their journey to allow Julia a few days to recline in an inn.

The weather, when at last the party reached the mountains, was abnormally cold and rainy. Birds were quiet. Bachman spent days vainly hunting for grouse and quail, which he thought might tempt Julia's failed appetite.

> I am just looking out of my windows on the grand, beautiful, romantic & lovely scenes around me in this sweet valley surrounded with mountains covered to their highest peaks with rich & varied foliage but alas how different in the scenes in the building round me—I hear coughing all day & through the long night—I meet with pallid faces & see the hectic flush on many a cheek—How terrible is consumption—Holding on with a deadly grasp—weakening the cords of life from day to day & relinquishing only its fatal power when life is extinct. How sad this beautiful garden of earth—deformed with graves & monuments of the dead. (JB to JWA, 28 July 1847, CMBA)

As she lay dying, Julia's fear left her and she took "the character of some superior angelic being." On her next to last day she asked, "Father when I am going to my heavenly rest pray at my pillow that I may ascent to my saviors home on the wings of my earthly Fathers prayers." The next morning she suddenly raised her hands. "My time has come Father pray." She died as he prayed, and Bachman exulted, "In the whole of my long ministry I have never witnessed so triumphant a death" (JB to Audubon "Friends," 8 September 1847, CMBA).

Lynch became "indisposed" on the way home. At first, Bachman "ascribed her symptoms to anxiety of the mind & hoped that a change of scene & rest would restore her." But at home the Charleston doctors "thought it advisable to produce external irritations," and applied leeches to her skin. They rubbed croton oil—a corrosive drug usually used as a purgative—on her chest until a large blister arose; repeated applications kept the blister going for weeks. Lynch suffered with weakness and depression. She could eat, but could hold nothing down. For a few months, she became neither better nor worse. Then, for no apparent reason, she got better, and gradually recovered. Perhaps, indeed, her affliction had been in her mind.

Expecting to follow her sisters in death, Lynch had played the role of dying to the edge of the grave (JB to VA, 28 October 1847, CMBA).

Once more seeking intellectual diversion from the relentless attrition of his family, Bachman begged Victor and John to give him the information he needed to continue writing the text for the second volume of *The Quadrupeds*. If Victor could not send the material to him, then John could gather books, field notes, skins—everything including the granddaughters—and come to Charleston. Bachman felt that six weeks with John could accomplish more than six months apart. "Perhaps your presence would divert my mind & thus relieve me from a load of oppression that I have been of late trying to shake off & cause the windows of my chamber once again to be opened" (27 October 1847, CMBA). His appeal was ignored.

Though the days were still chilly, robins were singing and building their nests when Bachman and two daughters, Lynch and Jane, visited Minnie's Land in May of 1848. One night, ignoring the din of the Audubon house, Bachman found a seat by the fire and put his foot on the fender to soak away the lingering pain of the first dog-bite. He drifted off—but woke suddenly to find that the girls, both Victor's and John's, had gathered round to tease him for loud snoring, and insist that he talk with them instead of napping (JB to MM, 11 May 1848, CMBA).

Just keeping up with who was who among the Audubon children had been a chore for Bachman and his daughters on a visit to Minnie's Land that spring. Bachman's Audubon granddaughters, Lucy and Harriet, had to explain to the Charleston relatives that Victor's brood were the little ones with light and curly hair, and that John's had dark straight hair (Harriet B. Audubon to Wilson Bachman, 1 April 1922, Claude H. Neuffer collection).

The adults kept busy at Minnie's Land; Victor with publishing *The Quadrupeds;* John with chores, feeding his many dogs, gathering hen eggs, and fussing about the garden; and Lucy Audubon with worrying about housekeeping and endlessly scanning the papers for job-wanted advertisements by maids. All the while, everyone suffered the tireless idiocy of "the poor old Gentleman." In his letter to Maria Martin of 11 May 1848, Bachman told of how Audubon went to bed, "having eaten his eleventh meal," offered snuff to all, "kissed all the Ladies & heard his little evening song in french after having seen that John had fed all the dogs."

Maria Martin Bachman, "our sweetheart." Courtesy of the
Charleston Museum, Charleston, South Carolina.

"His is indeed a most melancholy case," Bachman wrote to Maria Martin. "The outlines of his countenance & his general robust form are there, but the mind is all in ruins. . . . Imagine to yourself a crabbed restless uncontrollable child—worrying & bothering every one & you have not a tithe of a description of this poor old man" (11 May 1848, CMBA).

From Charleston, on 18 December 1848, Bachman sent pleasant news to Victor and John. Somewhat coyly, he announced his engagement to Maria Martin. "Now I shall entrust you all with a secret which you may entrust to your wives & which they may whisper in the ears of their particular friends with an injunction not to insert in the Herald," he wrote. "Maria has been weak enough to consent to take the old man with all his infirmities of mind & eyes for better & for worse & thus lawfully become his nurse & his scribe Decm 28th" (CMBA).

Nurse and scribe were exactly the roles the new Mrs. Bachman had to assume. The bridegroom fell into a decline. He suffered so much with his eyes that writing and reading were too painful to consider. He slept poorly, his bowels were irregular, and he lost weight. Maria finally gathered up Bachman, books, and papers and in June 1849 escorted them all to Madison Springs, Georgia, where hot baths and escape from church responsibilities restored him. Dictating to his bride, he began writing the second volume of *The Quadrupeds* by spending four hours a day. Before long, Bachman and Maria were writing twelve hours out of twenty-four. On 27 January 1851, with five months still to go before volume 2 of *The Quadrupeds* would be published, Audubon breathed his last breath.

Maria did much more than take down Bachman's words. Editing material Victor had sent, as well as script Bachman provided, she shaped the book. "She knocks to the right & left with your articles & mine—lops off corrects criticizes, and abuses & praises by turns," Bachman wrote. "She does wonders, but she has gained nothing in health & has no faith in the [hot spring] waters" (30 June 1849, CMBA).

By March of 1852, the need to write the third and publish the final volume of *The Quadrupeds* had become compelling. Burdened by debt, Victor finally agreed to travel to Charleston and "hold the pen" for Bachman. For six weeks they "were almost invisible" in Bachman's study.

As they were bringing the writing to a close, Bachman dashed off a sales letter to "a friend residing in Savannah, Ga." Taking the opportunity to describe how he and Audubon had divided the work, the pastor wrote, "The figures [paintings] were made by the Audubons," he wrote, "and the descriptions [scientific names] and letter-press [text] were prepared by myself." As to the importance of *The Quadrupeds*, Bachman wrote, "I will only add that in my department is summed up the result of investigations pursued through a long life, and, I think the figures have never been equalled in any publication either in Europe or America" (C. Bachman 1888, 279). Bachman was accurate on both counts. He had studied mammals almost as long as he could remember, and the drawings by Audubon and his sons were unmatched.

Bachman had recognized his own status as a scientist for at least twelve years. In 1840 he had assured Audubon that as to the quadrupeds, he, Bachman, would row naturalists "such as you, Harlan—Peale—Ord & the other Bipeds" up salt river. "I can show the whole concern of you & Richardson to boot," Bachman shifted metaphors, "that they have often been barking with cold noses on the back track" (15 January 1840, CMBA).

On 26 March 1852, Bachman wrote to Dr. Jared P. Kirtland, who, like Bachman, had a rare warbler named for him, "The last animal on hand was described five minutes ago. I threw my hat to the ceiling, kicked books, papers, rabbit and squirrel skins and bats about the room, and felt that the nightmare of some years was off my breast" (CPL). Victor dotted the last period, and Bachman, not to mention Victor, "could breathe again" (Bachman 1874, 194–96).

Chapter 13

THE UNITY OF MAN

*J*UST BEFORE CHRISTMAS 1847, the second disabling incident involving a dog and Bachman took place. The dog had mange. Ensconced in his study, his refuge from a world of trouble, Bachman filled a pot with lard, sulphur, and one-half-pound of gunpowder, the standard mange remedy, and passed the container to "Sam our little servant" to take it outside where he could bathe the ailing animal.

Then Bachman settled in his chair by the fire, his mind on writing, his feet toasting on the fender. Once his pen touched the paper, he lost touch with his surroundings and, absorbed in thought, failed to notice that instead of taking the pot outside, innocent little Sam had seen fit to melt the lard by putting it "on the fire about 18 inches from my nose" (JB to VA, 13 December 1847, CMBA).

An explosion "like that of a cannon," sent Bachman sprawling, his hair, eyelashes, and brows singed to the roots, and his face, with the exception of circles shielded by his eyeglasses, badly burned. The glasses saved him from blindness. He spent the next ten days on his back, his face poulticed with freshly grated, raw potato. A premature emergence in the light proved too much for his eyes and he retired to his darkened room for five more days, coming out just in time to keep an appointment with Louis Agassiz for a long conversation in the study. Agassiz, a distinguished scientist, had come to Charleston to address the Philosophical Society (JB to VA, 13 December 1847, CMBA).

Bachman had first met Agassiz in 1838 at the convocation of scientists in Freyburg. There the paleontologist had delivered a landmark address on fossil fish that deeply impressed the pastor. Now, a decade after their meeting, they sat together in Bachman's study, probing each other's minds. Agassiz had become famous for his work on glaciers, and had come to the

United States in 1846 to assume a post at Harvard University. No one could dismiss Agassiz lightly—he had a way about him. His lectures, to give one example of the power of his delivery, were embellished by beautiful chalk drawings swiftly executed with both hands as he talked.

Agassiz spoke highly of volume 1 of *The Quadrupeds* during the conversation in Bachman's study, bestowing praise on both drawings and text. Nothing produced in Europe, Agassiz told Bachman, could equal it (Happoldt 1960, 77). This bold assertion inspired Bachman to write Victor that he prized Agassiz's opinion "more than [any man's] in America" (13 December 1847, CMBA). Bachman wrote to Victor that he was looking forward to questioning the scholar about a number of puzzling mammals scheduled to appear in volume 2 of *The Quadrupeds*—which Bachman hoped to begin writing any day.

Elements of the conversation, however, were unsettling. To Bachman's distress, the great man revealed surprising gaps in his knowledge. "Alas Agassiz cant help me," Bachman bemoaned, "he knows scarcely one of our animals & not those of his own country—he knows nothing of Quadrupeds" (JB to VA, 6 January 1848, CMBA). Worse was Agassiz's support of the contention that each human race represented a separate species of man.

Bachman, who rejected this idea, was sadly disappointed, but Agassiz did not stand alone in his belief. The notion that numerous human races meant multiple human species was resonating nationally with strong religious and political overtones, and debate about it had spread rapidly from scientific into public arenas. If African Americans and Native Americans were separate species from caucasians, the argument went, then the caucasian enslavement of African Americans and extermination of Native Americans became easier to rationalize.

It was ironic therefore, that Bachman, who owned African American slaves and held Native Americans in contempt, took the opposing position that there is only one species of man. And ironic, too, that in the enlightened Northeast so many men of science and politics would unite against Bachman, leaving him almost alone in his defense of the doctrine of the unity of the human race. After much thought, Bachman defined his position in an exhaustive book by that name. It took him but one month to write it late in 1849, and to publish it in Charleston early in 1850.

The idea that mankind comprised several separate species had been brought vividly to the attention of Charlestonians in April 1844, in the person of the fast-talking, charming George Robins Gliddon. Gliddon had arrived in the city to present to the Philosophical Society his popular lecture on the ruins left by human species of ancient Egypt. He had arrived in town buoyed by an advance copy of Dr. Samuel George Morton's *Crania Aegyptiaca,* which its author had dedicated to him, thereby "handing me to posterity," as the showman proudly put it. The endorsement gave a measure of credibility to the thesis of Gliddon's lectures, that each human race constituted biologically distinct species (Stanton 1960, 52).

Gliddon, an Englishman serving as U.S. vice-consul at Cairo, had already traveled far toward launching Morton's second book on the subject. The skulls of ninety-three Egyptians, "grinning horribly their ghastly smiles," stared through empty sockets at Gliddon and his uneasy servant from perches all around in his Egyptian residence. His macabre dwelling had become a way station for skulls traveling between violated tombs in the Sahara and Morton's tidy museum cabinets in Philadelphia (45).

Gliddon contributed more than empty skulls to *Crania Aegyptiaca*. He told Morton, who never strayed far from Philadelphia, of unequivocally dated three-thousand-year-old Egyptian temples decorated with carvings of faces recognizable as Africans, Jews, and caucasians (Egyptians were considered caucasians). Most scientists of the day, relying in part on the biblical chronology worked out by Archbishop Usher, thought the Earth was about six thousand years old. But after subtracting the age of the Egyptian carvings from Usher's date of six thousand years, it seemed to many students of the subject that too few years remained for Earth's existing life forms to have evolved at all. Before long, Gliddon's compelling lectures completely undermined Morton's faith in the archbishop (50).

In the face of the new evidence, Morton dropped the notion that reproductive isolation was necessary for speciation, and confidently asserted that new species were created by crossbreeding (the opposite of reproductive isolation). He claimed, for instance, that the domestic horse was a cross of four wild species of the horse family (127).

Bachman was ill when Morton's *Crania Americana* was published, but he was already familiar with its contents as he had subscribed to receive installments of the work two years before it appeared in book form. Lavishly illustrated with haunting plates of nearly one hundred skulls, and replete with data, it presented among other things Morton's system for measuring volumes of human crania. He would fill each skull with white pepper seeds, then pour the seeds into a container of known volume. He later improved the accuracy of the measurement by substituting lead shot for seeds. The measurements seemed to support Morton's claim that caucasians had more capacious crania than Native Americans; therefore, they thought, caucasians were intellectually superior to the other races (31–32).

Two considerations, however, kept Morton from publishing these conclusions right away. First, infertility of offspring from crossbreeding was generally accepted by scientists as evidence that the parents were of different species, and yet Morton knew that crosses among the races of man were fertile, indicating that they were of one species. Second, it was widely accepted on religious grounds that all men were descended from Adam and Eve and thus were a single species. So reasonably argued, so exquisitely illustrated, and written by a scientist of such high repute, *Crania Americana* was widely read and roundly praised.

John Bachman, following an approach he adopted early in his intellectual life, chose to debate Morton entirely on the scientific evidence, setting aside—but not rejecting—biblical authority. He believed that because scientific and biblical truths were equivalent, the scriptures and science could not contradict each other. If a fact of nature seemed at variance with the Bible, Bachman maintained, the interpretation of the scriptures should be reexamined (Bachman 1850, 1).

The argument between old friends—Bachman and Morton had been colleagues since Harlan pirated Bachman's rat—became a debate on the origin of the species. Morton defined species as a "primordial form" (Stanton 1960, 131). Freed by Gliddon from Usher's restrictively young Earth, Morton claimed that many contemporary species had arisen through hybridization of primordial forms.

Bachman, for his part, described a species as belonging to "one stock that produce fertile offspring by association." He had kept birds in his aviary for decades, and perhaps had bred and studied more hybrids than any other scientist up to his time. He had also seen enough variation in domestic and wild animals to know that varieties turned up regularly and for no obvious reason, especially in domesticated animals. Occasionally, a wild variety that could reproduce more successfully than its progenitors would appear and ultimately displace the old population (Bachman 1855a, 8–9).

Bachman defined "permanent varieties" variously in his writing. Many, he contended, were stable, evolved forms "as permanent as the species themselves" (Bachman 1850, 14). This amounted to accepting *two* kinds of species: a stock dating from creation "that produces fertile offspring by association," and, second, permanent varieties that having once arisen "do not change their characteristics unless they breed with other varieties." By recognizing two sets of species, one consistent with his religion and the other with natural selection, Bachman created intellectual space for both faith and science (Bachman 1855a, 9).

Morton died in 1851, leaving his collaborators, Gliddon and Dr. Josiah Clark Nott of Mobile, Alabama, to carry on the debate. Bachman held up his side of the quarrel, countering, in articles published between 1850 and 1855, the claims of Gliddon, Nott, and even Agassiz. As scientific debate, the controversy had proceeded about as far as it could go without the introduction of new ideas or information. Morton and his allies were wrong, and Bachman knew only part of the truth. Not until the concept of extinction won wide acceptance, and the age of the Earth was determined to be not thousands but millions, even billions of years old would evolution win over most of the best minds in science.

Confident that all men are of one species, Bachman stood firm, even when his loyalty to the South was questioned; many southerners regarded defenders of "the unity of man" to be traitorous abolitionists. Morton's supporters, meanwhile, berated Bachman for their mentor's death.

The political question of slavery and the scientific question of the unity of man both moved toward resolution as the 1850s drew to a close. Darwin published his *On the Origin of Species* in 1859. A year later, the southern states, with South Carolina in the lead, began seceding from the Union. Committed to the Union, and loyal to the South and the institution of slavery, Bachman faced an excruciating choice: should he support the southern states—or the Union. There was really never any question which choice Bachman finally must make, but he delayed and agonized, debating his stand in many letters exchanged with Victor. After the election of Abraham Lincoln in 1860, with secession a foregone conclusion, Bachman was at last forced to choose the South.

He did so from the pulpit of his church on Archdale Street, preaching a watershed sermon a week before South Carolina seceded. He returned to his home distraught. To take Bachman's mind off the crisis, a visitor mentioned Darwin's sensational book and for the moment Bachman brightened, recalling his chat in England with the young Darwin who had just returned from his voyage on the *Beagle* (*News and Courier,* 25 February 1874).

Unlike many scientists and most clerics of the day, Bachman had reason to welcome publication of the *Origin of Species,* having come so close to formulating evolution himself that a few slight adjustments of his view of speciation might have led him to accept Darwin's thesis wholeheartedly. In fact, Darwin later quoted from Bachman's long essay of 1855, "An Examination of Prof. Agassiz's Sketch of the Nat. Provinces of the Animal World," to bolster his argument in *The Descent of Man* explaining the origin of the species in terms of evolution.

The diverting chat with the solicitous visitor was short-lived. Bachman's face clouded and he abruptly broke off. "My mind is not upon these things. I have this day done the saddest act of my life; I have preached a sermon against the Union, and upholding the secession movement of our people. My father fought in the Revolutionary War. I was taught from my earliest childhood to venerate my country's flag." His voice choked with sorrow, Bachman pointed to the United States Arsenal Building visible through the window, barely a block away. The flag of the Union still flew there. "Many and many a time have I looked upon that flag with pride. It grieves me that I can do so no more. I love the Union, but I must go with my people" (*News and Courier,* 25 February 1874).

Chapter 14

THE LAST OF THE JOSTLES

ACHMAN'S INVENTION, "The Jostle Family," was a metaphor—
on the surface lighthearted, at heart serious—for his friendship with Audubon. Within a few months of meeting his friend he assigned Jostle titles not only to Audubon and himself, but also to Audubon's wife and sons. It was the Jostles, not Audubon unaided, who pushed *The Birds of America* to completion in the 1830s, and later, in the 1840s, the junior Jostles compensated for Audubon's insidious physical and mental decline by working as a team in the production and publication of *The Quadrupeds.* As a unit, the Jostles had no choice but to continue to work together, however bruising the exchanges between Bachman and Audubon's sons. The incomes of the Audubons depended on the successes of their publications, and all told, John Woodhouse ultimately was responsible for the support of nine children, and Victor Gifford for six. The projects of the Jostles were sustained after Audubon's death and the completion of *The Quadrupeds.*

To shelter themselves and their progeny both Victor and John built houses at Minnie's Land. Victor, it is said, fell in a stairwell in his new house, and incurred a disabling injury to his spine. John launched the full-scale American republication of *The Birds of America* in 1860, about the same time that Victor died of his injuries (Herrick 1968, 295).

The republication was a disaster. John had printed a large number of plates by the time that war loomed between the North and the South, discouraging subscribers. John could not pay the printers, fell hopelessly into debt, succumbed to a bronchial infection, and died in February 1862.

With the advent of the war, which led to a sustained bombardment of Charleston from the Union-occupied forts in and around Charleston harbor, Bachman became deeply involved in organizing and working in Charleston hospitals, filled with sick and wounded Confederate soldiers.

In the wards, Bachman encountered two soldiers ill with measles. He took them home, and his wife, Maria, cleared for the soldiers the "painting-room," where thirty years earlier Audubon had portrayed many of his birds.

Charleston was constantly under fire. On several occasions, the bombardment became so intense that Bachman and Maria fled to Columbia to take refuge in the homes of friends. Bachman and Maria and several of Bachman's grandchildren were in Columbia during the last week of December 1862. To explain to the children why they received so few toys, Maria composed one of her songs:

Old Santa Claus, a merry wight,
Is far away in sorry plight,
Compelled to stay in Yankee land,
Because his wares are contraband;
He tried to run the *vile* blockade,
And many a desp'rate efforts made
But all in vain, and now he stands,
With down-cast eyes and *empty hands*.

The Bachmans again spent Christmas with Columbia friends in 1863. Maria was not well and slept poorly. Two nights after Christmas Bachman rose from his bed and went to fetch a physician. A "simple remedy" was ordered, but Maria died before Bachman "could take in the thought" (C. Bachman 1888, 374–75).

Bachman lived eleven more years, suffering several serious strokes that confined him to his bed. He outlived many of his friends and wondered why he should live so long. "I have buried my early friends, and am left like a pelican in the wilderness," he remarked plaintively (378). He died on 24 February 1874, at the age of eighty-four.

Meanwhile, the financial collapse of the Audubons just before and just after the beginning of the Civil War forced Lucy Audubon to resume teaching. She rented her house, and ultimately sold it. For about ten dollars each she sold more than four hundred of the original *Birds of America* paintings to a museum. In 1863 she moved in with a granddaughter, and spent her last days in Kentucky with another granddaughter. It was in Kentucky that she died six months after the death of Bachman, the last of the Jostles.

BOOKS AND ARTICLES

Audubon, John J. 1900. *Audubon and His Journals*. 2 vols. Edited by Maria R. Audubon. New York: Scribner.

—————. 1929a. *Journal of John James Audubon Made During His Trip to New Orleans in 1820–1821*. Edited by Howard Corning. Cambridge, Mass.: Club of Odd Volumes.

—————. 1929b. *Journal of John James Audubon Made While Obtaining Subscriptions to His "Birds of America," 1840–1843*. Edited by Howard Corning. Cambridge, Mass.: Business Historical Society.

—————. 1965. *Audubon Watercolors and Drawings*. Introduction and data on pictures by Edward Dwight. Utica, N.Y.: Munson-Williams-Proctor Institute.

—————. 1966. *The Original Watercolor Paintings by John James Audubon*. Introduction by Marshall B. Davidson. Notes about paintings by Edward H. Dwight. New York: American Heritage.

—————. 1967a [1840–44]. *The Birds of America*. 7 vols. New York: John J. Audubon. Reprint. Introduction by Dean Amadon. New York: Dover Publications.

—————. 1967b *The 1826 Journal of John James Audubon*. Transcribed by Alice Ford. Introduction and notes by Alice Ford. Norman: University of Oklahoma Press.

—————. 1969 [1930]. *Letters of John James Audubon, 1826–1840*. 2 vols. Edited by Howard Corning. Kraus reprint. Cambridge, Mass.: Club of Odd Volumes.

Audubon, John J., and John Bachman. 1846–54. *The Viviparous Quadrupeds of North America*. 3 vols. New York: John J. Audubon and V. G. Audubon.

—————. 1989. *Audubon's Wildlife, the Quadrupeds of North America*. 1 vol. Retitled edition of *The Viviparous Quadrupeds of North America*. Stanford, Conn.: Longmeadow Press.

Audubon, Lucy. 1869. *The Life of John James Audubon, the Naturalist*. Introduction by James Wilson. New York: Lucy Audubon.

Bachman, Catherine. 1888. *John Bachman*. Charleston: Walker, Evans and Cogswell Co.

Bachman, John. 1827. "Journal of Rev. John Bachman, 9 August to 25 September 1827." Manuscript Charleston: Charleston Museum.

————. 1832. "Mr. Audubon." *Charleston City Gazette and Commercial Daily Advertiser,* 6 June 1832, pages unnumbered.

————. 1834a. *An account of some experiments made on the habits of the Vultures inhabiting Carolina, the Turkey Buzzard, and the Carrion Crow, Particularly as it regards the extraordinary powers of smelling, usually attributed to them.* Charleston: John Bachman.

————. 1834b. "The Author's Original Manuscript Account of His Experiments with Buzzards: 'Notes on some experiments made on the Buzzards of Carolina— Cathares aura & C. atratus. . . .'" CMBA.

————. 1850. *The Doctrine of the Unity of the Human Race.* Charleston: C. Canning.

————. 1855a. "Characteristics of Genera and Species." *Charleston Medical Journal and Review* 9, no. 2 (March): 201–22. Charleston: James, Williams and Gitsinger.

————. 1855b. "An Examination of Prof. Agassiz's Sketch of the Nat. Provinces of the Animal World." *Charleston Medical Journal and Review* 9, no. 4 (July): 482–534.

————. 1855c. *Continuation of the Review of "Nott and Gliddon's Types of Mankind."* No. 2. Charleston: James, Williams and Gitsinger.

————. 1874. "Letter to Jared P. Kirtland." *Proceedings,* 1845–59, pp. 194–96. Cleveland: Cleveland Academy of Natural History.

————. 1929. "Some Letters of Bachman to Audubon." Comment by Ruthven Deane. *The Auk* 46:177–85.

Bost, Raymond M. 1963. *The Reverend John Bachman and the Development of Southern Lutheranism.* Ph.D. diss., Yale University, Hartford, Conn.

Bull, Elias. 1969. "A Man Who Loved Roses." *Sandlapper* (May): 72–77. Columbia, S.C.

Cantwell, Robert. 1961. *Alexander Wilson, Naturalist and Pioneer: A Biography.* Philadelphia and New York: Lippincott.

Darwin, Charles. 1871. *The Descent of Man.* London: John Murray. Reprinted 1960. New York: Random House, Modern Library edition.

Ford, Alice. 1951. *Audubon's Animals.* New York: Studio Publications, Inc.

————. 1988. *John James Audubon: A Biography.* New York: Abbeville Press.

Fries, Waldemar. 1973. *The Double Elephant Folio: The Story of Audubon's Birds of America.* Chicago: American Library Association.

Hammond, E. A. 1963. "Dr. Strobels' Account of John J. Audubon." *The Auk,* 80 (October): 462–66.

Happoldt, Christopher. 1960. *The Christopher Happoldt Journal.* Preface and biographies of Christopher Happoldt and John Bachman by Claude H. Neuffer. Charleston: Charleston Museum.

[Haskell, John B.?] 1874. "John Bachman: The Death of the Distinguished Naturalist and Divine." *Charleston Courier,* 25 February 1874, pages unnumbered.

Herrick, Francis. 1968. *Audubon the Naturalist.* 2 vols. 1917, Appleton. 1938 and 1968 editions, New York: Dover Publications.

Irving, John. 1842. *A Day on Cooper River.* Charleston: A. E. Miller.

Ridge, Davy-Jo. 1985. *A Load of Gratitude: Audubon and South Carolina.* Columbia: University of South Carolina.

Rose, Jennie. 1927. "John Bachman at Home." Manuscript. Charleston: St. John's Lutheran Church.

Sanders, Albert, and W. Ripley. 1985. *Audubon: The Charleston Connection.* Charleston: Charleston Museum.

Savage, Henry, Jr. 1970. *Lost Heritage.* New York: William Morrow.

Stanton, William. 1960. *The Leopard's Spots.* Chicago: University of Chicago Press.

Stroble, Benjamin. 1963. "John J. Audubon." *Charleston Mercury,* June and July 1832. Reprinted by E. A. Hammond in "Dr. Stroble's Account of John J. Audubon," *The Auk* (1963): 80:464–66.

Strobel, Martin. 1825. *Jacob Martin and Elizabeth Pennington.* Charleston: Martin Strobel.

Thomas, Clayton. 1981. *Taber's Cyclopedic Medical Dictionary.* Philadelphia: F. A. Davis Co.

Townes, Ellen. [No date.] "The Genealogy of the Hard Family." Manuscript. Greenville, S.C.: Greenville County Library.

Welty, Joel. 1979. *The Life of Birds.* Philadelphia: Saunders College Publishing.

Yarrell, William. 1838. *Proceedings.* Part 6, pp. 85–105. London: Zoological Society of London.

MANUSCRIPT COLLECTIONS

American Philosophical Society Library, Philadelphia
The Charleston Museum, Bachman and Audubon
Library of the College of Physicians, Philadelphia
Library of St. John's Lutheran Church, Charleston
The South Caroliniana Library
William Coleman Family, Charleston
Yale University Library

179, 181; courtship and marriage of, 166, 167, 168, 172; in Charleston, 166, 167–68, 171–72; and wife's illnesses, 171, 183, 184; and *The Quadrupeds* Volume I (Audubon & Bachman), 172, 186, 191–200, 203; and Maria's Audubon's illness, 177; at Minnie's Land, 187, 217; and *The Quadrupeds* Volumes II and III (Audubon & Bachman), 203, 204, 205, 207, 210; children of, 207; financial responsibility for family, 217; injury and death of, 217

Aumack, Jacob, 57, 58

Bachman, Catherine (daughter), 87, 172
Bachman, Clara (daughter), 40
Bachman, Cordelia (daughter), 40
Bachman, Ellen (daughter), 40
Bachman, Eva (mother), 18, 20, 41, 43, 120
Bachman, Eva (sister), 18, 41, 43, 120
Bachman, George (grandfather), 18
Bachman, Harriet (daughter, later Harriet Bachman Haskell), 175, 203
Bachman, Harriet Martin (wife): in preparations for JJA's first visit, 6; first meeting with JB, 36; family history of, 36–37; birth of, 37; courtship and wedding of, 39–40; married life of, 40, 45; children of, 40, 81, 87, 172–73 (*see also names of children*); JB's letters to, 42, 46; and JB's illnesses, 46; illnesses of, 81, 95–96, 104, 149, 184, 195, 197, 202–3; relationship with JJA, 82; and daughter Eliza's marriage, 167; trip to New York and Philadelphia, 170, 171; and Maria Audubon's illness, 176, 178; death of, 203
Bachman, Henry (brother), 18
Bachman, Henry (son), 40
Bachman, Jacob (brother), 18

Bachman, Jacob (father), 18, 19–20, 38–39, 40–41, 43
Bachman, Jane (daughter), 172, 175, 176, 184, 207
Bachman, John: first meeting with JJA, 4, 6–7; and JJA in Charleston during first visit, 4, 6–12, 73–79; portrait of, 5; and Wilson, 6, 8, 24, 25, 29, 30, 32, 150; contributions to *The Birds of America* (Audubon), 7–8, 25, 81, 91–92, 98–99, 101–2, 105–7, 121, 156, 217; and John Woodhouse Audubon, 11, 32, 74, 110–11, 117–18, 121, 150; birds raised by, 12–14, 40, 80, 91, 104; birth of, 18; family history of, 18; childhood of, 18–20; youthful interest in nature, 19–20, 23, 24–25, 26–28, 29; education of, 19–21, 26, 27; religious education, 20, 27, 28–29, 30, 32; in Philadelphia as youth, 20–25, 26, 28; on song for bird identification, 23, 93, 115; illnesses of, 26, 33–34, 43–47, 81, 135, 138, 140–41, 155, 156, 159, 164, 165, 172, 183, 205, 209, 218; mammal studies by, 26–27, 110–12, 118, 121, 128–30, 141–42, 147–48, 155, 160–61; as teacher, 29–30, 32; as pastor at Gilead, 32–33, 34, 39; as pastor at Charleston, 34, 35–36, 38, 165, 216; journey to Charleston by, 35; and War of 1812, 35, 37–38; physical description of, 36; courtship and wedding of, 39–40; married life with Harriet, 40, 45; children of, 40, 81, 87, 172–73 (*see also names of children*); and father's estate, 40–41, 43; Erie Canal/Great Lakes voyage by, 41–43; letters to wife, 42, 46; fieldtrips with JJA, 73, 74–78, 92, 145–47; personal relationship with JJA, 73–74, 82, 98–99, 131–34, 181–82, 217; and JJA's misdesignation of eagle, 76–77; as agent for *The Birds of*